MW01231998

Jerome Cardan. The Life of Girolamo Cardano, of Milan, Physician

JEROME CARDAN.

THE LIFE

OF

GIROLAMO CARDANO, OF MILAN,
PHYSICIAN.

BY HENRY MORLEY.

IN TWO VOLUMES.
VOL. II.

LONDON:
CHAPMAN AND HALL, 193, PICCADILLY.
MDCCCLIV.

ES

CONTENTS TO VOL. II.

CONTENTS.

JEROME CARDAN.

CHAPTER I.

HOW CARDAN, PROSPERING, DENIED HIS SERVICE TO THE POPE AND TO THE KING OF DENMARK.

D'Avalos dying in the year 1546, Ferrante Gonzaga became governor of Milan. He was a prince, according to Jerome, of the harshest temper, but one who favoured virtue and good men[1].

The governor of Milan was the one particular great man whose friendship Cardan, as a Milanese, having property within the province and desiring quiet, held to be essential. In 1546 the money difficulty with the Barbiani family was brought to a happy issue. Jerome received all that was due to him. In the same year he brought also to a successful end the last of the family lawsuits that had followed on his father's death, that with the heirs of his godfather, Domenico delle Torre[2]. His fame

[1] Dialogus Tetim. Opera, Tom. i. p. 671.
[2] De Vitâ Propriâ, cap. iv. xxv. xxx.

was great as a physician. He was to suffer no more
poverty. He desired to work in peace, and keep all
danger at a distance. Throughout his life he abstained
wholly from political disputes that were very profitless, a
fertile source of trouble, and of risk that he was quite
coward enough to shun; they would, moreover, clog his
labour for the acquisition of a lasting name. The man
behind whom he could shelter himself best against all
enemies—who could best cause his property and time and
life to be respected—was the governor of the province;
his favour, therefore, the philosopher sought, and as he
had obtained D'Avalos for a cordial patron, so also he
desired the friendship of his less worthy successor. Gonzaga had, indeed, no taste for the society of learned men,
but he could be taught to reckon the well-known physician among friendly citizens over whose lives and liberties
he would be properly disposed to watch, and in those
days of anarchy that was, in Jerome's case, a point worth
gaining.

While the Professor of Medicine was writing indefatigably at Milan, during the year of absence from his duties
in the university of Pavia, the year of his wife's death,
there was a brilliant offer[1] made to him, which he refused.
The friendship of the Cardinal Sfondrato had confirmed

---

[1] Details on this subject are given in De Vitâ Propr. cap. iv. De
Libris Propriis (1557), p. 23.

and strengthened high respect for Cardan in the mind of the learned Cardinal Morone. Morone was one of the most notable of the great men who had a home in Milan, stood high in the favour of the Pope, and was at that time president of the Council of Trent, with the history of which famous conclave his name is throughout associated intimately.

Morone the elder, father to Jerome's friend, had been one of the shrewdest and most unscrupulous of Italian diplomatists ; he was chancellor to the last Sforzas, and closely, though by no means creditably, mixed up with Milanese public affairs when Jerome was a boy. His career in Milan closed with capture and imprisonment under the custody of Constable Bourbon. That check to his career was trifling. When Bourbon wanted money for his troops, and raised it by ransoms, Hieronimo Morone bought his liberty for twenty thousand florins, and moreover attached himself very adroitly to his late enemy, so that he became his counsellor and secretary. He even played a selfish game so well, that, after the death of Bourbon before the walls of Rome, he kept his own position in the army. This shrewd man had been one of the chief mediators in obtaining the liberty of the Pope Clement VII, and, in gratitude for that service, his son Giovanni received, at the age of twenty, and just before his father's death, in the year 1529, the bishopric of Modena.

Giovanni Morone, who was both able and liberal, prospered in the Church. He after a time resigned his see, and was engaged in the negotiations preceding the establishment of the Tridentine Council ; then he was made a cardinal, appointed the Pope's legate in his second capital, Bologna, and was selected, in 1545, to preside over the Council of Trent, then opened. Such was his rank and standing in the world in the year 1546. In later years his liberal dislike of the new Roman Inquisition exposed him to the enmity of one bigoted Pope, and even to imprisonment. The shadow, however, quickly passed over his life, and in his last years he was again to be found effectively using his ability and moderation to promote the peace and real well-being of the Church. Once he was almost elected Pope, having received twenty-eight votes in the conclave. This Cardinal Morone then, who was eight years younger than Cardan, made to the philosopher, in the year 1546, a brilliant offer. There was a fine opening in Rome if he would go and practise there; entering into the service of the Pontiff, who would liberally pension him.

The Pope Paul III. was he who, as cardinal, had begun the building in Rome of the splendid Farnese Palace. In his habits he was magnificent and liberal, an easy man, who, although worldly, was beloved of many, and was always an encourager of learning. When it was proposed to Cardan to go into his service, this Pope, Alexander Farnese, had for twelve years occupied St. Peter's chair, and was seventy-nine years old. He was a scholarly and courteous old man, who discoursed in a low tone of voice, and in a prolix way, picking his words deliberately, because, whether he spoke Italian, Greek, or Latin, he would be careful to use no expression that did not become the refinement of a learned man. His speech was also civilly ambiguous ; he went through an intricate political career, getting promises and giving none, in great as in small affairs always avoiding the simplicities of yes and no. By this Pope, Jerome would have been appreciated. His infallibility was wholly subject to the influence of stars, and dreams, and omens. He entered upon no undertaking or matter of common business without proper astrological or other safe authority. An union with France, most earnestly desired, was very long delayed by him, because he could not get a right accord between a couple of nativities. How great a treasure would Cardan, therefore, have been to that old man !

Jerome declined the Cardinal Morone's offer, though it involved conditions not to be despised. The Pope, he said, is decrepid; he is but a crumbling wall; and shall I quit a certain for an insecure position ? He did not then,

he tells us, fully understand the probity of Morone, or the
splendour of the Farnese house. The new governor;
Gonzaga, was as hostile to the Pope as the old governor;
D'Avalos, had been friendly, and out of Rome his Holiness
was more freely known as a man immersed in political
business speculations, than by his home character as a
kind and liberal old gentleman. The year 1546, too, was,
indeed, the beginning of his end. He had laboured, upon
public grounds, to effect peace between France and Spain,
to subjugate the Turks and Protestants, and had worked
even more zealously for the aggrandisement of his own
family. After the Turkish war, he had obtained Camarino
from the hands of a woman by an act resembling rob-
bery, and given it to his grandson Ottavio. He had got
Novara with its territories for his son Pier Luigi. He
worked up domestic alliances with France and Spain, and
nearly obtained for his grandson Ottavio, who had married the emperor's illegitimate daughter, Margaret, the
whole duchy of Milan. For your imperial highness, said
the Pope to Charles, had better not keep the duchy; you
should not think of being a count, duke, or prince, but
should be only emperor. You have not prospered since
you became Duke of Milan. When you hold such titles
men distrust you, for they fear that you desire to enrich
yourself by the possession of such towns. You will do
well, therefore, to give up Milan to some other person.

But to whom? Surely not to your French rival. I see nothing better than that you should give it to my grand-son, your son-in-law; give it to him, with his wife, Margaret. This idea the Pope carried so far, that he prevailed upon his friend the Marquis d'Avalos[1], who was rather credulous, to perfume himself and go to court as governor of Milan, with a prettily turned speech, there to do homage to Margaret, and to propose that he should bring her home to Milan as his future mistress. It may be that this visible participation in the projects of the Pope made it not difficult for the enemies of the Marquis to perplex his last days with imperial disfavour.

Covered or open there was almost always a breach between the Pope and Emperor. The disaffected throughout Italy looked upon his Holiness as their most powerful protector. The imperialists—men like Gonzaga—hated, or at least distrusted the whole family of the Farnese, of which the younger members were assuredly concerned in a great deal of plotting. Chief mover among them was the Pope's son, Pier Luigi. He was the working spider that had charge of the whole cobweb of Farnese diplomacy. It is not necessary here to tell how, by the removal of the council of Trent to Bologna, and the withdrawal of his

[1] In Ranke's History of the Popes, to which I owe some of these particulars, I find stated in a note, that the MS. life of D'Avalos, referred to in a previous page (156), is in the Chigi library at Rome. It is said to contain amusing matter, and must merit publication.

troops in the autumn of the year 1546, the Pope wilfully, and
through jealousy, checked the emperor in the full stream
of his success against the Protestants. It is enough to add,
that his son and family manager, Pier Luigi, was assassi-
nated, chiefly at the instigation of Ferrante Gonzaga; and
that he himself being compelled into a policy that for a
time was hostile to the interests of his immediate family,
the family that he had laboured all his days to aggrandise,
his own blood turned against him.   After an angry inter-
view with the Cardinal Alessandro Farnese, in which he
had been enraged greatly at his selfishness, the old man
died.   There were found, it was said, three drops of co-
agulated blood in his heart, a fatal distillation caused by
the sharp throbs of anger.   That is a cause of death that
may be questioned, but of the effects of anger, it is certain
that the old man died a little more than three years after
Cardan had declined to pass into his service.

On the whole, then, there can be little doubt that the
physician, in refusing the Pope's offer, decided prudently.
Had he gone to Rome he would have been drawn into the
current of political affairs, and have identified himself with
one of two contending parties.   The Pope, with all his
liberality and splendour, was, indeed, no better than a
crumbling wall for a philosopher to lean upon.

Jerome desired, also, to retain the position that he held
as a professor in the University of Pavia.   It suited his

habits as a student, it enabled him to renew with energy, under the best conditions, that study of his profession which he had suffered to become lax at Milan, and a far more important advantage attached to it was, that it placed him in the best position for the education of his eldest son; Gianbatista then was of an age to study medicine, and a young relative, Gaspar Cardan, worked with him under Jerome's supervision. His love for his studies and his love for his son, alike bound the new professor to the lecture-table[1]. He had quitted Pavia only for a time while trouble made the university a bankrupt, but he did not remain absent longer than a year. In 1547 he returned to the duties of his professorship, and in that year was tempted by another dazzling offer[2].

Jerome had gone to Pavia with great honour, accompanied and lauded by his former teacher, Curtius, whose fame he was already surpassing. It was probably at Pavia that he had the opportunity of establishing a friendship with a very famous teacher, the bold founder of modern anatomy, Andreas Vesalius. Vesalius was thriving rapidly. He had defied the prejudices of his age, and based the study of the human frame on actual dissection of the divine image. He had contra-

[1] De Lib. Prop Lib. ult. Opera, Tom. i. p. 131.
[2] Authority for the details of the succeeding offer, and the reasons given for its refusal, will be found in chapter iv. De Vitâ Propriâ, and in the last book of De Libris Propriis. Opera, Tom. i.

dicted Galen on a thousand points, to the disgust and
alarm of the whole body of rule of thumb physicians,
who, with Sylvius of Paris at their head, attacked him
furiously.   Vesalius had studied under Sylvius, an easy-
going and most eminent professor of the old school, who,
in teaching Galen to his pupils, skipped all the hard
passages, and illustrated his doctrine by demonstrating
from limbs of dogs dissected out for him by an assistant.
He became so angry, that he absolutely raved at the pre-
sumption of Vesalius, who was not thirty years old when
he overthrew the ancient system by the publication of his
book upon the Fabric of the Human Body.   Around
Vesalius, however, the young men of the profession
gathered; curiosity and admiration brought throngs to
his lecture-rooms, and he was sought as a star by rival
universities.   He was Professor of Anatomy in three or
four Italian towns at once, giving a short winter-course
at each one in succession.   In that way he came to
Pavia[1], but although the friendship established between
himself and Cardan was very intimate, it seems to have been
maintained exclusively by written intercourse, for Cardan
says that, friends as they were, they never met[2].   There

---

[1] Details concerning Vesalius are drawn from the life prefixed by
Boerhaave and Albinus to his Corporis Humani Fabrica, and from his
own treatise De Radice Chinâ, which is full of autobiographical
matter.   A sketch of his career, founded upon that and other authority,
was given (by me) in *Fraser's Magazine* for November, 1853.

[2] De Lib. Prop. Lib. ult. Op Tom. 1. p. 138.

was every reason why two such men should be friends. They were both famous: one eminent in mathematics, the other in anatomy; both physicians, yet with no clashing of interests to make them disagree.. They both loved pleasure; and although Vesalius indolently wasted at the court of Madrid the mature years of his life, that time was in the future; when he taught at Pavia, his taste for luxury had not yet marred the polish or the keenness of his wit. Again, they had both triumphed in a battle with the world. Vesalius was a man thirteen years his junior, whom Jerome knew how to respect. On the other hand, the young anatomist, over whom old practitioners were groaning, who was compelled by the prejudices of society to plunder churchyards, and to keep dead bodies concealed sometimes even in his bed, probably would like Jerome all the better for the persecutions he, too, had experienced, and for his bold carelessness about conventional respectability. Certainly the professors of anatomy and medicine were friends; to that fact one testifies by statements and allusions scattered through his works; and to that fact the other also testified on the occasion that has caused his name to appear in the present narrative.

Christian III, King of Denmark, wished to secure long life for himself by attaching to his court some very eminent physician. Since, however, Christian had behaved in but a heathenish way towards the Roman

Church, it was not likely that his patronage would be
desired by any but a bold man who was not afraid of
venturing upon complicity with heretics.   Christian's
accession having been heartily opposed by the bishops,
and the beginning of his reign having been much confused with civil war, his majesty, when he had been three
years upon the throne, in defiance of his pledged faith,
seized by force every bishop in his dominions, and
abolished totally the Roman Catholic form of worship.
The bishops after a time were liberated, on condition that
they would submit to the new order of things.   One
only preferred to die in prison.   This act of perfidy or
piety had been committed about ten years before Christian
wished for an Italian physician to his household.   His
dominions during his reign had been at no time free
from intestine strife; and though he had been so good as
to assassinate Danish Catholicism, he had not proved an
enlightened ruler.   He had bribed his nobles by securing
to them every just and unjust privilege; and among
others, power of life and death over their vassals.   All
that he had done the public only dimly knew in Italy,
for news from Denmark must have found its way only in
the shape of strange rumours and legends to the people of
the south of Europe, at a time when it was not even easy
for a man in Milan to know accurately what was being
done in Venice.

The offer of the King of Denmark was made through his ambassador in the first instance to Vesalius, a physician, who was at the same time eminent and bold. He was habitually acting in defiance of Church bigotry, and was therefore perhaps not likely to object on theological grounds to a royal patient. Vesalius, however, had a different career before him. He already possessed good private means, had several lucrative professorships, and a large practice; his father also was apothecary to the emperor, and held out to him just expectations of advancement at Madrid. He therefore, of course, declined the King of Denmark's offers. Being requested then to name some other illustrious physician whom he would advise the ambassador to seek on the part of his master, he named Jerome Cardan.

The ambassador went therefore to Cardan, whom it had taken fifteen years in the beginning of his career to acquire the art of hoping for nothing, and upon whom society had then at last begun to shower its pecuniary blessings. He had achieved at last his conquest of the world; that done, he had only to receive homage and collect his tribute. On the part of the King of Denmark, there was offered to the prospering philosopher a yearly stipend of three hundred and six Hungarian gold crowns, in plain cash, and a share in the revenue accruing from a tax on furs, which would probably be less punctually received, and the amount of which would fluctuate, but which might be said to make, together with the other sum, an income of eight hundred crowns. There was offered to him, in addition to this salary, free maintenance for himself and a household of five, together with allowance for three horses. That he would have from the king, and more he might receive as a physician, from the courtiers or other Danes who came to him for counsel.

Jerome was not to be tempted. He remained at Pavia. The climate of Denmark, he said, was cold and moist, and would not suit his sickly constitution. The people of Denmark he considered to be almost barbarous, a race of turbulent men, not more congenial to his mind than their soil would be to his body. In Denmark he seems to have felt that he would have been almost banished from that republic of letters in which he had always hoped to become a laurelled citizen. He urged strongly the heresy of the Danes, that they used rites and precepts very different from those of Rome, and that he should be compelled either to give up the religion of his country, which he certainly would never do, or to live openly at variance with those about him, and estranged from the consolations of his Church. He took no part in the quarrel between Catholic and Protestant, and he philosophised upon eternal things with a surprising boldness; but though he ran the risk of being called by his own Church an impious man or an atheist, still Cardan held with the whole force of his superstition to its mystical pretensions. By the dark side of his own fancy he clung firmly to the dark side of his Church's faith. Church and philosopher so joined were never to be parted. His opinion of the Protestant cause he incidentally expressed in comments on the horoscope of Luther. The heresy so widely propagated would, he said—and the stars said—fall to pieces of itself ; for "it would rear up an infinite number of heads, so that, if nothing else convicted it of falsehood, yet by that very multitude of opinions it would be shown that, since truth is one only, in plurality there must be error[1]."

Another reason, urged by him with equal emphasis, against acceptance of the Danish offer, was his duty to his children. His eldest son was of an age to require university education ; Jerome was proud of him, and loved him with a beautiful devotion. While he was teaching medicine at Pavia, he could most readily secure for him all requisite advantages. His other children, too, were recently left motherless. He would remain at home. Neither for Pope nor heretic would he move out of his appointed path.

---

[1] " . . . . solvitur in seipso—infinitaque reddit capita, ut si nihil aliud errorem convincat, multitudo ista opinionum ostendere tamen possit, eum Veritas una tantum sit, plurimos necessario aberrare." De Exemplis centum geniturarum. Op. Tom. v. p. 465.

CHAPTER II.

THE stipend attached to the professorship at Pavia was liberal. It consisted in the first year of two hundred and forty, and in the year 1547 was increased to four hundred gold crowns[1]. Pavia was the same university which Cardan had first entered as a neglected youth, when at the age of nineteen he escaped from bondage in his father's house. The honours that were at last paid to him there, the profitable medical reputation that accrued to him from his prominent position as a teacher of his art, and the wide difference between the actual salary he was receiving, and the few crowns paid to him as a Plat lecturer upon arithmetic, made up a sum of worldly good fortune, so unexpected, that Jerome felt for a time, he says, as though it had been all a dream!

Vesalius was perhaps the only medical teacher in Italy who was then able to fill his lecture-room. He had a stimulating subject. His dissections of real human bodies attracted the curious as much as the inquiring. He was a

_____

[1] De Lib. Prop. Lib ult. Op. Tom. i. p 108. Geniturarum Exemplar (ed. Lugd. 1555), p. 80.

man of the world too, strong-willed, and perhaps overbearing in his temper, but of courteous habits ; young, handsome, well-dressed, affable, and a fluent speaker, master of an admirable style.   Jerome Cardan had nothing in his body calculated to win for his learned expositions of Hippocrates the accident of popularity.   He was a sickly man, rather small of stature, thin-armed, narrow-chested, lean, and gouty.   His teeth were beginning already to fall out.   He was a fair-complexioned man, with yellow hair, having bald protuberant temples, and a luxuriant beard under the chin.   The massive temples, indicating as we now say Ideality, indicated as he then said the influence of Taurus at his birth.   He had an ugly scar upon his forehead, small grey-blue, weak, short-sighted eyes—his left eye, since the first attack of gout, watered habitually,—and a pendulous lower lip.   He was not trim of dress or suave of manner.   He had a harsh, abrupt voice, and a slight stutter in his speech ; he stooped when he walked, and was ungainly in his gesture.   Furthermore, his whole skin had been subject to an eruption since he was twenty-four years old, and did not become sound again till he was fifty-one[1].

[1] This personal description of Cardan is taken partly from the chapter De Vitâ Propriâ, and chiefly from the account of himself in the third and longest dissertation on his own horoscope. Geniturarum Exemplar (ed. Lugd. 1555), pp. 57—140.

VOL. II.   C

On the other hand, he was renowned for learning; he
was very earnest ; students would like his eccentricities,
and he worked indefatigably in his calling. For he devoted
himself exclusively at Pavia to the study of his profession,
because he was determined to work down the old belief
that he was properly versed only in mathematics and
astrology[1]. His public teaching in the university is partly
represented by the written Commentaries on Hippocrates,
at which he laboured with the heartiest good-will. Into
them he endeavoured to put the whole pith of Hippocrates
and Galen, adding such free comments and elucidations
as should cause the complete work to represent also the
whole pith of the medical science of his time.

Whoever may desire to ascertain what sort of teaching
was contained in the lectures delivered on the Principles
and Practice of Medicine by a first-rate professor in the
middle of the sixteenth century, should turn to Cardan's
Commentaries on Hippocrates. In the opinion of their
writer they excelled his other works. They were written,
he said, in the years of his complete maturity, when he
had also the advantage of full leisure. Though treating of
his art generally, they embraced all that was in it. They
were filled with the divine opinions of Hippocrates, and

---

[1] De Libris Propriis (ed. 1557), pp. 56, *et seq.*, for this fact and
succeeding details concerning literary work done while Cardan was
at Pavia.

they were written, he added, with the noblest purpose—
namely, to increase health among men.

Upon that work, and upon three others, Jerome,
towards the close of life, rested his assurance of immortal
fame. The other three were : first, the Arithmetic (including the tenth book—that on the Great Art) already
discussed in these pages ; next, a book on Astrology; and
finally, a systematic work on Music. He claims to have
been the first among moderns by whom an attempt was
made to restore the art of music to its true position as a
science. To those four books he was disposed to add his
work on Physiognomy. His other writings, he said, might
become more popular, as they were more attractive to the
multitude, but those were the firm pillars to the temple of
his fame.

Of them, too, the Commentaries on Hippocrates were
most to be relied upon, because they would be most
widely read. The art of healing, he said, concerns
all men ; the name of its great author, therefore, will be in
eternal honour, and his doctrine sought by thousands.
For his other great works, Jerome expected a much more
restricted circle of appreciating readers. His mathematical writings could be comprehended only by the learned.
Astrology was falling into undeserved discredit, and the
study of it was confined to a small number of men,—great
lords or princes, and philosophers. Then, as for music,

they who did not practice it would scarcely care to read
about its rules and principles, while they who did, had not
the wit to comprehend them. Still, for their originality,
and because they advanced four sciences, Cardan believed
that the four treatises here named—all, except that upon
Arithmetic and Algebra, written at Pavia—would be
known and esteemed by future generations—be "eternal as
the human race[1]."

Physicians now no longer quote Hippocrates. Astrology
has given place to an exact science of Astronomy. Music
has attained in all its forms a new development, and few
musicians send their thoughts back to Cardan. Only the
mathematicians, occupying ground that has long been
highly cultivated, look back to him in their traditions as
a famous pioneer.

For his ingenuity, Jerome was called by his friend
Alciat a man of inventions. The works just named, and
the treatise upon Subtle Things, belong, with a few others,
to a distinct period of his literary life, which commenced
when he removed to Pavia, and ended in the year 1552.
Upon his writings during that period more will be said
presently.

Andrea Alzate, Latinised Andreas Alciatus, the great
jurist of his age, was another of the professors in the
University of Pavia when Cardan was summoned thither,

---

[1] De Libris Propris (ed. 1557), p. 70.

and he was not less ready than Vesalius to recognise the greatness of the Milanese physician and philosopher. Jerome, on his part, seems to have admired Alciat —who was eight years his senior—more than any other of his literary friends; he was even moved to write a brief sketch of his life[1]. Alciat, the only son of a noble family, was born in a village of the Milanese from which he took his name—Alzate, near Como. He studied at Pavia and Bologna. He became doctor of laws, and having noble birth and a rich patrimony, as well as very great ability and eloquence, his talents were acknowledged early. Already at the age of twenty-two he was a professor at Pavia, where he wrote his Legal Paradoxes—"Paradoxa Juris." That was a work which created uproar among all old-fashioned commentators upon jurisprudence; it expounded with new vigour the best principles of Roman law, and laid the strong foundations of its author's fame. Alciat in Italy, and Zase in Germany, are indeed still remembered as the first liberal exponents of the Roman jurisprudence. At the beginning of his practice, this shrewd jurist had made himself remarkable when, as advocate in a certain witch-process, he opposed with all his energy the barbarous custom of extracting con-

[1] Vita Andreæ Alciati. Opera, Tom. ix. pp. 569, 570. In the sketch of Alciat given above, the personal details are all taken from the notes left by Cardan. Whatever is there said more than Cardan tells, will be found in Ersch und Gruber's Allgemeine Encyklopädie.

fessions by torture from presumed witches.   All that such
people assert about themselves he declared to be nothing
but fantastical invention.   He set himself also against
astrology, and declared later in life, when his opinion was
heard with respect by every prince in Europe, that men
practising astrology should be severely punished.   Cardan
took his opinion on that head very good-humouredly, and
retaliated upon his friend by calculating his nativity, and
printing it in a small book of horoscopes, cheerfully pointing out at the same time the liberty he took.

From Pavia the law professor was induced by the offer
of high pay to remove to Avignon.   A proposed reduction
of his salary caused him to leave Avignon when he was
twenty-nine years old, and go to Milan, where he practised
and acquired great fame and profit.   He was placed in
charge of the provisioning of the town during the following years of distress and famine.   From Milan, Alciat was
called to Bourges, where Francis I. gave him a salary of
twelve hundred ducats, and honoured his lectures sometimes even by personal attendance.   The dauphin, before
one lecture, made him a present of four hundred ducats.
Students came from foreign lands to hear his brilliant
and profound expositions of the laws, and his renown increased so much that he was to a certain extent contended
for by rival princes.   A man profoundly versed in law,
and an acute counsellor whose wit was marketable—
for he loved money as much as fame, and both inordi-

nately—could prompt and aid very substantially any king in quarrel with his neighbours. At the same time, he could give still more important aid in the establishment of a sound system of home polity, if any king then reigning should desire so much. Francesco Sforza, Duke of Milan, knowing these things, used his power over Alciat as territorial lord, and commanded him, on pain of forfeiting his patrimony and all property belonging to him in the Milanese, to leave the King of France, and teach again at Pavia. He was not to receive less there than was paid to him at Bourges. The lawyer went again, therefore, to Pavia.

Disturbed in his teaching by the wars, he removed, in 1537, from Pavia to Bologna. Home troubles abating, and the duchy of Milan having been bequeathed to Charles V, Charles also used his influence, as Duke of Milan, in compelling Alciat to teach at Pavia, with a salary of one thousand two hundred ducats. Renewed disturbances impoverished that university, and the purchasable jurist was enticed to Ferrara by Duke Hercules II, with the promise of thirteen hundred and fifty ducats yearly. In 1547 he was again fetched back to Pavia, where Cardan also, recently a widower, was lecturing; there finally Alciat lived and lectured—maintaining at the same time another house at Milan—until he died, in 1550, fifty-eight years old, and to the last unmarried. Jerome had been forewarned of his friend's death in a dream.

All the compulsions put upon Alciat had been profitable to him.   The Emperor had made him a Count
Palatine ; the Pope would have created him a Cardinal,
but that honour being incompatible with the continued
practice of his very lucrative profession, he did not at all
see why he should hurt his income by accepting it.   He
became, therefore, an apostolic protonotary instead.

In 1547, when Cardan was at Pavia with two such
men as Alciat and Vesalius for friends and colleagues, the
jurist was arranging a complete edition of his works.
He had come to the end of those wanderings which he
had himself boastfully compared to the travels of the sun,
who traverses all parts to light and warm them.   He was
tormented with gout, not the result, as in Cardan, of a
bad constitution, but the price of his great dinners, for
he was a mighty eater.   The two gouty professors could
condole together.   Alciat suffered most.   He was at last
wholly unable to walk, and was afflicted in his hands as well
as feet ; but the immediate cause of his death was a fever.

If he had not been tortured by the gout, Jerome thinks
that his friend must have been the happiest of men.   He
surpassed in his calling all predecessors, and was entitled
to Cicero's praise of Scævola as the best orator among
lawyers, the best lawyer among orators; that praise, too,
the physician observes, was not only true, but also
undisputed.   Apart from the gout, his felicity was
without equal; he had incomparable erudition, stores

of books, universal fame in his own lifetime, influence
with every prince in Europe, troops of attendants on his
lectures, large salaries, great wealth, and an eloquence so
singular, that men when he spoke might believe they
were hearing a new Cicero.

Alciat cultivated friendships ; he was smooth, cheerful,
even gay in his manners—perhaps that is one reason why
he passed through life unenvied and unopposed—he often
laughed while he spoke : a practice which, says Cardan,
is detestable in most men, but in him had a certain grace.
He was of middle stature and broad-chested, with large
features, great eyes, nose, lips, and ears, so that, adds
Jerome, he was, as one might say, bull-faced, but in such
a way that even all those who did not know who he was,
when they saw him freely gave him their respect.

Jerome was engaged at Pavia not only in the writing
of books, the delivery of lectures, the cultivation of
friendships, and the practice of his profession—in 1547
he cured, among others, the wife of his friend Annibale
della Croce[1], who had long suffered from a diseased hip—
but he had the education of his eldest son and of his
young relative Gaspardo Cardan[2] to superintend. A pupil
who had lately attended him at Milan, Giovanni Battista
Boscano[3], does not seem to have followed him to Pavia.

---

[1] De Ut. ex Adv. Cap. Lib. iii. cap. 2.
[2] De Vitâ Propriâ, cap. xxxv. p. 156.
[3] Ibid. p. 157.

The young Gaspar had been entrusted to him by another Cardan of the same name, one of the relations who remembered him in his prosperity. Jerome had a great many relations on his father's side, for the Cardans, as before said, were long-lived and moderately prolific. There was even a second Jerome Cardan[1], also a physician, who, when Jerome the philosopher was at Pavia, had established for himself a low practice in Milan, where he curried favour with the druggists, and became a thriving man. He will not again be mentioned in these pages.

Gian Battista, Jerome's eldest son[2], was studious and quiet, but he had, like his father, some strong passions, and was aided less by example than by precept in the regulation of his mind. Clara was a good girl, of strong constitution; she had not been without maternal training, and after her mother's death was guided by her grandmother Thaddæa. Her father's oddities lay quite out of her sphere; she was a good daughter, and when she became marriageable, married. In her whole life she gave no trouble to her father more than belonged to the payment of her dowry; that he gave ungrudgingly as a home debt, to the payment of which,

---

[1] Synesiorum Somniorum (ed. Bas. 1562), p. 262.

[2] The account here given of Jerome's children is taken from statements made by him in his last essay on his own horoscope and the horoscopes of his household, in the Geniturarum Exemplar.

by her good conduct, she had become justly entitled.
Aldo Urbano, the last born, who had come into the world
under a most flattering configuration of the planets, to
whom the stars promised lavishly talents and all their most
glittering rewards, grew up a clever child, but a decided
scapegrace. By his mother he had been known only as
an object of solicitude. He had been born on the 25th
of May, in the year 1543, three years before Lucia's
death, and during those three years he had been afflicted,
first with convulsions, then with dysentery, then with
what his father called an abscess in the brain; also with
six months of fever. He was three years old before he
learned to walk. He grew, however, into better health,
and under irregular training in a house not free from the
rattle of dice, and too much visited by men of low intellect and morals, whom Jerome himself despised while he
took pleasure in their voices, the quick boy learnt evil
ways. Cardan confesses and deplores the hurt that he did
to his children by the bad example that he set in his own
house[1]. They felt none of the toils from which the hard-
working philosopher came for relaxation to the dice-table,
or to that refreshment of music which could then hardly
be attained except in company with men who were, for
all other faculties that they possessed, to be despised and
shunned. To the children, Jerome's hours in the study

[1] De Vitâ Propriâ, p. 62.

were the hours during which they had no father to watch
over them; for, as Cardan has properly said, the man who
writes and is intent upon his writing, is for the time
being unable to see beyond his table; blind, therefore,
and also deaf and dumb[1].

But the philosopher was not neglectful of his charge.
In 1547 he was called to see a patient in Genoa[2], and
after his return from that journey made some amends to
his children for his absence by the composition of a little
Book of Precepts[3] for their use. Into it he put in a condensed form what he took to be the elements of wisdom,
wording it in proverbs, among which are some taken,
like the chief part of the learning of the time, from the
ancients, as from Cicero, Seneca, or Publius Syrus; some
were Italian proverbs current in his day, but the greater
number were his own, for he was apt at writing pithy
sentences, and freely scattered them about his works.
Where they have been taken from others they were not
unfrequently adapted to his use before they were adopted
by him.

The little Book of Precepts to his children is important
to this history of Cardan's life, because it is in the highest
degree characteristic of the writer. If we keep in mind

---

[1] De Subtilitate. Lib. xiv.

[2] De Libris Propriis. Lib. ult. Op. Tom i. p. 109.

[3] Hieronymi Cardani Medici Mediolanensis Libellus Præceptorum
Filiis.

the events of his career thus far detailed, in order that we may put the right construction upon some of his half-wise, half-bitter words, that otherwise can easily be misinterpreted, we shall receive a very distinct notion of Jerome's personal character—we shall see that he was at heart a gentleman as well as a philosopher, and a man of the world according to the temper of the day in which he lived. They will help us also to form a just measure of the quality of his mature intellect, obviously much riper when he wrote them than it was when he wrote the books on Consolation and on Wisdom. Incidentally, also, they serve to illustrate, sometimes in a very striking way, the temper of the days in which he lived; the chapter upon travelling, for example, is in that respect extremely curious. The following selection from these precepts contains about one-fourth of the whole. I have retained the original form of the tract, and have endeavoured to retain also its exact spirit, at the same time preserving a fair balance between the trivial and the weighty matters discussed in it. The Preface and Conclusion have not been abbreviated. Comment upon these precepts would be impertinent ; but I have, for the convenience of the reader, prefixed asterisks to those sayings which illustrate most effectively either the life of Cardan or his times.

CARDAN'S COUNSEL TO HIS CHILDREN.

"PREFACE.

Many, my sons, think that the chief part of happiness depends on fortune; know that they are deceived: for although fortune does contribute something to it, yet the chief part of it lies in ourselves.

Chapter the First.—ON THE WORSHIP OF GOD.

Give thanks to God daily, if you can. You will become better by doing so. Speak of Him seldom, using His name only in reverence.

* Never swear to keep a secret, if, being free, you would not become slaves.

When human efforts are of no avail, seek help from God.

It is temerity to beg that God will do for us what we can do ourselves.

Whoever would be taught of God, must keep his spirit free from vice, his body free from grossness.

* Do not labour at interpretations of the sacred page, for they are manifold, and there is danger in that work.

Receive, as from God, all good that happens to you.

* Do not believe that demons speak to you, or that you see the dead; but never seek experience upon the matter: for many things lie hidden from our sight.

Chapter the Second.—On the Observance due to
Princes.

Next to God, you must take thought of princes that
you give them no offence.

Be gentle before them, or be silent.

Passionate or jealous princes do not serve, and do not
live within their reach.   Power joined to anger or suspicion, begets lightning.

Do not wilfully court princes or governors; such practice is suspicious.   He who is pleased with more than
ought to please him, wants more than he ought to want.

* Do not resist princes, or men in great power, or the
populace, even though you are on the side of justice.

* Never do what will displease a prince.   If you have
done it, never fancy that you are forgiven.

* Time governs princes, princes govern men.   Look
for the end to time.

Chapter the Third.—On Life.

After these two, study most your way of life, for that
lies at the beginning of all.

Sleep should precede labour, labour should precede
food, food should precede drink and exceed it.

Be content with food of one kind at a time, lest you
become gluttonous.

Prefer water to wine; and among wines prefer the white.

Avoid war, plague, and famine, for they spare few and slay many.

Do not eat mushrooms, snakes, or frogs, or anything that grates upon the teeth; and do not drink two kinds of wine.

Eat only twice a day, and only once of meat.

* Never take choice morsels from strangers, or without knowing whence they come.

* When you are invited to a feast, if you must go, take heed of the faith of those who bring the cup to you.

Never sleep on feathers.

Dismiss all careful thoughts when you retire to bed.

* Hold hyacinth[1] in your hand to promote sleep and protect you against plague and lightning.

Chapter the Fourth.—On Journeys.

* Never leave the public road except of necessity, for safety or for any useful purpose.

* Never spend much time in a lonely inn, or ride into it at night.

* Avoid travelling alone, or walking through a town, for many things may happen to you.

* When you are on the road, think of the road and nothing else.

* Never walk under the eaves of houses; acting upon

---

[1] Or jacinth—the mineral, a gem of a fine purple red, the original of Milton's "hyacinthine locks."

this rule, I have twice escaped being killed by falling tiles.

* Do not cross unexplored water on horseback, or stormy water in a boat.

* Do not run your horse into deep water unless you are obliged.

* Never associate with a stranger on the public road.

* Stand out of the way of running men, or of wild animals.   The mad dogs always go straight forward.

Chapter the Fifth.—ON THE VIRTUES, AND FIRST ON FORTITUDE.

All virtues are fair and honest, only by fortitude we become like the immortal gods, and happy.

Know that a good humour in an ill event bears half the weight of ill.

Live joyously when you are able; men are worn down by cares.

What cannot be altered trouble yourself not about.

Be firm always; obstinate never.

Chapter the Sixth.—ON PRUDENCE IN GENERAL.

Next to fortitude, nothing secures happiness so much as prudence.

Though nothing hinders you from knowing what cannot concern you, do not seek to know it.

* Do not put faith in dreams; but do not scorn them, especially because they are peculiar in our family.

Predict nothing uselessly.

Four good mothers have begotten four bad sons: Truth—Hatred; Joy—Mourning; Security—Danger; Familiarity—Contempt.

* It is more prudent to spend money usefully than to lay it by, for more results come of the use of money, which is action, than of the preservation of it, which is rest.

When the mind is perturbed, never deliberate.

Say little; among many words some are imprudent.

* Never giggle; laughter abounds in the mouth of fools.

Great prudence and little wit is better than great wit and little prudence.

Fortune is more easily to be found than got; more easily to be got than kept.

* There is no necromancy; it is better for you that you put no faith in alchemy: avoid what is in bad repute.

Do not talk to other people of yourselves, your children, or your wife.

Let your dress be clean and elegant, but never costly.

You will know wise men by their works, not by their words; you may know fools by both.

* When you talk with a bad or dishonest man, look at his hand, not at his face.

Chapter the Seventh.—ON PRUDENCE WITH REGARD
TO MEMBERS OF A HOUSEHOLD.

* Remember that a family is held together, not by fear
or by love, but by mutual respect.

* Love children, honour brothers; parents and every
member of the family love or turn out of doors.

Chapter the Eighth.—ON PRUDENCE WITH REGARD TO
A WIFE.

The care of a wife is before the care for wealth. A bad
wife makes the rich man wretched, but a good wife makes
the poor man happy.

Do not marry a woman without moderate possessions.

A woman loves or hates; she has no middle humour.

Never irritate a wife, but give her counsel.

Do not marry one who is quarrelsome, she will not
obey you once.

Take no wife from a witless family, or one infected by
a constitutional disease; you perpetuate sorrow by so
doing.

Before other people, neither flatter your wife nor slight
her.

* A woman left by herself thinks; too much caressed,
suspects : therefore take heed.

Chapter the Ninth.—On Prudence towards
Children.

Children chiefly follow the nature and constitution of
their mother.

* Never let your children have a stepmother; if you do,
never put faith in her as their accuser.

* Educate a bastard as if he were legitimate, for he is
your own blood.

* Trust schoolmasters to teach your children, not to feed
them.

* You owe to your children agreeable names, knowledge of a useful art, good manners, instruction in music,
arithmetic, and writing.

Chapter the Tenth.—On Prudence with regard to
Wealth.

Wealth comes by inheritance, by favour of princes, by
the laborious exercise for payment of a difficult art.

* He who wishes to grow rich should undertake no
journeys except for certainty of gain.

Do not waste or despise wealth: it is the instrument of
all good.

Never display money or jewels.

Know how to be mastered and to lose; sometimes that
is profitable.

Count your gold twice, weigh it, and ring it.

* Little gold is got in a long time and with much labour.   Much gold is got with little time and trouble.

* Never complain of a father who has left his children poor, if he has left them victuals and the knowledge of a trade."

Chapter the Eleventh is on Prudence concerning Honours ; Chapter the Twelfth on Prudence in Business; from which it will suffice to quote one precept :

" Deeds are masculine and words are feminine. Letters are of the neuter gender.

Chapter the Thirteenth.—ON PRUDENCE TOWARDS PARENTS, BROTHERS, AND RELATIONS.

Love a just parent.   If he is unjust, bear with him or quit him.

Be the best friends among yourselves, but before others quarrel.

Chapter the Fourteenth.—ON PRUDENCE TOWARDS FRIENDS.

Have as many good friends and neighbours as you can; they strengthen reputation, and give comfort.

* If necessary, slip out of the tie of friendship, never break it.

Never desert a friend at the bidding of a relative or flatterer.

Speak only on compulsion of a friend's crime, never of an enemy's misfortune.

Chapter the Fifteenth.—ON PRUDENCE TOWARDS
ENEMIES.

Never talk about your enemies.

Speak fairly to enemies who hide their designs, even
though you may intend to be revenged upon them.

If you hate a man, though only in secret, never trust
him, because hate is hardly to be hidden.

* With enemies do not speak personally, but through
messengers.

Chapter the Sixteenth.—ON PRUDENCE IN SOCIETY.

Avoid those who are wicked, envious, foolish, talkative,
passionate, proud, given to laugh at others, or ungrateful.

Do not be querulous, meddlesome, morose, or too in-
quisitive.

* Put no trust in a red Lombard, a black German, a
blinking Tuscan, a lame Venetian, a tall, thin Spaniard, a
bearded woman, a curly-pated man, or a Greek.

Avoid nothing so much as men who speak well and act
wickedly.

* It is a part of happiness to mingle with the happy;
diligently avoid, therefore, the company of the unfor-
tunate.

* Whoever calls you gambler, calls you a sink of vices.

Contemn no man for a bodily deformity; the mind is
the whole man.

Delay is the handle to denial.

Visit nobody while he is eating, or while he is in bed.

The misfortunes of others, if they do not tell you of them, do not seem to know."

Then follows a short chapter on Wisdom, and then a chapter entitled "What Books are to be Read." It is remarkable that from this chapter he omits some of his own favourites, but he is putting down his precept, not his practice.

" * These authors only are worthy to be read, because the life of man is long enough to read them in ; but, if more be taken, some of these have to be left, and so there is made an exchange of gold for brass.

In Poetry : Homer, Virgil, Horace.

In Grammar : Priscian.

In Rhetoric : Cicero, Quintilian.

In History : Xenophon's Anabasis, the Catiline of Sallust, Suetonius, Argentonius, Voyages to the Indies, Plutarch's Lives, and Cario's Compendium.

In Mathematics : Euclid, Apollonius, Archimedes, Vitruvius, Ptolemy.

In Medicine : Hippocrates, Galen, Avicenna, Rhases for his copiousness; Dioscorides, Pierre Bellon, Gesner, Vesalius.

In Physics : Aristotle, Theophrastus, Plotinus, Plutarch.

Miscellaneous: Pausanias, Pliny, Athenæus; works of Pierre Bellon, Hieroglyphics of Pierius, Mythology of Natalis, Cœlius Rhodiginus, Cœlius Calcagninus, Stories of Boccacio, Polyphilus, Thesaurus of the Latin language.

Beyond these you should not go; by using them you will economise your time, become richer in information than you could otherwise be, save much cost of book-buying, and want nothing in the way of solid learning, elegant composition, or amusement."

Chapters the nineteenth to the thirty-sixth and last, are very short, some of them containing in the original not more than a line or two. The following are some of the remaining sentences:

" Take care that you are better than you seem.

Envy is to probity as shadow to the flesh; so do not fear it.

* Be more ready to help friends than to hurt foes.

* Play for relaxation, not for money.

* Never lie, but circumvent.

* A liar either is a fool, or else he differs little from a thief and traitor.

* Take heed that you never weaken a true cause with falsehoods.

* To avoid falsehood wear truth as a habit, occupy yourself only on worthy things, and do not argue.

Have no horse, or a good one.   Never leave him loose upon the road.

* Do not spend upon animals more than a thousandth part of your income."

How much Jerome himself had spent on them we ought not to inquire: many of the precepts here cited have been manifestly warnings to his children against doing that which he himself had done.   Having ended his compendium of precepts, he appends to them the following

" CONCLUSION.

Observation of all these rules is not necessary to happiness, but he will be happy who observes them.

It is, however, much easier to know these things than to do them."

CHAPTER III.

THERE is no fault in the parent, said Cardan, that we
may not hope to see amended in the child. "What may
we not hope of children? We are old and they are
young; we sick, they sound; we weak, poor, despised,
they robust, rich, and of much esteem ; we bearing envy
and enmity, exiles, they grateful among friends and in
their home. There is nothing that the parent suffers of
which he may not hope that it will not be suffered by his
child[1]."

The first joy of the parent[2], said the philosopher, than
whom no father ever was more fond, the first joy of the
parent is when a child is to be born. Then let the mother
be well cared for, let her eat this and not eat that, and let

---

[1] De Utilitate ex Adversis Capiendâ (ed cit.), p. 248.
[2] Ibid. pp. 975—983, for the account of the six joys of parents in
their children, and for the succeeding details, where no other reference
has been appended.

her never lift her arms over her head. The second joy is
when the child appears. At once let it have some fine
honey, with a few grains of powdered hyacinth or emerald.
It may be weaned when the first teeth appear, but long
lactation is a good thing; Plotinus is said to have been
suckled until he was seven years old.

But it is when infants first begin to use their feet that
they first become delightful, and this is the third joy of
parents. As the joy increases, greater still becomes the
fear: for they are both one feeling. And as the fear increases, greater still becomes the solicitude and watchful
care. If they become frightened, let them at once be
steadied by the helping nurse." Surely we have here an
insight into Jerome's heart!

Let the young child, he further says, be shut out from
the sight or hearing of all ill. When he is about seven
years old, let him be taught elements of geometry to cultivate his memory and his imagination. With syllogisms
cultivate his reason. Let him be taught music, and especially to play upon stringed instruments; let him be in-
structed in arithmetic and painting, so that he may acquire a taste for them, but not be led to immerse himself
in such pursuits. He should be taught also a good handwriting, astrology, and when he is older, Greek and Latin[1].

[1] The preceding summary is taken from Cardan's Proxenata, seu

It is the fourth joy of parents to see the mind expand within the growing child. He should be placed under a master who is a married man[1], and who, if it can be afforded, should have charge only of a single family. The discipline should be severe. If children are to become well trained, and firm in virtue, Jerome, in one place, says that they should be entrusted to a severe and even cruel teacher, who would train them up in familiarity with blows, with hunger, toil, the strictest temperance, and subject them to a sharp despotism outside the doors of home[2]. That, however, he gives as one strong expression of a general faith in the importance of rough training for a boy. Elsewhere, in many passages, his creed assumes a milder aspect. Home discipline must not be too severe, the father must not be lost in the master; and it is one use, Jerome thinks, of a schoolmaster, that the necessary whippings may come only from his hand, and the hatred of the children fall only upon his head. He would encourage in boys the use of the most laborious games, and teach them to regard nothing as more atrocious than the use of dice, that render the rich man of the morning the beggar of the night.

---

de Prudentiâ Civili—Liber recens in lucem protractus vel e tenebris erutus.—Ludg. Bat.—Elzevir. 1627, p. 695.

[1] De Ut. ex Adv Cap. p. 981.
[2] Proxenata, pp. 691—694, for these and the next details.

Again, advises the philosopher, choose those men for masters who both know how to teach and really wish to do it[1]; for great are the weariness and labour that attend the task. Flatter not the pupils; above all, flatter not the teacher; do not flatter, but reward him solidly[2]. The expense of a good teacher is not light, but there is nothing better than to incur it if you would train up good youths, and sound. Children should be trained to take written notes of what is taught them, and to answer questions instantly. The manner of teaching should be pleasant, mixed with jests that must not pass the bounds of decency. All things may be taught merrily, says Jerome, except Greek and Latin[3]. And, after all, he inclines most to believe that kindness in the teacher will do more than force, and that in using force blows are to be avoided. For, he says, though by the aid of these the children may be made to learn, yet, the brain being filled with lacrymal matter, they are apt to turn out fools or rascals[4].

It is evident that he sways curiously between two opinions. By nature, Cardan was very kind, and shrank

[1] "Eos eligas qui sciant docere, et qui hoc velint: magnus enim labor, tædiumque majus." Loc. cit.

[2] "Absint denique blanditiæ omnes, et maxime ab educatoribus. Eorum loco perpetua sint benefacta."

[3] De Ut. Adv. Cap. p. 251. Proxenata, p. 695.

[4] Proxenata, p. 696. "Meliores sunt in universum blanditiæ vi, et in vi fugere oportet verbera: nam etsi perficiant ex his, ubi defecerit ætas, impleto cerebro lacrymali materiâ, stulti aut improbi evadunt."

from cruelty[1]; but his age had faith in the rod, and his reason succumbed to the opinions of Solomon. Fear, he knew to be wholesome, and hunger useful to a boy, by keeping down his passions and begetting sober ways; confinement, also, is good, but not unless coupled with low diet[2]. All these constraints were to be put upon a son in love, for he must be watched over with anxious tenderness; and, "whenever doubts arise," says the father, "we must risk all wealth, though it were of a hundred thousand Spanish crowns, rather than risk the safety of our children[3]."

When the son has attained the age of twenty comes the fifth joy of his parents, for then they may see him governing his own actions while he remains obedient to themselves. After the age of twenty, but not sooner, give daughters in marriage. When a child marries, the sixth joy of the parents is complete, and dear to them is the hope that they will see their race continued. Such thoughts disclose to us the vulnerable spot in the strong heart of the philosopher.

With these fatherly reflections some astute sayings are mingled. His own children he meant to train as students, but he advised fathers, who had sons to put out in the

---

[1] "A crudelitate fui semper alienus." Geniturarum Exemplar (ed. 1555), p. 87.
[2] Proxenata, p. 696.　　　　[3] Ibid. p. 691.

world, that those who were courteous and able should be put with princes, those who were active and laborious with rich merchants, those who were ingenious with great artificers, those who had ingratiating ways, and even tempers, with the sons of rich men, as fellow-pupils, with people hating their kindred and the like, with old men especially, and misers[1].

There were fatherly dreams also. One night, in the year 1547, Jerome, whose wife had not then long been dead, dreamt that there remained to him but a single son. In the morning he went out thinking of this, and was pursued by the nurse, who told him that his son, Aldo, was convulsed, that his eyes were distorted, and that she believed him to be dying. The vision of the night had warned him of necessity for energetic measures, if he would preserve his child. He ran home, therefore, without delay, to watch over him. He administered a powder composed of pearl and gems. It acted as an emetic. He administered another. It was kept upon the stomach. The boy slept, perspired, and in three days was well[2].

Another dream[3] was yet more curiously ominous, and really seemed like a shadow thrown before by the calamity, of which a portent had appeared at Gianbattista's birth. In the year 1550, Cardan being then at Milan,

---

[1] Proxenata, p. 694.   [2] De Vitâ Propriâ, cap. xxxvi.
[3] Synesiorum Somniorum Lib. p. 264.

one day in May, between the hours of three and five in
the afternoon, when he had dropped asleep, because it
happened to be Sunday, he dreamt that he had married
a second wife, and was reproaching Lucia with the fact
that his new wife was quieter than she had been.   Lucia,
who stood by, replied to him only with sad looks and
silence.   The new wife soon disappeared, Lucia remaining.—That phantom was the only second wife taken by
the philosopher, who held stepmothers in dread, and
frequently warned fathers against them, quoting even,
in one place, the harsh line—

Lurida terribiles miscent aconita novercæ.

He did not marry again in the flesh.—The second wife
of his dream having disappeared speedily, and Lucia remaining, whom he knew to be dead, she asked him for
five masses; then she touched him, willing to be touched,
and having touched him, fastened a label on his forehead,
which he bore unwillingly, because he feared its import,
and it soon fell off.   Then it appeared to him that his
mother came to them, and although she also was dead,
and had died, indeed, ten years before his wife, he thought
her to be living.   And lo! between the two dead women
stood his eldest son!   They had between them Gianbattista,
not as he then was, a youth of sixteen, but as he had been
when he was a child of seven years old.   Jerome feared
that Lucia would take her son away with her into the

shades, and he entreated, therefore, of Clara, whom he
thought to be alive, that she would hold him by the hand.
She did not. Then he turned to Lucia and besought her
not to touch the child. She bade him be of good cheer.
At last they departed, and the boy was forced away from
his father by one of the women over a small bridge.

Two or three facts may be here set down out of a large
mass of detail concerning household economy[1] contained
in Cardan's works. He gives minute directions for the
management of servants. Boys—who are to be preferred
—may be corrected by the stick, but when they have grown
up, they must not be struck or treated as if they were
slaves. A man's nurse is to be regarded with as much respect as a superior. A bad servant may be at once known
by his carrying of fire. There is nothing needing so much
care in a household as fire, nothing that will grow so immoderately when it is not wanted, or fall into ashes so
perversely when it is required. A servant who carries it
behind him is to be dismissed at once. If he hold it at
his side, occasionally looking at it as he goes, he is to be
regarded with distrust. The good servant carries fire in
a straight line before him. Great watch is to be kept over

---

[1] These domestic details are chiefly taken from chapters xxxviii.
and xxxix. of Proxenata (pp. 155—199), entitled respectively, Res
Domestica et ejus Conservatio: Œconomica distributio et Præcepta.
A few facts among them are extracted from the fourth book De Ut.
ex Adv. Cap.

servants. The practice usual in cardinals' houses of lock-
ing them in from the outside after dark, is inconvenient,
because, if one should be ill in the night, none can go out
for assistance, or in case of accident, escape is difficult.
Jerome recommends systems of dissimulation and espial,
by the adoption of which any man suspected of secret
ill-doing may be tricked into betrayal of himself. Has
anything been stolen, call the household together suddenly, and let each take a tremendous oath, involving
death upon himself within twelve months, if he be guilty.
Make a sign upon each man's breast, as he swears, in con-
secration of his vow; in so doing, the thief will be detected by the movement of his heart. It is well, if one
has three or four good servants, to let some one watch
while they are eating, not to stint them, but to prevent
theft. It is a common thing for servants, when their food
is given out, to simulate an extraordinary appetite, and,
after eating for two or three days a very large allowance,
to make good their claim, set by what is given to them
in excess, and sell it out of doors, or take it to their sweet-
hearts. The usual daily allowance for a servant is two
pounds of bread, four measures of flat wine, and for other
victual seventeen farthings.

Frangible vessels in a household must be left to princes,
but there is need to take care that the vessels used do not
corrupt the food that is put into them. There should be

two wine-cellars, and everything should be kept locked, there being to each lock a duplicate key. Jerome invented a lock that would betray any one who opened it by stealth, and also a contrivance, of which he gives a picture, for the more effectual securing of a bedroom door. Since it is very customary to steal linen at the wash, he recommends that it be marked very distinctly in one corner, and since that mark may by chance be obliterated, and a false accusation might thereupon be brought against the laundress, he advises the addition of two small and apparently accidental marks upon some other portion of each piece. The practice of marking linen probably was then not general, for Jerome gives a diagram in explanation of his meaning. There are—as it may be guessed from the character of these examples—few facts connected with the social history of Italy in the sixteenth century of which illustrations are not to be found in Cardan's works.

It was thought prudent by Jerome that men should keep not only their own papers, but all writings addressed to them, even sheets of empty words and begging letters. Use might arise. He had in his study four locked cupboards—one for literary papers, one for bills and papers touching upon money affairs, one for the courtesies and compliments of life, and one for waste.

Now, therefore, we have come back to the physician's

study, and there arises a fit opportunity for giving some additional account of the pen work done by him during these years of his professorship at Pavia.

Some of the works not yet specified as having been written between the years 1546 and 1552 may be mentioned briefly[1]. After his return from Genoa it has been said that he wrote the little book of Precepts, but on his return he had brought home with him a work that had been written on his journey to and fro, namely, four books on the Preservation of Health—first, in the case of young and healthy people ; secondly, in the case of old people ; thirdly, in the case of diseased people ; and, fourthly, in particular trades. Afterwards he wrote also ten books of explained problems upon all sorts of subjects, classified, and an Italian popular treatise meant to be both instructive and amusing, " De le Burle Calde."

Of the Commentaries on Hippocrates and Galen, it is enough to say that they form about an eighth part of the whole mass of Cardan's published writings, and would fill about twenty-five volumes of the magnitude of that now in the reader's hand. They are as much extinct as the megatherium, although the author himself rested his hope of fame chiefly upon them. In his day they were valuable, and they still have a kind of fossil value, but as they con-

---

[1] De Libris Propriis. Lib. ult. Opera, Tom. i. pp. 71, 72, is the authority until another reference occurs.

tain little matter that has any biographical interest, it is not requisite to speak more of them here.. It is enough to state their bulk. The work on Music was divided into five books. The first treated of general rules and principles; the second of ancient music, rhythms, hymns, choruses, and dances; the third of the music of the writer's own time; the fourth of the mode of composing songs and counterpoint; the fifth was on the structure and use of instruments, being an account of the various musical instruments then commonly in use. This, too, was at the time a valuable work, and in many respects original; it may be said also that there were one or two Italian tracts on music left among his writings. Of the works hitherto-undescribed, the one concerning which Cardan himself would most wish a biographer to speak fully, is that upon Metoposcopy[1], a kind of physiognomy invented by himself, or rather amplified so largely from a few existing hints, as to rank practically as a new invention. Melampodius had written upon the mysteries of warts upon the face; the study of them is a part of Metoposcopy, but that science is concerned chiefly with the lines—not the furrows—upon the forehead. There are fine lines upon.

[1] "Hieronimi Cardani Medici Mediolanensis Metoposcopia, Libris xiii. et octingentis faciei humanæ eiconibus complexa. Lutetia Parisiorum. Apud Thomam Jolly, 1658." That was the first published edition of the book; from it are taken the succeeding statements.

the forehead as there are upon the hand ; Jerome applied
Astrology in a minute and systematic way to the elucidation of them.

This important work was written at Milan in the year
1550. Until that year all had gone well in Pavia, but
then the professor's salary of two hundred and forty gold
crowns being again stopped by the troubles, he remained
in Milan[1]. In the succeeding year he resumed his lectures.
During the vacation year 1550, then, Cardan wrote
thirteen books of Metoposcopy, illustrated with a great
number of plates; but it was not until one hundred and
eight years afterward that they were first partially made
public by a bookseller in Paris.

A few words will explain the nature of the science. Of
lines upon the forehead, it is necessary for the metopos-
copist to observe the position, the direction, length, and
colour, and the observation is to be taken at a proper
time; that is to say, in the morning, when the subject of
it has not broken fast[2]. The forehead was mapped out by
Cardan as an astrologer, much as the head has been since
mapped out by Gall as a phrenologist. Seven lines drawn
at equal distances, one above another, horizontally across
the whole forehead, beginning close over the eyes, indicate
respectively the regions of the Moon, Mercury, Venus,
the Sun, Mars, Jupiter, Saturn. The signification of

[1] De Vitâ Propriâ, cap. iv.   [2] Metoposcopia, p. 6.

each planet is always the same, and forehead reading is
thus philosophically allied to the science of palmistry,
already discussed. Jerome presents head after head,
marked upon the forehead with every combination of
lines that had occurred to him, and under each writes the
character and fortune which, by his system, he discovers
such a combination to betray. Thus, if a woman has a
straight line running horizontally across the forehead, just
above the middle—in the region of Mars—she will be
fortunate in life, and get the better of her husband[1]; but
if the same line be crooked, it betokens that she is to die
by violence[2]. A waving line, like Hogarth's line of
beauty, over one eye—in the region of the Moon—assures
to the possessor good fortune upon water and in mer-
chandise; women with this line will be fortunate in
marriage and in all their undertakings[3]. It is also excellent for a man to have a perpendicular line running from
the nose half-way up to form a T, with a line not quite
horizontal, but running obliquely, so that it begins in the
region of Mars, on the left, and ends on the right hand,
in the region of the Sun. He will be brave, strenuous,
and noble—victor in all his undertakings; and a woman
with such lines will be generous and fortunate[4]. Con-
figurations that by no means flatter their possessor form

[1] Metoposcopia, p. 34.   [2] Ibid. p. 37.   [3] Ibid. p. 11.   [4] Ibid. p. 33.

the majority, but I cite none of these; let it be enough to add concerning warts, that a woman who has a wart at the root of the nose, between the eyes, is a most atrocious monster, guilty or capable of the worst crimes that a foul imagination can conceive, and that she is destined to a wretched end[1]. A woman with a wart upon her left cheek, a little to the left of where the dimple is or should be, will be eventually poisoned by her husband.

The published work is but a fragment of the entire treatise, which in other books was made to explain on the same principles the meaning of lines upon the knee, arm, navel, and foot, they being discussed and illustrated as minutely as the lines upon the forehead[2]. Such was the result obtained by building one false science on another. Astrology based upon astronomical observations—error based upon truth—had in it some tangible matter; but Metoposcopy based upon Astrology—error based upon error—is one of the most unsubstantial speculations that was ever built up by a scientific man.

The books on Subtilty occupied Cardan during three years at Pavia, and were, in part, first published at Nuremberg; shortly afterwards, more fully, at Paris, in the year 1551[3]. They acquired great popularity, and

---

[1] Metoposcopia, p. 188.

[2] De Libris Propriis (ed. 1557).

[3] "Hieronimi Cardani Medici Mediolanensis De Subtilitate, Libri xxi.

were soon reprinted at Lyons and at Basle. These books, we are told, were first suggested to their author in a dream, wherein it appeared to him that he saw a book in twenty-one parts, containing various treatises, and about the middle a little geometry, written in the most delightful style, not without some agreeable obscurity, wherein there were revealed all the secrets of the world about him. In it was made clear whatever was dark in all the sciences, and he derived such pleasure from the contemplation of this book, that when he was awake the delight abided with him, and he remembered even its form and plan.

There is something within us, he says, commenting on such a dream, something besides ourselves[1].

Then there arose in him a great desire to write such a book, though it was larger and more ambitious than any that he had yet attempted, and he could not hope to make a mortal work so perfect as the one of which he dreamed. He began then to write it, and for three years, not only was writing it by day among his other labours,

Ad Illustrem Principem Ferrandum Gonzagam Mediolanensis Provinciæ Præfectum. Parisiis. Apud Jacobum Dupuys, 1551." Dupuys had for his emblem and sign "The Samaritan Woman," that Scripture subject being chosen because it introduced the image of a well, and the idea of his own name. This is the edition cited in succeeding references.

[1] De Subtilitate, Lib. xviii. p. 299, for this account of the first conception of the work, compared with statements in De Lib. Prop. Lib. ult. Op. Tom. i. p. 71.

but also often reading it, and seeing it in dreams by night.
He saw in dreams its title, the number of the books, and
the order of their contents. He dreamt that it was
printed, and that there were two or three copies in town
—an admirable work, larger than his own, and by another
author. When it really was first printed at Nuremberg
he never dreamt of it again. The treatise on Subtilty
was followed up in the same vein by another upon the
Variety of Things[1]. Dreams had stimulated him to the
production of that treatise also. The object of both was
the same, and the two together very perfectly fulfilled his
purpose, which was to take a comprehensive and philosophical survey of nature—according, of course, to the
philosophy of his own century; to point out, as well as
he could, the subtle truths which underlie the wonderful
variety of things which fill the universe; to describe the
circle of the sciences, and (expressing each by those of its
facts which were most difficult of comprehension) to
apply his wit, or his acquired knowledge as a philosopher,
to the elucidation of them. With these works Jerome
took great pains; that on the Variety of Things cost him
more trouble than anything he ever undertook. It was
repeatedly rewritten and remodelled, and many parts of it
were transferred into the books on Subtilty. The books

---

[1] " De Varietate Rerum, eorumque Usu." It was published five or
six years later.

on Subtilty were so exact in their method as to exclude very many topics for which there was room found in the other treatise, which is to be taken as the sequel or appendix to it.[1]

These productions attained great popularity, and contain many isolated specimens of ingenuity, applications of knowledge to common life, as to the raising of sunken vessels, the cure of smoky chimneys, the manufacture of writing ink and such matters; for, as the reader may have perceived, Jerome's quick wit was ready to apply itself to any topic ranging between speculation on the Cosmos and the management of washerwomen. His generalisations upon nature do not, however, rise above the level of the knowledge current in his time among philosophers. He and his neighbours taught what they had learnt from Aristotle, Pliny, and Theophrastus; where they differed from such guides, it was not often to good purpose. The poor potter, Bernard Palissy, of whom the world then knew nothing, and who, at the crisis of his fate, was building his own furnace at Saintes with bleeding hands, while Cardan wrote upon subtilty at Pavia, Palissy knew more truth about those ways of nature that he had observed than had been perceived by Aristotle, or than was taught by all the learned of that century—I might almost add of the next. Cardan's fame as an author was

[1] De Libris Propriis. Lib. ult. Opera, Tom. i. p. 74.

at its height when his work on Subtilty appeared at Paris;
whatever he wrote was sought eagerly; it was in the
hands of all men, and was so much quoted and copied,
that he says: "I do not know whether I was most read
in my own works, or in the works of other people[1]." A
copy of it was obtained by Bernard Palissy[2], and another
fell into the hands of Julius Cæsar Scaliger. All the
world witnessed Scaliger's attack upon it, in a thick book,
weak, scholastic, trivial, of which, and of the resulting
controversy, we shall hereafter be compelled to speak.
Cardan himself, probably, never heard of Palissy, or saw
the few sentences written in nervous French, which not
only pointed out the incorrectness of his theory concerning mountains and the structure of the globe, but for the
first time promulgated, upon such subjects, true and philosophical opinions.

In the work on Subtilty, Cardan at the outset defines
subtle things as those which are sensible by the senses, or
intelligible by the intellect, but with difficulty comprehended[3]. Then he treats of matter which he supposed—as
we suppose now—to be composed of ultimate parts, minute,

---

[1] "Cum primum in publicum prodiere, statim in omnium manibus
esse cœperunt· et tot eruditorum testimonio comprobari: ut nesciam
an in propriis an in alienis libris nostra magis leguntur." De Lib.
Prop. p. 79.

[2] See the Life of Bernard Palissy of Saintes, vol. ii. pp. 173, et seq.

[3] "Est Subtilitas ratio quædam, qua sensibilia a sensibus intelligi-
bilia ab intellectu difficile comprehenduntur."

hard and eternal, out of which things have been created according to their form and nature. In their creation the Divine Being has produced, he says, the best combination that was possible of an existing material, eternal like Himself[1]. Having discussed matter and first principles, cold and heat, dryness and moisture, the book passes on to the description of a few mechanical contrivances—of a wonderful lamp, pumps, siphons, Jerome's contrivance for the raising of sunk vessels, levers, scales. He teaches that there are but three elements, air, earth, and water ; fire he excludes, because nothing is produced out of it. He treats further of fire, of lightning, of artillery, shows how to know those cannons that will burst, as one burst at Pavia during the All-Saints' procession, and destroyed six men. He endeavours to explain why fire can be struck out of a stone, why a string will not burn when it is tied round an egg, why heat breeds putridity, and so forth. He treats of air, of the cause of plague, of tides, of the origin of rivers; they have, he says, many sources, but the chief is air converted into water. The true theory of springs, as of most other processes of nature, was unknown to him. Its first discoverer was Bernard Palissy.

Of the earth, in that part of Cardan's work to which

[1] Compare the statements in book i. with the dictum in book xi. "Divina igitur sapientia in unoquoque fecit optimum quod ex tali materiâ poterat excogitari."

Palissy directly alludes,. we find it stated, that "the earth is entirely stable, round and in the middle. of the world: these things are demonstrated. by mathematics. For the whole earth is no more able to stir from its place than the heavens are able to stand still[1]." And of mountains, he says, " their origin is threefold. Either the earth swells, being agitated by frequent movements, and gives birth to mountains as to pimples rising from a body, which is the case with a mountain called La Nova, near the lake Averno, in the Terra di Lavoro ; or their soil is heaped up by the winds, which is often the case in Africa.; or, what is most natural and common, they are the stones left after the material of the earth has been washed away by running water, for the water of a stream descends into the valley, and the stony mountain itself rises from the valley, whence it happens that all mountains are more or less composed of stones. Their height above the surrounding soil is because the fields are daily eaten down by the rains, and the earth itself decays ; but stones, besides that they do not decay, also for the most part grow, as we shall show hereafter[2]." The notion that earth taken from stone leaves mountain, that a Salisbury Plain would be a Mount Salisbury, if all the soil were taken out of it, and only the

[1] De Subtil. Lib ii p. 60. "Terra toto stabilis est, rotunda atque medio mundi: hæc autem a mathematicis demonstrantur. Nec enim plus tota terra loco moveri potest, quam cœlum quiescere."
[2] Ibid. p. 59.

stones left, was so far curious, but as it was the orthodox
belief, it passed into Cardan's mind, with other science of
the same kind, as learning that was not to be disturbed.
He had no taste at all for revolutionary work, except in
medicine.   In other sciences he took all that was taught
with a few quiet modifications, and that formed the body
of his learning.   No man of his time knew so much that
had been taught about so many things.   From the points
at which his learning ended in each separate direction he
endeavoured to go on.   In mathematics he was left with
his face turned in the right direction, and he made a
great and real advance; in the natural sciences he was
placed by his learning commonly with his face turned in
the wrong direction, and he went on into Metoposcopy
and other nonsense.

.. The philosopher having discussed the subject of mountains, proceeded to consider why the earth is higher than the
sea.   There were seven reasons then current, one of them
being that the earth was lifted and held up by the stars.
Of the heavens, and the stars, and light, the work next
treated, giving a right reason for the twinkling of the
fixed stars, inquiring into the composition of stars, the
soul of the universe, comets; rainbows, parhelia; discussing burning glasses, mirrors in which future or distant
objects are revealed, shadows; inquiring why it is that,
when we travel, moon and stars seem to go with us.   The

book upon Light is, on the whole, more than usually accurate in its philosophy. Jerome's father had, it may be remembered, studied the subject, and been the first editor of Archbishop Peckham's Perspective[1]. There was a good deal of correct knowledge then afloat concerning optical laws, and by its aid Jerome was ready to correct some popular errors, such as the belief that trees emit sweet odour when the end of a rainbow rests upon them. He knew that rainbows belong to the eye, and have not out of the eye a substantial, separate existence.

The treatise next passes to substances compounded of the elements, to metallic substances, earths and gems, inquiring, among other things, why amber attracts straws and other light substances, of course without any idea of electricity. He attributes the phenomenon to the fatness and warmth inherent in the constitution of the amber. He then, in his sixth book, treats in detail of the seven metals, and in the seventh book of stones and gems, pointing out how to tell those that are false, and using some of the knowledge that he formerly obtained from his friend the jeweller, Guerini. He treats also of the properties of gems, and describes three remarkable agates in his own possession. One of them, which he had found to display great virtue in promoting sleep, had incorporated in its substance a profile nearly resembling that of the Emperor

[1] Vol. i. p. 4.

Galba[1]. He gives a fac-simile thereof, which is here
reproduced.

The eighth book is botanical, the ninth treats of the
animals generated from putridity, and of their propaga-
tion; how from the putrid matter of oxen we get bees,
from that of horses wasps, and hornets out of mules.   In
this book, treating of the power of warmth as a principle
of life, Cardan quotes Joannes Leo, who related that in
Egypt the executioner cuts criminals in half, and that the
upper half being then placed upon a hearth, over which
quicklime has been scattered, will understand and answer
questions for a quarter of an hour.   The next book treats
of perfect animals, and in this is contained, under the head
of sheep, the praise of English wool, not less renowned
than was the Milesian in the days of Virgil. " Now,
therefore," says Jerome, " is Britannia famous for her
wool.   No wonder, when there is no poisonous animal in
the country, and it is infested now only by the fox, and by

[1] The figure was added in a subsequent edition, and recopied into
the works.   Tom. iii. p. 466.

the wolf formerly; but even the wolves now being exterminated, all the flocks wander in safety." Then he goes on to state how the sheep in England slake their thirst upon the dews of heaven, and are deprived of every other kind of drink, because the waters of the land are deadly to them[1]. He adds that the moist grass of England is quite full of worms, and assigns that as the reason why the air is full of crows that feed upon them. There are no serpents on account of " the immense cold."

From other animals the philosopher rises in the next book to man and the creation of him. There are three kinds of men, he says—the divine, which neither deceive nor are deceived; the human, which deceive but are not deceived ; and the belluine, which cannot deceive but are deceived. Men who deceive and are deceived belong to a compound sort ; they are part human and part belluine. The same book treats of man's religion, of his form, shows how, if you would have black-eyed children, you must entrust them to a black-eyed nurse; treats of education, and the proportion between different parts of the human body. The nature and temper of man is discussed in the next book. Cardan inquires why chil-

---

[1] De Subtilitate. Lib. x. p. 192. " Ergo nunc Britannia inclyta vellere est. Nec mirum cum nullum animal venenatum mittat, imo nec infestum præter vulpem olim et lupum, nunc vero exterminatis etiam lupis, tutò pecus vagatur; rore cœli sitim sedant greges, ab omni alio potu arcentur, quod aquæ ibi ovibus sint exitiales," &c.

dren resemble parents, why the drinking of potable gold procures long life, touches upon the admiration of beauty among other things, and in the next book—upon the Senses—proceeds to inquire what beauty is, and for what reason we delight in it. The sense of hearing suggests a discussion upon hydraulic organs and upon music. The sense of smell suggests the question, why is it that men who smell well rarely are far-sighted and are more ingenious than other people? In this chapter is also explained why people who have sharp eyes are slow to fall in love, and by a just connexion with the main subject there is also room found for an inquiry why thorns grow with roses, and for instructions how to catch birds and fish, and how to keep flies from horses.

From the senses of man the theme rises to a consideration of his soul and intellect, to a survey of his wisdom and his passions and his faculties, including an artificial and a passive memory. Here we meet with a few shrewd definitions, as that Bashfulness consists of Hope and Fear; —Envy is a thin Hate;—Suspicion is a little Fear, just as Audacity is a vast Hope[1]. It needs not to be said that through all former chapters of the work good sayings have been scattered, as for instance, that the shadow of princes is the cap of fools, a proverb taken, perhaps, from the ver-

[1] "Verecundia ex spe constat et timore."—"Invidia vero odium tenue est."—' Suspitio vero timor est parvus, velut audacia spes maxima." De Subtil. p. 246.

nacular, and that it needs more courage and impudence to
deny a falsehood attested by a great number of witnesses,
than to sustain a truth against which so many witnesses
declare that it is false,—a very nice but very just distinction.

The fifteenth book upon Subtilty discusses miscellaneous
curiosities. The sixteenth is upon Sciences, especially
geometry and music, and includes an exposition of the
signs of the weather. The next book is upon Arts and
Mechanical Contrivances, in which book are explained a
method of writing in cipher, a method of fortifying a
town, and a method of telegraphing and of talking by the
use of torches. It contains, also, scientific expositions
upon pulleys, wheels, and screws. The next book is upon
Marvels; one of them is rope-dancing. Here occurs the
consideration why is it that the eye of a black dog held
in a man's hand hinders all dogs in his neighbourhood
from barking, and how useful such an eye must be to
thieves. Here is a place also for the narration of dreams.
The nineteenth book is upon Demons, and their truth;
charms are discussed, and one for headache given, which
the author has found useful. There is a special inquiry
into the Telchinnes, subterranean demons, who vexed
treasure-hunters. The next book treats of Angels and
Intelligences,—giving their names. The twenty-first and
last, of the Universe and the Divine Being, who is in-

voked thus by the philosopher in his concluding sentences: " Thou, therefore, Most High God, from whom all good things flow, by whose nod all things are moved, whose empire has no bounds, infinite clearness, who alone affordest the true light, complete in Thyself, known to Thyself only, whose wisdom exceeds all thought, one and incomparable, out of whom there is nothing, who hast led me as a worm of the earth under the shadow of knowledge, to whom I owe all truth that is here written : pardon in me the errors which my ambition and my rashness and my haste have bred, and by illuminating my mind out of Thine unwearied goodness, guide me to better things. And though Thou needest nothing, and I can add nothing to the voice of Heaven, and all heavenly powers, the sea and earth, and all the corners of the world[1], I pay to Thee incessant thanks for the innumerable benefits that I have received at Thy hands."

The work described in this brief summary was in its

---

[1] " Tu igitur altissime Deus, a quo omnia bona profluunt, cujus nutu cuncta moventur, cujus imperium nullis finitur limitibus, claritas infinita, qui solus lumen verum præbes, solus vere æternus, totus in teipso, tibi soli notus, cujus sapientia omnem excedit cogitationem, unus atque incomparabilis, extra quem nihil est, qui me velut terræ vermem in umbra scientiæ direxisti, cui quicquid veri hic scriptum est debeo: errores, ambitio mea, temeritasque ac celeritas pepererunt, ignosce mihi, mentemque meam illuminando, pro tuâ indefessâ liberalitate ad meliora dirige. Cum vero tu nullis indigeas, nec quicquam addere possim, quod cæli, cælorumque potestates, quod maria terraque faciunt, universæque ipsius mundi partes, gratias perpetuas pro innumeris erga me beneficis ago."

time regarded as a monument of wisdom, and being very
entertaining, was extremely popular. Jerome himself did
not count it among the works upon which he relied most
for immortality; it was of a kind, he said, to please the
public, but there were other of his writings more likely to
satisfy the wise[1]. These Twenty-one Books upon Subtilty
were dedicated by the prudent citizen to the governor of
his province, Ferrante Gonzaga, whom he praises most for
a late negotiation which he had conducted, and which had
justified some hope of peace.

The hope was not fulfilled. In 1550, Jerome, as before said, stayed away from Pavia because the university
was unable to pay his salary. In the succeeding year he
again lectured there, but a cat of the most placid character[2]
having been left at home one day, dragged out upon the
tiles some of his written lectures (written after delivery,
he taught extemporaneously[3]), and tore them upon the
house-top. The book upon Fate, which lay more ready
to her claws, she had not touched. Who can doubt what
followed ? At the end of the year, quite unexpectedly,
his lectures ceased, and his professorship was not assumed
again for eight whole years.

His reason for retirement[4] was again the turmoil in the

---

[1] De Libris Propr. Lib. ult. Tom. i. p. 72.

[2] De Vitâ Propriâ, cap. xxxvii., for this story of the cat's conduct
and its consequences.   [3] Ibid. cap. xii.

[4] De Libris Propriis. Lib. ult. Op. Tom. i. p 81. "Gallo rege

district.. The King of France was pressing with war; Italy, Switzerland, and Turkey were convulsed; and while all men were awaiting ruin, he abandoned his professorship, thinking it better so to do, and safer. It proved to be well that he did so, for Pavia was in the midst of perils; there were no salaries paid in the year after he left, and moreover, there died out of the senate two presidents—one of them the Cardinal Sfondrato—who had been friendly to Cardan, and who had been accustomed to watch over his interests.

Of the Cardinal Sfondrato, to whose friendship Jerome had been much indebted for the recognition that he ob- tained from the Milanese physicians, and who had assisted in securing for him the professorship at Pavia, Jerome has left a sketch in an essay on his horoscope[1]. The substance of it is here stated. He had begun life as a private man, had been professor of civil law in Pavia at the age of thirty, and after a few years had been called to the senate by Francisco Sforza, Duke of Milan. He had married, and become the father of two eight-month boys, whose lives were preserved with difficulty. It was by care of one of them that Cardan earned his friendship. They did, after all, together with four girls, survive their father. (One of the boys became a pope.) When

urgente commota est Italia, Elvetii, Turcæ Omnibus ergo ad interitum spectantibus deserui legendi munus, melius esse ratus, quod etiam tutius esset." The other considerations connected with the same sub- ject form the continuation of the passage.

[1] Geniturarum Exemplar, p. 50.

Charles V. became Duke of Milan, Sfondrato had
been made a member of the secret council. In the
year 1541 his wife died, and he was appointed, as we
have seen, governor of Sienna. There he remained
eighteen months, and obtained from the townspeople a
good-will that had not been earned by others in the same
position. In the year 1544 he went to Rome and was
ordained a bishop; directly afterwards he became archbishop and cardinal. When Pope Paul III. died at the
end of the year 1549, he was almost elected his successor.
He was then fifty-six years old, and he died in the summer
following of a weary disease, that some, of course, attributed
to poison. He was a big man, tall, frank-looking, fat and
rubicund, genial, elegant, joyously disposed, not without
wisdom and erudition. In business he was cautious, prudent, prompt and successful. He delighted in gambling,
and that, too, for large sums. He was passionate and
somewhat prejudiced. He believed in fate, and in the
Sortes Virgilianæ, of which he testified that he had often
found them true.

In addition to the motives that have been assigned,
Cardan had other reasons for retiring from his post at
Pavia. He considered that he had attained his end
as a professor; he had recalled his mind thoroughly
to the pursuit of medicine, had written a great body
of professional matter, and had obtained fame as a
physician. He had also completed the university edu-

cation of his eldest son, and of the young relative, Gaspar, who studied with him. Gaspar having obtained his degree, finally went to Rome and practised physic. Gian Battista had only to go through the requisite formalities which should obtain for him admission into the profession. Cardan, therefore, by retiring from a profitless and dangerous post, hoped to indulge himself with what seemed to be at that stage of his life the most desirable thing—literary leisure, and to increase and yet more firmly to establish his great fame by assiduity in writing.

With these hopes, Jerome, at the end of the year 1551, abandoned his professorship in Pavia and went to Milan, not intending to remain there. It is probable that he was coward enough to desire a quiet and safe place in which to enjoy the literary leisure upon which his heart was set, and as the King of France sent war out into other countries, there was chance that he had none at home. There might be peace for him in Paris, and, perhaps, prosperity. He may have desired at any rate to go to France and try the ground there. I do not know from his own telling that he was actuated by these motives. He himself says no more than that, after quitting Pavia, he had meant to go to France, even if he had no business to take him thither[1]. Having that design, then, he went back to Milan.

[1] De Vitâ Propriâ, p. 18.

CHAPTER IV.

CARDAN'S JOURNEY TO PARIS.

BY the end of November in the same year a letter[1] reached Cardan through the hands of merchants. It had been about two months upon the road, the messenger by whom it was despatched having been hindered in his progress through a country thoroughly confused with war. This epistle contained matters of importance, and came from a brother physician, who talked in a most edifying way the science of his time, and seems to have been a perfect master of the ponderous scholastic style. I have not space here, and no reader would have patience, for the whole of Dr. Cassanate's composition; shortened, however, by the omission of a few masses of surplus verbiage, it must now form a portion of this narrative. How great would be the consternation of an active literary man

---

[1] De Libris Propriis (1557). The letter itself is given in the same work, and extends there from page 159 to page 175.

or hard-working physician in our own day who should receive a business letter such as this!

"Health to you.

"Since it is important in all new conjunctions of events, most learned man, to understand how they arose, and by what recommendation friendship comes to us from strangers, I think it right to give the reason of this letter to you from me, a man unknown to you indeed, but by whom you have been diligently studied.

"To many the source of the most delightful friendship is a certain sympathy and a similitude of disposition. To others, that friendship seems to contribute not little to the pleasantness of life, which is induced by a similitude of studies. For nothing excites more desire than likeness to oneself, and there is no claimant more ready than nature. Nevertheless it happens easily that the web of friendship of this kind is broken. Especially when together with education, language, and commerce, customs also vary, similarity of study may then easily be changed into a cause of difference. I think with Cicero, that the best basis of friendship is a faith in character; because it is the property of virtue to conciliate to itself the minds of men, and to unite them in its service and in friendship with each other: For in her lies the fitness of things, in her lies their stability, in her is constancy, and when she goes abroad, and extends her light, and has seen and recognised the same light in another, she enters to it, and in turn receives into herself that which was in another, whence there arises between them love or friendship. Whence we see that there is nothing more to be loved than virtue, nothing that more attracts men into friendship.

So that on account of their virtue and probity we even love those whom we have not seen, and so great is virtue's force, that (what is more) we even love her in an enemy.

"Wherefore, by as much as we despise those men who are useless to themselves or others, in whom there is no work, no industry, no care,—so it is our common usage in life to extol to the skies with fame and good-will those who have excelled in benefiting their own race. We elevate and bring our highest praise to those in whom we think that we perceive excellent and rare virtues, those by whom life is evidently spent on honourable and great matters, and in doing service to the State, whose virtue and whose studies are fruitful to others, but to themselves laborious, or dangerous, or by them freely given. In which respect you have as much surpassed the multitude by your very great fame, and not less great genius and erudition, as you have bound to yourself students of many arts by your unwearied zeal in writing. So much even he well knows who has admired but the least of your many monuments and labours, for I estimate the lion by his claw.

"I, out of the so numerous and important writings, the result of immense labour, of which you have edited a catalogue in your book 'De Libris Propriis,' have seen only the Books on Wisdom and upon Subtilty, with those upon Consolation, which were published with the books on Wisdom. The last were given to me in the year 1549, when I practised medicine at Toulouse, by a legal friend, very studious of the humaner letters; but the books on Subtilty were given to me by the same friend in this year 1551, in Scotland, where I am now practising. These alone out of so many are in my possession; from the reading of which there has proceeded so great a desire for the reading of the rest, that if I did not

hope some day, and that soon, to enjoy them, the want of
them would be felt far more seriously than it is.   For while
I think it worthy of the highest praise and glory to write
books that are worth reading and useful to the human race,
it is my utmost pleasure to enjoy the fruit of the vigils and
the literary toils of others; so that when I regret having
been without your works, and grieve at it and think it my
hurt, I console myself with the expectation of hereafter
reading them.   For your copiousness in writing, your
variety, your multifarious reading, your observation of things,
the ornate gravity of your sentences, your pure and chaste
method of narration, make it necessary that whoever com-
prehends the unfathomable depths of memory, the most
practised industry and the extreme acuteness of judgment in
your existing monuments, will praise you, honour you, and
venerate you.

   " But that which has delighted me most is, that in reading
your fifth book upon Wisdom, I saw that you cited just experience, when, among other things, you wrote as follows :—
' But what if the art itself yield not a livelihood, and there be
no passage to another calling, a new invention has to be
struck out (for the novelty of a thing always begets favour)
that in some particular shall be of certain use.   When we
ourselves long laboured in this city against envy, and our income was not so much as our expenses (so much harder is
the condition of a merit that is seen than of one that is unknown, and there is no prophet of honour in his own country),
we made many attempts to discover new things in our art ;
for away from the art no step could be made.   At length I
thought out the cure of Phthisis, which they call Phthoe,
despaired of for ages, and I healed many, who now survive.
I discovered, also, the method of curing aqua intercutis,

healing many. But reason should lead to invention, and experiment is a master and a cause of work in others. In experimenting, if there be danger, it should be attempted gently, and by degrees.' Now, by these two discoveries of yours, you have bound men to you not less than you have enriched our science. For if it is not a light thing to adorn an art with illustrious and magnificent works, and to add to it, with the course of time, increments of knowledge to which no wit or patience of those living before had penetrated, how much more in the art which is above all, and which is destined for the safety of the whole human race, is it of immense utility to fetch out something abstruse and recondite, remote from the vulgar method of philosophising and from popular ideas. Not a few are deceived in believing that the art of healing, discovered by the labour of the ancients, has been brought to perfection, and can make no further progress. They would have all posterity marching, as it were, in one file, and stepping in the same track, from which it shall be nefarious to diverge (as they say) by a nail's breadth.

      *   *   *   *   *

So, as I said to M. Fernel, the famous physician of Paris, they err as much who contend that all things have been thoroughly investigated and comprehended by the ancients, as they who deny to them the first knowledge of things, and reject them as old-fashioned in their practice. But perhaps I am more prolix than is needful in a letter destined to another kind of business. I, to return to the matter in hand, have felt myself so addicted and bound to you by your erudition, virtue, and wisdom, in the use of which you do not cease with assiduity of study to make yourself of value to all students of letters, that for a long time I have desired nothing more than that there might be offered to me an occasion of showing how grateful my mind is towards you. And this has happened, although later than I could have wished ; but now that a happy opportunity has offered itself, permit me not lightly to felicitate yourself and me. Myself on account of my reverend lord archbishop and patron's expectation of and petition for health from your aid only, as the one Æsculapius able to assist, and therefore, on account of the mutual, and by me, much desired enjoyment of intercourse between us to which I can now look forward. You, however, I felicitate, because this affair, I hope, will be of no little use to you, and will bring you a great increase of praise, the love of which (when glory follows virtue) is innate in generous minds as a spur always to greater deeds. Wherefore I am far from thinking that this matter will be unwelcome to you, I believe rather that it will meet your best desires. For of things to be desired, as Cicero testifies in his second on Invention, there are three kinds."—[Here the writer again gets into deep water.] * * *

" These three, admirable man, you may possess altogether in the present case without trouble, and with the greatest pleasure. For through this there will be a celebration of your virtue and wisdom even at the uttermost parts of the earth ; through this there will be no mean addition to your household means ; through this you will acquire the friendship of good men, and rise into incredible esteem. By which considerations it is fair to suppose that you will be moved—especially as we all seek the useful and grasp at it—nor can we possibly do otherwise, as is observed in Cicero's Offices. For who is he who shuns what is useful, or who would not prefer diligently to pursue it, most particularly when it is joined with dignities and honour?

" But to what all this tends, now hear. The brother of

the most humane prince, the regent of the kingdom of Scotland, the most illustrious Archbishop of St. Andrew's, whose physician I have been for about four years, was vexed, at the age of about thirty, ten years ago, with a periodic asthma." [The medical account of the case I must abbreviate a little, but the old theory of periodic asthma is too curious to be omitted.] "The first accession of the disease was a distillation from the brains into the lungs, associated at that time with hoarseness, which, by the help of the physician then present, was for the time removed, but there was a bad temperature left in the brain; it was too cold and moist, so that an unnatural matter was collected in the head, which was retained there for a short time, because the brain could neither properly digest its own aliment (especially since it was nourished with pituitous blood), nor had it power to resolve the vapours brought into it from the parts below. Things being left in this state by a preceding attack, it happens that, whenever the whole body is filled with a matter which as a substance vapour or quality, invades the brain, there is a fresh accession of the complaint, that is to say, there is a flow of the same humour down into the lungs. This periodical distillation, the signs of which I will pass over, is best known by the fact that it happens from an obvious cause, suddenly, to the patient apparently in good health, except for the signs accompanying properly the fever and the actual distillation. And this accession agrees almost accurately with the conjunctions and oppositions of the moon. Medical aid having been slighted, or at least not assiduously sought (so does the strength of the disease seem able, in course of time, to destroy the strength of the body), there is now danger, especially as there is now a constant flow, and most at night. The lungs are thus not slightly weakened.

The matter flowing down into the lungs is serous, limpid, watery, pituitous, and sweet or insipid. If it were acrid or salt, the lungs would ulcerate, and the disease would become tabes, or what the Greeks called phthoe. Thin at first and in small quantity it is expelled by violent coughing. Stirred by the cough, broken and divided by the expired air, the matter flows back into the lungs, afterwards digested and somewhat thickened—half thick, as it were—it is expectorated copiously by stronger efforts of the chest with gentler coughing. Being again reduced to a small quantity, if it is thick and got rid of slowly it is expelled only by the most violent efforts, because the too tenacious humour adheres to the lungs and does not even reach the throat. The consequence is dyspnœa, or difficulty of breathing, with stertor. Afterwards, when the obstruction has been overcome by which the respiration is made unusually great and vehement, and frequent (which is the cause of increased heat), there is a hot and burning breath out of the mouth, which causes the air to be rarer than is proper for health, and insufficient even when the chest is very much dilated. The arterial pulse is soft, small at the beginning of the attack, frequent and irregular, showing the constriction and pain in the respiratory parts, and the increase of the body's heat, for the air drawn in, on account of the narrowness of the road left for it, is not enough to cool the heart and lungs." [This is the main theory; then are added a few medical signs, and the writer states that the archbishop is so much reduced as to desire for himself some strong help against so serious a disorder.]

" You have here the whole theory of the disease, which hitherto I have laboured to assuage, and hinder from passing into worse. What remedies, what labour and industry I

have used, you shall hereafter learn, if it please Heaven.
For I have neither expected at any time his complete cure,
nor do I think that the most effectual help will ever bring it
about, partly because of the moistness of the air (which par-
takes somewhat of the saltness of the sea) and the strength
of the winds, partly also because of his distractions with incessant labours in state affairs, which hang wholly upon him,
as it were upon a thread; he is so worried night and day,
that in the midst of his vast responsibilities he can hardly
breathe, still less pay that attention to the care of health
which our good Hippocrates highly desired at the hands of
sick men and others, as well as of physicians.

"Now, however, leaving the great tumult of his cares and
undertakings, he is about to visit Paris—a city flourishing as
the seat of studies of all kinds, and especially of medicine—
entirely bent upon attending to his health. But since he
has frequently been informed by me of your eminent virtue,
your singular erudition and most abundant experience as a
practising physician, the archbishop most eagerly desires
your help as the most valid protection that he can obtain
against his malady (which faith is seen to conduce not a little
to recovery); so that he is persuaded that he will be healed
by you as if by the hands of a favouring Apollo. Therefore
he desires in this affair not only to receive your advice, but
he is so eager to profit by your presence with him, that he
would spare no cost that would attract you before some fixed
day to Paris. Therefore contrive, I beseech you, that
Lutetia (Paris), the nurse of so many great philosophers,
may behold you at least once, that you may be surrounded
and admired by so many scholars; that they may receive,
cherish, and venerate with fresh honour a man whose
writings have already had from them a worshipful reception.
For whatever time you wish to occupy upon the journey,

whatever escort you would have, or charge you would be at, take the necessary money from the hands of him who will deliver this. If the season and your health permit, and you are willing, means shall not be wanting to enable you to travel post; and if there be need of it, you shall have the safe conduct of the princes on the road, and the public faith of each country pledged to you.

"This one thing, lastly, be assured of, that you deal here with a most humane and liberal prince, from whom you may fairly expect not less advantage to yourself than he is expecting, on the other hand, from you. He expects gain to his body; you will receive gain of fortune: due not to fortune but rather the just reward of your labour, and of your singular learning and virtue.

"But if the season, your home studies, household, press of time, business, or the tie of friends, or anything else, make it impossible for you to go so far as Paris, at least travel to Lyons, which is less distant from you, and a famous town. This we entreat of you to do out of your humanity; we wish it for honour's sake, and for the sake of no mean good; for by so doing you will not only be serviceable to one most excellent prince, but rather put an entire state and kingdom under obligation to you. If, again (as we do not expect), you concede neither of our requests, then I beseech that you will send us, at full, your advice as to the opposing of the disease I have described (that is ready to pass over into Phthisis, or worse, which Heaven forbid), omitting nothing that you think may be done for its subjection, and take what you think proper as a fee. That all this will be done by you in good faith I do not doubt. * * *

"But now as I write the last words of this letter, there occur to me two passages published in your eighteenth book on Subtilty, which is concerning marvels. In one of them you bear testimony to a remarkable means of causing men to become fat; in the other, you assert that you have discovered a wonderful mode of relieving those who are without breath, or breathing painfully. We have succeeded in attaining neither of these ends, though either invention would be in no small degree convenient to our purpose. As for ocimum[1] and its qualities, Dioscorides, Galen, and Pliny, differ so much that I can in no way reconcile their statements.

" But enough has been said.

" Finally, the most illustrious lord archbishop has commanded me to fix the month of January as that in which, on some appointed day, you may be seen in Paris. I fear, indeed, that the winter may oppose some delay against your coming, or deprive you of the willingness tó come. But need, according to the precept of Hippocrates, begets urgency. Farewell, most excellent man. May the Lord of all men long preserve you, and increase daily your genius as a writer, so that you may long aid the study of medicine, and all that is good in literature, in that way earning an immortal name.— Edinburgh, the 28th of September, 1551. WILLIAM CASSANATE, Physician.''

Cardan replied to this letter that he would go to Paris —that, indeed, precisely suited with his previous humour, —and he required two hundred crowns as travelling expenses for the journey thither, which were paid to him in Milan.

The lord archbishop, on behalf of whom this letter had been sent by his body physician, William Cassanate,

---

[1] Ocimum has not been identified with any modern herb. Pliny states that it grew best when sown with cursing and railing.

was John Hamilton, Archbishop of St. Andrew's,—called
in Cardan's Latin Amultho;—Hamilton who was hung.
Cassanate[1] was the son of a Spaniard, settled at Besançon
in Burgundy.   He was fourteen years younger than
Jerome, having been born at six o'clock in the morning
of the 5th of October, 1515,—one is exact in dates
when there is a horoscope to draw upon for information.
Concerning this Cassanate, who has left behind him
nothing by which he is retained, however slightly, in the
memory of scholars or physicians, it would, indeed, be
difficult to give any particulars, if Cardan had not discussed his character in calculating his nativity[2].   He was
the only survivor of six brothers; a man very careful of
his own interests, time-serving, and most happy in the
atmosphere of courts.   He could change opinions as the
exigencies of the day required, and profit by political
confusion.   He had a decided taste for the admixture of
court business, as a meddler or negotiator, with his professional cares, and in that way may have rendered himself, by the use of a little tact, very agreeable to the
archbishop.   He was fond of the external good things

1 Cardan spells the name Casanate, but the usual spelling is adopted
in the text.   There have been several obscure scholars of this name.

2 His is one of the twelve horoscopes which illustrated Cardan's
commentaries on Ptolemy.   It is included in a little book entitled
"Hier. Card. Medic. Mediol. Geniturarum Exemplar.   Præterea et
multa quæ ad Interrogationes et electiones pertinent superaddita.   Et
examplum eclipsis quam consecuta est gravissima pestis. Lugduni.
Apud Theobaldum Paganum" (who has a Pagan or Saracen on horseback for his emblem), "1555."

of life; delighted in elegant company, in gaiety, and pleasure; and spent much of the great wealth that he knew how to scrape together, in expensive entertainments. He had a wife and one daughter when Jerome knew him, but the stars were promising him a considerable family. Cassanate had left his father, who was still living at Besançon, to settle in Scotland—a land rarely accepted as a home by strangers from the south; and there he had been, when he wrote to Cardan, attached for four years to the household of Archbishop Hamilton. He was then thirty-six years old.

The archbishop, who was so distracted by incessant labours in state affairs " that he could scarcely find time to breathe," since he is to become now a foremost person in this narrative, must be recalled in a few words to the memory. He was an actor in some of the most familiar scenes of our domestic history—the troubles that surrounded Mary Queen of Scots. Mary, who herself became one of Cardan's patrons, was only nine years old when that famous physician set out to meet John Hamilton at Paris.

It will be remembered that Mary's father, James V, having made no provision for the administration of his kingdom, left the office of regent open to be battled for after his death. The Roman Catholic party advocated the claim of Cardinal Beatoun to that dignity; to him there was opposed the brother of our archbishop, James Hamilton, Earl of Arran, who was next heir to the

queen. James Hamilton was declared regent by the
choice of Scotland. Mary was not many months old
when Henry VIII. demanded her as the future wife of
his son Edward, with a view to the extension of his own
rule over the Scots. The new regent agreed, on behalf
of Scotland, that the queen, when she became ten years
old, should be sent to London, and that six persons of the
first rank should at once go to the English court, and there
reside as hostages. This happened in 1543. Cardinal
Beatoun then seeing his opportunity, made the best of it,
dilated on the regent's weakness, and stirred up a host of
passions. The Scottish barons declared against the alliance
with England, and the cardinal then seized the persons of
the Queen Mary and her mother.

John Hamilton, at that time Abbot of Paisley, was
natural brother to the regent, and had a great influence
over his mind, which he began then very actively to
exert. The abbot was a warm partisan of the interests of
France, and a zealous defender of the established faith.
He was a man of strong will and great energy, one whom
it was not easy to overreach or intimidate; and, though
taxed by his contemporaries with various irregularities in
his private life, he displayed for a long time, in the fulfilment of his duties as a churchman, admirable temper and
great prudence. It was not until about six years after
Cardan's connexion with him ceased, that he acquired the
temper of the religious persecutor. John Hamilton,

Abbot of Paisley, used then his influence over his weaker brother so effectually, that James, on the 25th of August, ratified the treaty with King Henry, and declared the cardinal an enemy to his country, and on the 3rd of September following, met the cardinal at Callender, and declared for the interests of France; he even went so far as to abjure the Church of the Reformers in the Franciscan church at Stirling.

Then followed changes of leaders, wars, peace, and the murder of Beatoun. After the death of Henry VIII. in 1547, the Abbot of Paisley became Archbishop of St. Andrew's. Scotland was soon afterwards invaded by the Earl of Somerset, protector of the young King Edward and of England. The Scots turned to France for help; and by the advice of Mary of Guise, the queen-mother, offered their little queen in marriage to the dauphin, and agreed also to send her to the French court for education. The offer was made by the nobles assembled at Stirling, and hastily confirmed in a camp-parliament. In June, 1548, the child-queen, six years old, was, in fact, carried to France by a fleet which had brought over to Scotland six thousand French soldiers. There she was living when Cardan visited Paris. There followed at home the decline of Somerset's power, and the general peace obtained by France from the Earl of Warwick in March of the year 1550.

The queen-mother, Mary of Guise, was ambitious, and aspired to the regency. James Hamilton, alone, was no match for her arts. He depended for the retaining of his position, and for advice in all emergencies, upon the strong mind of his brother, the archbishop. In addition to his own ecclesiastical affairs, John Hamilton had virtually to manage all that was difficult in the affairs of Scotland, and to bring them into accordance with the right sustainment of the interests of his own family. The archbishop's health, however, failed from month to month, and at the end of the year 1551 the attacks of asthma, which recurred every eight days, and lasted on each occasion twenty-four hours, had brought him nearly to the point of death. The regent then, missing the support of his strong arm, promised to give up to the queen-mother his difficult position. So stood the affairs of the Hamiltons when the archbishop's medical adviser recommended that, as they had already sought advice from the physicians in attendance on the Emperor Charles V. and on the King of France, recourse should be had in the next place to Cardan. When Cassanate wrote to Milan, James Hamilton had not committed himself to a promise that he would resign the regency. Before the year was at an end, however, he had made that promise, and it was for the archbishop, if he could regain strength, to prevent him from fulfilling it. In such a crisis it was unsafe for John

Hamilton to trust his brother out of reach, and it became, therefore, impossible for him to go to France.

Jerome, having replied to Cassanate's letter, heard again from Scotland on the 12th of February; and receiving then the money asked for to defray his travelling expenses, he set out on the 23rd of the same month for Lyons, where it was understood that his journey possibly might end[1]. There it was possible that he might meet the archbishop; but if not, he was, at any rate, there to be met by the archbishop's physician, with a fresh remittance, in discharge of the cost of his journey on to Paris. He travelled by way of Domo d'Ossolo and the Simplon Pass, through Sion and Geneva, then from the Lake of Geneva straight to Lyons, reaching that town after a journey of not quite three weeks[2]. There he found neither archbishop nor archbishop's physician, and remained thirty-eight days without any further tidings of his patient. The illustrious Cardan, in Lyons, was not, however, suffered to be idle; patients flocked to him, he prescribed for many noblemen, and earned much

---

[1] See his own horoscope. Geniturarum Exemplar, p. 129.

[2] De Vitâ Propriâ, pp. 19, 20, and for the next facts. He says there, that he remained in Lyons forty-six days; but a correction of this and of some other slight inaccuracies of date has been made by reference to the Geniturarum Exemplar (written just after his return), where, in discussing his own horoscope under the head of Journeys, he is particular about all dates, and calculates the stars by which his incomings and outgoings were ruled.

money. Louis Birague, commander of the King's in-
fantry, whose good-will once, when he was at Milan, had
been sought for Jerome by young Brissac, as before nar-
rated, happened to be then in Lyons, and received the
great physician as a friend, offering him a stipend of a
thousand crowns a year, on the part of Marshal Brissac,
if he would consent to be attached to him, as his physician. Brissac's friends desired the presence of the
skilled physician; Brissac thought only[1] of the aid he
might have from his ingenuity in mathematics and
mechanics. That offer, however, was declined. Here,
too, we must name Guillaume Choul[2], a nobleman of
Lyons, king's counsellor and judge in Dauphiné, with
whom Jerome established an enduring friendship. M.
Choul was one of the most painstaking antiquaries of his
time, and wrote on medals, castrametation, baths, and
other Greek and Roman matters—works which have had
the honour of translation into Spanish.

At length Cassanate came, the bearer of a letter from
the archbishop himself, by which his physician was introduced formally, and in which his exact errand was stated.
The letter—written, of course, like all such documents,
in Latin—spoke of "serious, urgent, and inevitable business" that detained the archbishop at home, and its main
object was to persuade Jerome, if possible, to travel on to

[1] De Vitâ Propriâ, cap. xxxii.　　[2] Ibid. cap. xv.

Scotland. Cassanate was the bearer of three ·hundred crowns, payable to him for his travelling expenses between Lyons and Edinburgh, if he could be prevailed upon so far to extend his journey. Thus Hamilton wrote[1]: an oscillation in his style, between the familiar first person singular and the formal first person plural, has been left unaltered. ; The tone of the letter shows that the archbishop was a man of business:

" Your letter, written on the 23rd of November, was received three days ago by our physician, and read through by me. Inasmuch as you have therein, most learned Cardanus, equalled our opinion of your singularly recondite erudition and perfect virtue, you have also increased our expectation that the restoration of our health will proceed chiefly and certainly from you. Urged to that opinion already by the persuasions of our physician, I had thought that I must have recourse to you as to the Æsculapius most propitious and suitable for the quelling of my disease; not that I distrusted the help I received from the learned doctors, but that from your aid I promised to myself more. But though 'I myself, some months ago—as you have been very abundantly informed in the letter of our physician—had determined for that special reason to go to Paris, nevertheless, hindered by most serious and urgent and inevitable business, I was compelled to desist from my intention.

" Wherefore, because I wish to adopt the next best course, I have conceived the desire to send to you the man who is

---

[1] This letter is given by Cardan in his second book De Libris Propriis (ed. 1557).

the bearer of these, for the four last years my physician, one who is most studious of you, and who begot in us the opinion of you before expressed, that he, armed and equipped with your most prudent and (we expect, if God dispense it so) most healthful counsel, for which he has always thirsted, may inquire out the remedies against the disease, bring and administer them. He has written to you fully enough, at my command, upon my temperament, the origin and progress of the malady, and has set before you almost the whole manner of it, in my opinion, as plainly as if it were before your eyes. But since even this did not seem to himself sufficient, in order that we may do whatever belongs to the affair in hand with greater ease, correctness, and success, we have sent to you the said studious and faithful minister to our health, from whose discourse and from your mutual conversation, I hope that you will become so plainly acquainted with the whole theory of my disease, that afterwards you can fairly desire nothing to complete your absolute acquaintance with it.

"Nevertheless, because, as the poet says—

> Nec retinent patulæ commissa fidelius 'aures,
> Quam quæ sunt oculis subjecta,'

and what are seen are known more certainly than what are heard, and discoveries (as you most prudently say) succeed marvellously in the hands of their inventors, this one thing I seek out of your singular humanity and the good-will you have conceived towards us, that inasmuch as you were willing, according to the terms of your letter, to come as far as Paris, you will consent to come for once to Scotland also, upon any conditions that you please. The bearer of this will give you a safe conduct, and provide, also, for cost and attendance;

and will give, if there be any arrangement entered into between him and you, the guarantee of P. Francisco Resta, or
any other banker in Milan.

" This only, finally, I will promise you, best and most learned
Cardanus, with a true heart, that you shall incur no waste of
time and labour, for there shall accrue to you no moderate
increase of means, and the greatest harvest of fame and
esteem. I would have you, therefore, to persuade yourself
that I both wish and am able to do more things than I
promise. Which, without doubt, if you will take upon yourself so much trouble for our sake, you shall in very deed and
by experience discover.

" Farewell, most learned Cardanus, and visit our Lares to
find us not so much of Scythians as you perhaps suppose.—
Edinburgh, Feb. 4, 1552.

" Upon all matters not mentioned in this letter, confide in
William Cassanate, who delivers it."

A journey into frosty Scotland had by no means formed
part of Jerome's plan, and Cassanate used various persuasions, and held out many attractions, before the philosopher could be prevailed upon to go so far from home.
He believed that the archbishop had enticed him into
France, meaning that he should go to Edinburgh, but well
knowing that the proposal of a journey into Scotland
would have been refused, if sent to him at Milan[1]. Nei-

---

[1] Geniturarum Exemplar, p. 129. " Advocabant me in Gallias,
credo consulto veriti quod et futurum erat, me nullis conditionibus in
Scotiam, si eo me advocassent, deduci posse." The text shows, however, that the account given by historians of Hamilton's affairs fits so

ther Cassanate; he says; nor the money that he offered,
nor the hope of other profit, nor the wish to see new countries, persuaded him ; but the fear lest, when he got back
among his own people, some scandal, with a look of truth
about it, might be invented to explain his quick return;
est he might be disgraced and bespattered by the gossip
of his tattle-loving city.   Therefore, having received the
additional three hundred crowns, Jerome consented to
go on, and on the 18th of April the two physicians set
out, using the river Loire[1] for their highway as far as
possible, upon the road to Paris.   Just before quitting
Lyons, on the last day of preparation for departure,
advice was sought from the great Italian by a certain
schoolmaster; afflicted with a serious disease. He brought
money in his hand ; but Cardan declined to undertake
the case at such a time. The man said then that he could
show the way to a boy able to see demons in a pitcher.
By that offer Jerome was tempted; he went, therefore,
but found nothing worthy of a grave attention.   In the
mean time, he and his new patient had been talking of the
mirror of Orontius, which kindles fire, and which the

well into Cardan's narrative as perfectly to explain the real emer-
gency by which the archbishop was detained in Scotland. The next
citation is from the same authority (p. 130).

[1] De Vitâ Propriâ, p. 19; and for the succeeding anecdote, the same
authority compared with the fuller account given in the last book De
Libris Propriis.

scholar says, " I knew to have been one of the discoveries of Archimedes; he was led thus to show me a printed copy of Archimedes, as translated by Antonius Gogava into Latin. Then, as I looked over the volume, I saw that there were bound into it Ptolemy's Books on Astrological Judgments. I asked whether they were to be bought; he urged me to accept them, and I accepted them at length, for it was a saint's day, upon which it is not lawful to buy." Taking this book with him, then, to shorten his journey, he wrote commentaries upon it on the way to Paris, down the river Loire. These commentaries, forming a considerable work, were committed to a French printer, who gave Jerome occasion to declare that, of all printers, the French were the most dilatory. They were first printed, with the addition of twelve illustrative horoscopes, in 1555.

At Paris there was the heartiest reception ready for the Milanese physician. The only surly man among the *savants* seems to have been the Orontius just mentioned, in whom Jerome felt interest, and whom he says that he saw, but who refused to visit him[1]. M. Fine, who trans-

---

[1] De Vitâ Propriâ. " Ubi Orontium videre contigit, sed ille ad nos venire recusavit." A very brief account of his visit to the church of St. Dionysius, and of his dinner with the king's physicians, follows in the same place The general narrative of these incidents given in the text is amplified by reference to other mention of them in De Libris Propriis (ed. 1557), p. 138, and especially in the Geniturarum Exemplar.

lated his name into Greek, and was Oronce for literary purposes, certainly was a famous man, but he would have been more honoured than honouring in an exchange of courtesies with Jerome, for his fame had but an unsubstantial basis. When Cardan said that the glass of Orontius was taken from Archimedes, he touched upon a weak point in M. Fine. He was not an original man, though he did, indeed—labouring under a mistake—give out that he had squared the circle. He obtained much of his knowledge from the works of a heretical contemporary, Sebastian Munster. M. Fine, who was seven years older than Jerome, had gone very early to Paris from his native town of Briançon, in the Dauphiné, where he distinguished himself by mathematical tastes and a mechanical turn, making with his own hands several instruments that had not been seen before. He published works, at first translations, and taught mathematics, at first privately, then publicly in the College de Gervais. When Francis I. established a new college in Paris, Orontius was made royal professor of mathematics, and attracted many students. He wrote a Description of the World and a Description of France, and assumed a prominent position as a practical geographer. He was therefore sought and patronised by foreign princes who were in want of maps or charts. Sebastian Munster, a little man, robust, laborious, and wonderfully simple-minded, lay at the root of the reputa-

tion of Orontius.   Munster died of plague at Basle while
Cardan was sailing down the Loire to Paris.   He had
been teaching Hebrew and heretical theology in that
town for twenty-three years—in fact, ever since he gave
up the Cordelier's robe and became a Lutheran.   He wrote
an admirable Cosmography, besides an Organum Urani-
cum, and a great deal of Hebrew.   A scholar of Basle
delivered a Hebrew oration over him when he was dead,
but in the world he had not due honour.   Orontius was
far more widely celebrated.   Concerning Orontius, it should
be added, that he had once been imprisoned for discover-
ing bad omens for France among the stars, but that, with
that exception, fortune favoured him abundantly.   He
did not rightly use her gifts, for, though he had worked
for princes and been largely paid, he died in debt—
three years after Cardan's visit to Paris—and left a large
family of children destitute.

Orontius, then, in whom Jerome as a mechanist and
mathematician felt much interest, declined to become
acquainted with the new guest of the learned in the town.
Everywhere else, however, he was made to feel the greatness of his reputation.   At court he was flattered by the
desire of the king himself that he should kiss hands and
accept court service in France, with a considerable pension; but he was unwilling to offend the emperor, whom
he considered as his master, and who was at war with

France. He was called to attend the half-brother of
Mary Queen of Scots (probably the young Duke de
Longueville), and in the hope of service that he might
render an immense stipend was offered—but in too vague
a way—if he would become physician to her majesty.
Afterwards, when his treatment had been found successful
(the duke, however, if he was the patient, died about
that time), the offers were repeated, but they were not
determinate enough, and were, at any rate, refused[1].
Considering how beggarly a country Scotland was in his
opinion, Jerome took some pains to show how it was
that the queen could afford to make a lavish offer, and
attributed her means to wealth accruing from the royal
guardianship of estates, when the succession fell on
minors

It was not until they reached Paris that Jerome discussed terms with Cassanate ; but there was an agreement
then drawn up, which was afterwards destroyed as being
an instrument not necessary between a physician and an
honourable patient. Cardan was to have his travelling

---

[1] "Oblatas majores conditiones renui, unam Regis Gallorum, metui
Cæsaria nos offendere, cum inter eos principes desævirent bella: aliam
paulo post cum rediissem . . . . : aliam ante hanc locupletiorem
sed nimis dissitam, cum Scotorum Reginâ, cujus levirum curaveram;
et tamen spe sanitatis adipiscendæ. Post, cum sanassem, experimento
et gratiâ inductum . . . ." De Vitâ Prop. cap. iv. The reference of
the Queen of Scotland's wealth to the abuses of wardship, occurs
in cap. xxxii. of the same book.

expenses paid, and to receive ten gold crowns a day while in personal attendance upon the archbishop.

Hamilton's case having already been laid before the physicians of the King of France, Cassanate took the stranger to consult with them. Brasavolus he did not see. Brasavolus was a famous physician of Ferrara settled at the French court, and named Musa by the suggestion of King Francis. He is said to have been so devoted to his calling, that one day, when word was brought to him in the lecture-room that his house was on fire, he would not quit his class till he had finished his prelection. He then was absent from the gathering, but Jerome and Cassanate dined with Pharnelius and Sylvius, —that is to say, with Jean Fernel and Jacques de la Boë.

Jacques de la Boë was the Parisian professor of anatomy, and Jerome describes him as a merry little old man of seventy, quite bald, quite little, and full of jokes. He was the professor of the old school, who worshipped Galen, taught anatomy from small fragments of dog, and omitted from his teaching whatever was at all difficult even in the authority he worshipped. Sylvius, who was furiously endeavouring to hunt down his old pupil Vesalius, as an impious confuter of the word of Galen, followed him to Madrid with his hate, and sought to bribe the Madrid state physicians with the promise of a baby's skeleton if they would join the chase. Persecution of Vesalius had become the topmost thought of his old age, and he could not, of course, dine with a strange doctor without mounting on his hobby. " He was breathing animosity against Vesalius," says Jerome, " arising from I know not what cause. He professed, indeed, that it was for wrongs done to Galen ; and he demanded a most iniquitous thing, that I too should become his enemy."

Fernel[1], the other member of the little dinner-party, was a man entirely different in character. He was professor of medicine in the university, and the first court physician, in spite of his undisguised contempt for court society. His age Jerome considered to be fifty-five, but it

---

[1] The information about these learned men whose fame has departed, I have generally got from Zedler's Universal Lexicon. I have referred sometimes for it to the excellent Encyclopædia of Ersch and Gruber, and have had some aid, but not much, from Jocher's Gelehrten Lexicon. I have also, of course, been helped by Tiraboschi when the question has been of an obscure Italian author. The Biographie Universelle I have been unable to trust, and owe to it, I believe, nothing but a part of the sketch of Orontius. English biographical dictionaries, or the biographical part of English encyclopædias, I have found much reason to avoid. The Germans are the best encyclopædists. They study a man before they write even a few paragraphs about him. They are both accurate and full. The French are full, but much too careless about accuracy. The English are both inaccurate and meagre, wherever they have to put down any results of out-of-the-way reading. When, therefore, I have in this work had to rely, not on my own reading but on that of other men, I have preferred looking for information to the Germans. Even them, however, I have not trusted without comparing two or three accounts of the same thing by independent writers, and if I found on any point any discrepancy, have sought to ascertain what was the truth by reference to the original authorities.

was, in fact, not more than forty-six ; he was a pale, lean
man, who loved his study and his wife.   He had come to
Paris, when he was past the heyday of his youth, from
Clermont in Picardy, to study rhetoric and philosophy.
After two years he was offered a professorship of logic, but
he desired to learn and not to teach.   He gave up all the
pleasures of the capital, and withdrew himself entirely
from mere complimentary society to study Cicero, Pliny,
and Aristotle, and to perfect himself in mathematics.   He
was then teaching philosophy in the College of St. Barbe.
By the time he had attained great skill in mathematics he
had so much weakened his health that it became necessary
for him to retire into the country.   With restored health
he returned to town, received fresh lessons in oratory, and
resumed the study of elegant literature and of mathematics.
He was by that time married, and his wife, objecting to
the cost incurred for instruments by reason of his mathematical pursuits, he gave them up, good husband as he
was, and undertook to earn money instead of spending it.
He devoted himself then to medicine, and in that also, by
the power and the fineness of his mind, he attained rapidly
to eminence.   Patients flocked to him, and in his leisure
hours he explained Hippocrates and Galen.   He was
obliged soon, by the great increase of his private practice,
to abandon public teaching, but as he found leisure even
then to write on Physiology, the students forced him by

affectionate compulsion to expound that to them. A tract of his own on Venesection he was also perforce lecturing about, when he was interrupted by the command of Henry II, then dauphin, that he would attend on a great lady, whom he favoured, or who favoured him, in a case of considerable urgency. His effective aid secured to Fernel the dauphin's gratitude. The prince made him his chief physician, and the courtiers flocked about him, but he contemned a court life, and turned back to study : he refused to live at court. Nevertheless, the grateful prince did not withdraw from him the appointment or its salary. Again, in Paris, he was hindered from his studies and his duties as a teacher by the press of patients, for he never winnowed out the poor from among those to whom he gave time and attention. No poor sick man asked help of him and failed to get it. When, at last, Henry II. became king, Fernel was compelled, in spite of himself, to officiate as the first court physician. Among other incidents of his life, one of the most notable was the acquisition of the friendship of Catherine of Medicis, who believed that his skill had saved her from a state of childlessness, and on the birth of her first child gave him ten thousand dollars for his fee, at the same time ordering a like fee to be paid to him at the birth of every succeeding son or daughter. Fernel's pure student character will not be held in the less tender recollection

for the fact, that while still far from the extreme term of
life, six years after his dinner with Cardan, he died of
sorrow for the loss of the wife whom he had loved better
than his studies. He pined after her death, and in a few
months was buried by her side.

The two French physicians, De la Boë and Fernel,
with Cassanate and Cardan, formed the party assembled
to discuss the case of the archbishop. Jerome took great
pains not to commit himself. When the archbishop's
disease was talked about, he listened and said nothing.
He was asked at once, before dinner, for his opinion, but
declined to speak before the king's physicians, and objected, also, that he was quite unacquainted with the
patient. The matter was talked over also during dinner ;
but Cardan, when in courtesy he might have spoken, and
it was, perhaps, slightly discourteous to maintain reserve,
still abstained from committing himself formally to an
opinion.

Jerome saw sights also at Paris. To one of them he
was introduced by another of the king's physicians, Nico-
las Legrand, who has left little more than his name behind him, and who is barbarously Latinised, I do not know
whether by his own hand or by that of his friend, into Mag-
nienus[1]. He was an excellent man, says Cardan, studious

---

[1] Eloy's Dictionnaire Historique de la Médecine, not mentioned in
the preceding note, has helped me now and then, and coming to the

of mathematics, and a bustling man. He came to see me daily. He, being physician to the monks of St. Dionysius, took us to their noble church, distant about three miles from Paris, and famed throughout the whole world. There, when we had seen the sepulchres of kings, statues, and other marble ornaments, I studied carefully the horn of an unicorn that was suspended in the church[1]. He handled it and measured it, and he describes it carefully. More than once he refers to it. In another passage he records that, among the king's treasures in the church of St. Dionysius, there was nothing that appeared to him so precious as that rare and perfect horn.

Aimar de Ranconet was another of the eminent men in Paris by whom Cardan was particularly welcomed, and with him Jerome had correspondence after his departure. He was a lawyer by profession, but remarkably well versed in polite literature, philosophy, and mathematics. He was President of the Fourth Chamber of Accounts in the Parliament of Paris, and a student with a system. After a light supper, he would sleep for a few hours, and rising in the night at about the time when the monks' prayer bell was sounding,

---

rescue here when other help all failed, told me the real name of this gentleman. The barbarous Latinising of the names of persons and places, as of Hamilton into Amultho, Fernel into Pharnelius, the Simplon into Mons Sempronius, Duomo d'Ossolo into Dondosola, when any obscure person or place is the subject of it, makes a riddle.

[1] De Varietate Rerum (ed. Bas. 1557), p. 672.

put on a studying dress, not unlike a monastic robe, and
go to work. So he studied for four hours, profiting by the
silence of the night, and a stomach loaded, he said, with no
greater excess of humidity than could be spat away out of
his mouth. Then he returned to bed and worked again
after the second waking. A few scholarly and liberal words
spoken in parliament not very long after Cardan's departure caused Ranconet to be shut up in the Bastile on a
foul and absurd charge : there he died. His daughter,
it is said, died on a dunghill, his son was hung, and his
wife struck by lightning.

Of all the men that he saw in Paris, President Ranconet[1] was the one who won most on Cardan's affections.
He admired the immense store of his books, but he dwells
most on the acuteness and the liberality of his character;
he would despise none for poverty, contemn none for rude
speech, but judged them wisely and humanely by their
dispositions. " Then, said I to myself," Jerome observes,
" here is a rare bird, who looks into a thing perfectly,
and is deceived by no false show of right." Having it
in his mind to illustrate his lately written commentary
upon Ptolemy with a dozen horoscopes of eminent men,
he proposed to do homage to Ranconet, by placing him
and lauding him among the number. Ranconet begged
urgently that his horoscope might not be printed, but

---

[1] Geniturarum Exemplar, p. 42, for the following facts.

Jerome says that he refused him his request, because he
thought it unjust that the opportunity should be passed
over of celebrating the name of a man whose equal he
had not known in Italy, and for whose friendship alone it
had been worth while to visit France. The horoscope
was published therefore. It prophesied to him difficulty
in all affairs ; assigned to him a wife and children of illustrious character, some of whom would die by violence.
The melancholy fate of Ranconet fast followed the publication of these prophecies, and Cardan seems afterwards to
have wished that he had complied with his friend's entreaty, for he writes sadly when reviewing his past life :
" I injured those whom I proposed to praise, among them
the president at Paris, the most learned Aimar Ranconet[1].

Leaving good friends behind, the travellers proceeded
on their journey. Cardan carried away with him no pleasant thoughts of Paris as a town. Its general construction
had reminded him of Milan, but the streets he had found
always full of dirt, emitting stench, and the air unwhole-
some, the population being at the same time dense. Perhaps, he suggests, it is because of the dirt (lutum) that
the town has been called Lutetia, though, he admits, there
may be other derivations[2].

[1] De Vitâ Propriâ, p. 61.
[2] De Varietate Rerum (ed. Bas. 1557), p. 667. In the same chapter
of that work—" On Cities"—he characterises Rouen and Rome.

Again a river was the most convenient road, and the
two physicians travelled down the Seine to Rouen, which
town Cardan admired so much, that at the end of all his
travels there was none of which he spoke with like en-
thusiasm. Out of Rome, the Queen of Cities, he knew no
town so well built, so wholesome, and so handsome. Of
this journey through France into Scotland, Cardan relates
that it was not without peril, because there was the most
urgent danger then from war and piracy. For a serious
war was at that time raging between the emperor and
the King of France ; all things were being destroyed with
fire and sword; infants, women were being slain. "My
journey through France was made without the knowledge
of the emperor, even without any guarantee of public
faith ; yet so far was I from suffering any harm, that I
was received in the best spirit by the nobles. So much
was thought due to learning and good name by the French
nobility ; and truly it is splendid, liberal, generous, and
worthy of all praise, for in my utmost need and fear of
surrounding enemies, I was protected by it from the soldiers of the emperor. Marvellous chance, in truth ; the
enemy protects an alien lest he perish miserably in the
hands of his own people[1]."

[1] Geniturarum Exemplar, p. 131. The same authority covers the
next fact, but the date of Cardan's arrival is said to be the 3rd of July.
That is irreconcilable with the context, and falsifies the whole chro-
nology of the subsequent journey, as given by Cardan in three or four

For such protection, the governor of the coast provinces, when Cardan and his suite came to Boulogne, caused them to be attended by an escort of fourteen horse and twenty foot soldiers to Calais. From that point they took ship for England, and reached London on the 3rd of June.

separate works. By assuming July to have been misprinted for June, and allowing to the travellers a three days' rest in London, the accounts given are all made straight. Misprints abound in books of the sixteenth century, and they unluckily always abound most among names and dates.

CHAPTER V.

CARDAN IN EDINBURGH.

AFTER a rest in London of about three days, Cardan and his companions were conducted northward by Cassanate. The philosopher, journeying then in summer weather through the provinces of England, had an opportunity of acquiring a more accurate notion of this remote land than he before possessed. He did not, as he thought he should, see our sheep watered upon morning dew, nor did he find our sky very much darkened with crows[1]; what he did see, however, and think worth remembering concerning Britain, it will be more proper to relate when we approach the close of his experience among us. From London to Edinburgh was a journey of twenty-three days[2], and on the 29th of June the Milanese physician greeted personally his Scotch patient.

Cardan remained with the archbishop until nearly the

---

[1] *Ante*, vol. ii. p. 66.
[2] Geniturarum Exemplar, p. 131.

middle of September. He at first allowed Cassanate to act in obedience to the advice taken at Paris, and gave diligent trial to the remedial course suggested at the consultation held over the dinner-table with Fernel and De la Boël[1]. From this course no deviation was made during forty days, although his study of the case soon led him to form a view of it extremely different from that on which its first treatment was founded. Cassanate had placed at the base of the disease a cold brain; Jerome traced all evil to a hot one, and differed—with much courtesy—from his friends in other essential respects.

At the end of forty days John Hamilton became impatient, and by that time also Jerome was becoming much troubled by the five Italians who had accompanied him on his journey. One of them caused great scandal by his conduct in the town: he was a greedy, envious, lawless man; another, named Paolo Paladino, being very anxious to get back to Milan, urged his chief to take at once some active steps. The archbishop, who during all this time wasted in body, had become extremely restless and dissatisfied. Cardan then, at last, felt that it was proper to explain to the reverend lord his own professional position, to point out the fact that he himself dissented from the course of treatment hitherto pursued by Cassa-

[1] Consilia Medica. Opera, Tom. ix. p. 124; and for the succeeding facts, De Vitâ Propriâ, p. 193.

nate under the advice of the Parisians, and to suggest
what he took to be the true theory of the disorder, and
the proper way of trying for its cure. The consequence
of this explanation was, of course, that the archbishop (an
irascible man) was indignant at the body physician, and
the body physician was indignant at Cardan. Cassanate,
too, feared Jerome as a tale-teller, and the archbishop
reproached him for the time he had lost before coming to
a right understanding, being not the less annoyed at such
delay when the new system of cure was found to give
relief.

The whole opinion of Cardan upon his case was written
out for the archbishop at great length, as a help to those
doctors who might afterwards attend upon him. It
is included in a volume of professional opinions, carefully
drawn up after the manner of the time, whereof Jerome
kept copies, and which were subsequently given to the
world. A few notes from this document will not only
be found amusing, but will suggest, I think, a very clear
notion of the state of medical science in the sixteenth
century, and of the kind of practice in which the philosopher, whose life we are here tracing, was engaged[1].

In the first place it should be stated, that in conversa-

---

[1] The following are notes from the fifty-second opinion in the Consilia Medica, which occupies twenty-four double-columned folio pages
in the ninth volume of Cardan's works, pp. 124—148.

tions with Cassanate, on the way to Edinburgh, Cardan
had learnt, in addition to the facts mentioned by him in
his letter, one or two particulars. These were, that the
archbishop's periodical attacks did not agree always, but
only generally, with the changes of the moon; that sometimes, when he took care of himself, he might get through
fifteen or twenty days without them. That the duration
of each attack seldom exceeded twenty-four hours, but
that sometimes it remained upon him twice as long. That
his grace slept well, but that, on account of the urgency of
his affairs, he never took the quantity of sleep requisite to
free himself from crudities, especially since he was a great
eater and drinker. That he was irascible enough, had a
skin that exhaled freely, a chest of fair size, and rather a
thin neck.

Upon the case, after he had personally studied it, Cardan's opinion resembles a long clinical lecture. It is a
very acutely reasoned study of asthma, based upon principles laid down by Galen. Wonderfully absurd seems
now its medical philosophy, but in the year 2154 what
will be said even of our physic? Let us be modest in our
treatment of the physic of Cardan. He did not believe
with Cassanate that the matter finally expectorated had remained in his grace's brain as it collected there during the
intervals between the attacks. If so, he thought that the
operations of the intellect must be impeded, and that the

lord archbishop would not have, as he had, the red complexion of a healthy man; moreover, the matter so collecting and long standing in the head would turn corrupt[1]. He believed that the thin fluid discharged was partly serous humour, partly condensed vapour, which descended from the brain into the lungs, not through the cavity of the windpipe,—for if so, it would be coughed out during its downward passage,—but through its coats, as water soaks through linen. This thin humour and vapour he supposed to be originally drawn into the brain by the increased rarity in the substance of that organ, caused by undue heat. Heat makes all things rare; and rarefaction in one part of the body, to express the idea roughly, produces suction from another. The thick expectorated matter was formed, Cardan thought, from the food[2].

These notes, though they do not contain the whole of Cardan's diagnosis, are enough to indicate the kind of reasoning he used. He reasoned in the manner of the faculty, but he excelled other physicians of his time in shrewdness; and although perfectly obedient to authority, he used a skilled obedience, and was very willing to receive instruction from experience that he acquired. He

---

[1] Cons. Med. p. 128.

[2] A century later medical science was but little more advanced. This is the kind of reasoning that Molière burlesqued. The comments of Cassanate and Cardan on Hamilton's case illustrate perfectly Sganarelle's theory of Lucinde's muteness in the Médécin Malgré Lui. Act ii. sc. 6.

watched his cases very closely; and since, as we have before seen, he knew the harm that may be done by medicine, and had freed himself from many dangerous absurdities of practice, since he also dreaded misuse of the lancet, and relates candidly how in his early days he lost patients by bleeding them[1], there can be no doubt that he was in his day, what he was believed to be, one of the safest advisers to whom a sick man could apply for help.

Applying theory to practice, the basis of the archbishop's cure, in as far as diet was concerned, Cardan said must depend on the use of a food as much as possible cold-natured and humid.   The cold-natured food would resist the attraction of the brain, for it is the nature chiefly of warm things to exhale and to ascend.   Humidity, he said, would obstruct the soaking down of matter from the brain through the coats of the windpipe, so compelling it to descend by the main channel, whence it could be coughed out during its downward passage.

It was his opinion that the chief object of the cure by medicine should be to attack the root of the disease, namely, the unhealthy temperature of the brain.   With that view the head should be purged, and before that was done, there should, of course, come purgation of the body. Purgation of the head, he explained, was to be effected

---

[1] De Vitâ Propriâ, cap. xxxii'

through the palate, the nose, and the sutures of the skull, especially the coronal suture.

Applications to the palate he did not much like, as approaching too near to the seat of the disease.

An admirable prescription which he would recommend for the procuring of a good discharge by the nose was the following:—Take of goat's or cow's milk and of water, of each half a pint, mix and dissolve in them two grains of elaterium ; let this be drawn through the nostrils when the patient has an empty stomach.

As a valuable application over the coronal suture, which itself had cured an asthma of seven years' standing, the physician recommended an ointment to be applied over the shaven crown composed of Greek pitch and ship's tar, white mustard, euphorbium, and honey of anathardus, which might be sharpened, if requisite, by the addition of blister fly. This cerate, he said, sometimes fetches out two pints of water in the four-and-twenty hours, and sometimes only three or four ounces. It was no easy nightcap to suggest to an archbishop. Another remedy that he would recommend, was water from the baths of Lucca, freely drank for eight days, and on the eighth day dropped upon the head for half an hour, over the coronal suture.

---

[1] Elaterium is a sediment from pulp yielded by a plant called the Squirting Cucumber. It surpasses all drugs in its power of producing watery discharge from the mucous membranes. Two grains of elaterium, as prepared carefully in these days, would be a fearful overdose.

He advised also the use of the shower-bath, as he was himself in the habit of employing it, upon the hint of Celsus. In a well warmed bedroom, first wash the head over with hot water, containing a few ashes, then let a pail full of water, quite cold from the well, be dashed upon it suddenly—the beginner can rise gradually from the pitcher to the pail—then, after a brief pause, begin to rub the head with cool, dry cloths, and go on rubbing until there remains not a trace of moisture. Remain in the warm chamber for two hours before going out into the air. By this habit, says Cardan, the brain is kept to a natural temperature, and its substance rendered firm and dense.

As applications useful—but less useful—he suggests also the dropping, from a height, of certain warm medicated waters over the coronal suture.

Next to the correction of the brain, the most important care of the physician, in a case like that of the archbishop, must be to prevent the generation in the body of the peccant matter. With this view, it was advised that pains should be taken to promote good digestion, and to give food that would not pass into thin humour and vapour. Vapoury winds and moist air would be injurious; his grace should walk under the shade in tranquil weather, and be careful never to go out in rain or night-air. He should make use of a perfume-ball, because perfumes are drying; but among perfumes used by him he should not include roses; for by the scent of roses some brains are made warmer. The reverend lord should not sleep upon feathers, but upon unspun silk[1], and be particular upon that point. The heating of the spine and vena cava on a feather bed would cause matter straightway to ascend into the head. If one silk mattress proved too hard a couch, several might be placed upon each other. The patient, too, should lie never on his back, but on his face or side; by lying on the face, it was to be remembered that he might obtain relief, from a loss, during the night, of water by the mouth. The pillow should be of dry straw, finely chopped, and if that seemed to his grace too hard, it might be stuffed with well dried sea-weed; by no means with feather.

In matters of hygiène, whatever may be said of Cardan's theory, his practice was, on the whole, extremely sensible. His just hatred of feather beds, and his vigorous use of the shower-bath, may have done much to lengthen out the later years of his own life, in spite of all the ineradicable evils of his constitution.

The great physician further advised that the archbishop's pillow-case should be of linen, not of leather, and should be sprinkled at night with a drying perfume, made to the prescription which he gave. His grace was not to go to bed immediately after eating, but to wait at

---

[1] "Stupa serici." Cons. Med. p. 134.

least an hour and a half. Having retired, he was to sleep
with his hand upon his stomach; for, added Jerome;
whose words I now quote, " that helps much to good
digestion; let the sleep be for from seven hours to ten,
and let the reverend lord believe that there is nothing
better than a stretch of sleep; let him, therefore, take
time from his business and give it to his bed; or, if that
be impossible, let him subtract it from his studies: for
that should be the chief care of his life, without which
happy life is quite impossible[1]."

Upon rising, if his body chanced to be irregular in action,
it was advised that his grace should take a compound of
conserve of peaches and sugar of violets, waiting afterwards five hours for breakfast, and then breakfasting
lightly. He was to avoid purgatives, since they hurt
all people who have any tendency towards consumption,
and by disordering the stomach, injure the digestive
power. Instead of them, if necessary, he was directed
to drink from two to four pints of new ass's milk in the
morning, at one dose, or in several doses, but the whole
quantity taken never was to be divided into draughts
with intervals of more than an hour between them. That,

[1] Cons Med. p. 135, where the reverend prelate is also admonished
" de venere, ubi contingat necessitas debet, uti ea inter duos somnos;
scilicet post mediam noctem, et melius est exercere eam ter in sex
diebus, pro exemplo ita ut singulis duobus diebus semel, quam bis in
unâ die."

said Cardan, would serve his purpose, nourish his body
and his lungs, allay the excess of heat, be grateful to the
palate, and help also to avert consumption. When taking
this, the patient should not at the same time eat much,
especially should eat nothing very corruptible, as fish or
fruit, should use very gentle exercise, and keep his mind
as quiet as he could. The ass, whose milk he was to use,
should be well fed, and provided with mild herbs, such as
mallow, beet, and the blossoms of roses She should eat
corn and barley, have foaled recently, and it might be
better if the foal were not a male. Ass and foal should
live in freedom, and run daily together in the meadows.

His grace, having performed his first morning duties,
ought next to comb his head with an ivory comb, by
which the brain is comforted, rub well his extremities,
anoint his spine and chest with oil of sweet almonds, and,
being fully dressed, walk for a short time in some pleasant
spot, not sunny.

He should avoid all immoderate excess and repletion,
taking care also not to be immoderate in abstinence. In
discussing whether breakfast or supper should be the chief
meal, Cardan, having first decided that in every man's
case an established custom ought not to be interfered
with, proceeded to give a long series of curious, minute
directions upon food and cookery. He prescribed many
articles of diet as particularly proper to be used by the

archbishop, and added his advice upon the preparation of such things as would tend especially to make those fat who eat or drink them. Chief on this list is tortoise or turtle soup (what say the aldermen of London?); tortoises were to be preferred, the largest being the best. The whole animal, except the shell, was to be stewed down with water till he was as nearly as possible dissolved, and the flesh being eaten, and the juice being drank, no other food or drink being used for about twenty days, great fatness would follow.

Another excellent thing, of the efficacy of which Cardan had personal experience, was the water distilled from the blood of a young full-grown pig and coltsfoot leaves. Two ounces a day of this distilled water, taken with a little sugar for about fifteen days, would fatten a man rapidly, and be found able sometimes to bring back a hectic person from the gates of death.

He advised also distilled snails; but when there were so many pleasant things that might be used, he wondered who would employ frogs as they had been employed by some in Italy, though he confessed that even they might find a place in the kitchens of the Britons, cut off as that people is from the whole world. Having said so much, he begged pardon for jesting, and proceeded to name more provocatives of fatness. Among others, he gave the receipt for a capital thing, with which, at the outset of his career, he

had dieted and cured the Prior Gaddi, who was afflicted
with a skin disease. This was a mixture of thick barley-
water with chicken-broth, flavoured with wine and a little
cinnamon or ginger. It is easily digested, fattens, and
dilates the chest[1].

Cardan sought also to moderate the emotions of his
patient's mind. He suggested methods of shutting him
up, when in-doors, from the air of which he was afraid.
He advised strongly the use of the bath. He added a
great number of medical prescriptions, to be used habitually or on various emergencies, closing the list with the
recommendation of an issue under each knee, to be established only as a last resource, if other remedies should fail.
Finally, he added to his own elaborate advice a selection
of prescriptions suited to the case, culled from the chief
authorities in medicine, Greek, Roman, and Arabian.

The strictness of Cardan's regimen, if not the efficacy of
his medicine, the strong check that he put upon the archbishop's appetites and passions, the despotic limitation of
his hours of business, the lengthened period of rest, the
wholesome bed, the weekly shower-bath, the daily exercise, strict fast enjoined during the whole period of an
attack, and other such reforms in the archbishop's mode
of life, soon told upon his health. It improved very de-
cidedly, and his lordship, who was recovering his flesh,

[1] Cons. Med. p. 141.

was by no means content to part with his good friend and helper. Jerome remained in Edinburgh thirty-five days after the commencing of his own treatment of John Hamilton; but his fame as a practitioner was near its topmost height, and his skill was not bestowed on the archbishop only. Scottish nobles flocked to him, and paid so liberally for his advice, that, as he tells us, he made out of two of his prescriptions only, nineteen gold crowns in one day[1]. His chief patient, also, was a princely paymaster. Then there came to Cardan letters from Ranconet to tell of nobles whom his fame had brought to Paris. Many were coming in from the provinces that they might have the good fortune to be in the capital and obtain advice from the illustrious physician as he passed through to Milan. There were forty nobles who arrived in Paris on that errand, and there was a prince there offering a thousand gold crowns as his consultation fee, rather than lose the chance of profiting by Cardan's counsel. So Jerome was told afterwards; but all the tempting report sent to him by Ranconet was sent in vain. He had despatched Gaspar Cardan to France, and Gaspar, who had himself fallen among thieves, sent an ill report of the condition of the country. It was overrun by bands of robbers, bred out

---

[1] De Libris Propriis (1557), p. 181, for what follows, except the specification of the presents, for which see the last book De Libris. Opera, Tom i. p. 137.

of the war, by one of which, a foreign traveller in France, known to have much money with him, might fairly expect to be attacked. Jerome determined, therefore, not to seek the wealth awaiting him in Paris, but to travel home through the Low Countries.

There had come to him also an invitation to the court of London. The young King Edward VI, weakened by measles and small-pox, laboured under an affection of the lungs which baffled his physicians. It was for his reputed skill in treating such diseases that Cardan had been at great cost brought to Edinburgh, where he had confirmed his reputation. John Hamilton seemed to have been raised from a death-bed. It was most desirable, therefore, that the Italian physician should be persuaded to go home through London and see the king.

Jerome returned more suddenly than the archbishop desired. It was painful to him to be absent from his children[1]. By the first leaves that fell he was reminded that he should not like to face the rigours of a Scottish winter. Cassanate plagued him with his jealousy. The conduct of his one lawless follower also distressed him. Early in

[1] Some of the following considerations are recorded in the Geniturarum Exemplar, p. 106. For the day of leaving Edinburgh, see the same book, p. 131. It tallies with the statement, several times made, that he remained there 75 days; once he wrote, or it was printed, 68. If he had not reached London till the 3rd of July, all this part of the story would be wrong. The correction of July into June, giving three days for a rest in town, 23, as we are told, for the journey to Edinburgh, and 75 for the stay there, brings us to the 12th of September very exactly.

September, therefore, he begged for permission to depart. The archbishop—who had lent some of his renewed strength already to his brother, and got from him a retractation of his promise to resign the regency—the archbishop said that he was relieved, not cured, and lamented that his help should fail just when he had begun to feel its value. Cardan's stay, he reminded him, was short, in proportion to the great length of the journey he had undertaken. Nor was it then a safe time for departure; war was everywhere. Finally, the archbishop pleaded, that if his physician would wait with him six months more,—until April,—he should be detained no longer. Gold had no power of temptation. "The love of my sons," Jerome says, "urged me." With difficulty, therefore, the consent of the archbishop was obtained, and on the 12th of September, Cardan and his followers quitted Edinburgh to retrace their way to London.

On the night before his departure, Jerome supped with his reverend patron, and received many gifts from the archbishop and his friends. His grace paid him for his visit eighteen hundred gold crowns, of which fourteen hundred went to Cardan himself, the rest to his attendants. This payment was much in excess of the stipulated ten gold crowns a day. There was presented to Cardan, also, a gold chain worth a hundred and twenty-five crowns; and, among other gifts, was the welcome one of an ambling horse, upon which he could set out comfortably for his ride through England. His attendants also received gifts.

In return for all this liberality, the physician, at his departure, left in the archbishop's hands a document distinct from the long written opinion already mentioned ; it was a careful and elaborate paper of directions for his lordship's private use. This has been published among Cardan's works[1]. It gave careful and minute directions for the patient's management of himself, laid down a regimen, in which changes of season and other accidents were not left out of sight, and was meant as a substitute for his own presence in Edinburgh. No contingency could arise that had not been foreseen and provided for in one or other of the documents. The directions left with the archbishop tallied, of course, with the contents of the professional opinion to which reference has already been made ; they omitted scientific details, and gave practical results in the form of precise directions. It will be enough to show how Jerome in this paper planned out the archbishop's day, taking an average day, and omitting reference to the contingencies of state of health, season, and weather.

He was to begin every eighth day with the shower-bath already described. When he came out of his chamber in the morning, prepared after the manner recom-

---

[1] It is inserted also among the Consilia Medica. Opera, Tom ix. pp. 225, *et seq.*

mended in the other document, he was to proceed to
his quiet and shady promenade with a couple of tears of
mastic between his teeth, chewing them to promote a
beneficial flow of water from the mouth.

At nine o'clock he was to breakfast ; he was to eat first
the liver of a fowl, with two or three grains of ginger ;
after that, take some bread soaked in gravy, and squeezed
free from excess of moisture ; then about two ounces of
white wine. Next, he might proceed to eat more at his
discretion chicken roasted or stewed, and he might drink
wine four or five times, but he ought not to drink in all
more than ten ounces. After breakfast he was to rest and
amuse himself.

The four hours after twelve o'clock were recommended
as his lordship's hours of business, during which, however,
he was to write no letters with his own hand, and was to
avoid as much as possible all trouble.

At four o'clock he was to go out for an hour's ride on
horseback. Having returned, he was to sit, also to re-
cline now and then upon his bed, while he gave audience to those who desired speech with him. He was by
no means to be out of doors at twilight.

Having left a space of nine or ten hours between the
two meals, towards seven o'clock his lordship was to sup.
His supper should be like his breakfast, only lighter, and
should be commenced by the taking of a spoonful of pure

honey.   It would be well if he would sup often on bread
and goat's milk.   There was a cardinal in Milan advanced
in years who derived much benefit from two goats that he
kept.   Ass's milk, however, would do as well, or even
better.   At eight or half-past eight his lordship was advised to go to bed.   The nature of the bed he was to use
has been described already.   In it he was to secure to
himself ten hours of continued sleep.

For the better assurance of punctuality in the carrying
out of the system thus laid down, Jerome suggested to his
grace the usefulness of a good clock.   He therefore recommended him to get such a thing ; it was but respect-
able ; " for," he said, " every Italian prince has many, and
good ones[1]."

All the advice left by Cardan, Archbishop Hamilton
resolved to follow, and promised that at the end of two
years—when the new system should have had a full and
perfect trial—he would send a report of its results to
Milan.

[1] Consilia Medica.   Opera, Tom. ix. p. 228.

CHAPTER VI.

CARDAN IN LONDON.

SUMMONED to the king on his return to London[1], Jerome continued to grow rich.

His visit to King Edward VI. is mentioned in most histories of England. In Bishop Burnet's History of the Reformation, it is recorded thus under the year 1552:— "This summer Cardan, the great philosopher of that age, passed through England. He was brought from Italy on the account of Hamilton, Archbishop of St.Andrew's, who was then desperately sick of a dropsy. Cardan cured him of his disease: but being a man much conversant both in Astrology and Magic, as himself professed, he told the archbishop, that though he had at present saved his life, yet he could not change his fate; for he was to die on a gallows. In his going through England, he waited on King Edward, where he was so entertained by him, and observed his extraordinary parts and virtues so narrowly, that on many occasions he writ afterwards of him, with

---

[1] Geniturarum Exemplar, p. 133. "Londinum in Angliâ reversus, vocatus ad regem, dona accepi."

great astonishment, as being the most wonderful person he had ever seen[1]."

It was not until October that Cardan had audience of the king, and he had then, as we have seen, not cured the archbishop of a dropsy, but had taught him how to fortify himself against the attacks of asthma. The statement that Jerome had prophesied to Hamilton his death upon the gallows, is perhaps founded on a popular tradition. It is incorrect. He calculated his nativity[2]; and inasmuch as he was born at ten in the morning, on the 3rd of February, 1512, found that he would attain his felicity through much anxiety and peril (as any man could see that he was doing when the prophesy was made), and that if he lived over the year 1554, he would be in great danger from passion of the heart[3], or poison, in the year 1560. He was taken in the capture of Dunbarton Castle, condemned in a summary way, and hung four days afterwards at Sterling, in 1571, being the first bishop in Scotland who died by the hands of an executioner. Of that certainly the stars told nothing to Cardan. He was perfectly in earnest as an astrologer, and perfectly sincere.

---

[1] Burnet, vol. II. p. 208 (ed. 1681). In his appendix of documents, as many readers will remember, he quotes in illustration a passage from Cardan's Horoscope of Edward.

[2] Geniturarum Exemplar, p. 26.

[3] Or shall we translate "Passio Cordis—suffering by the cord," to make good the fame of the astrologer.

What he saw on earth he found in the heavens, deceiving
himself with a surprising ingenuity; but astrology could
tell him no truth that was hidden from his neighbours.
One of his luckiest predictions, of which he makes special
boast, was his discovery by the stars in the year 1548,
that in 1549 and the three following years he should
acquire great wealth. "Whence it will come, or can
come," he said then, "I do not know[1]." Of that prophesy, the events of the year 1552 were a fulfilment; and
he adds, after the fact, that if in 1548 he had read
Ptolemy's Judgments, he should then have discovered
that the wealth was to come through a journey. The
impression made upon Cardan by the young king was,
indeed, very great. "It would have been better, I think,
for this boy not to have been born," he says, "or that
being born and educated, that he had survived. For he
had graces. Quite as a boy, he was skilled in many languages; Latin, his native English, French; and he was
not unversed, I hear, in Greek, Italian, Spanish, and
perhaps, yet others. He was not ignorant of dialectics,
or of natural philosophy, or music. In his humanity he
was a picture of our mortal state; his gravity was that of
kingly majesty, his disposition worthy of so great a prince.
The boy of so much wit and so much promise was by a

---

[1] Geniturarum Exemplar, p. 91.

K 2

great miracle being educated to a comprehension of the
sum of human things. I do not here adorn the truth,
with rhetoric, but speak below the truth[1].   *   *   And
there was the mark in his face of death that was to come
too soon. Otherwise he was comely, because of his age
and of his parents, who had both been handsome[2]."   ;

Cardan, most probably, was introduced at court by the
king's tutor, Sir John Cheke; for it is Cheke with whom
he lodged, and whom he seems to have regarded as the
most familiar of his English friends. He calculated also.
Cheke's nativity, and published the result. He was born
at seventeen minutes past five in the afternoon on the 16th
of June, 1514[3]. That being set down, the reader probably
has learnt more of the date of Sir John Cheke's birth than
he knows of his own. I need scarcely recal the fact, that
Cheke early became a Protestant, and was professor of
Greek at Cambridge. There he taught a new pronuncia-
tion that was forbidden by the chancellor, Gardiner,
Bishop of Winchester, and so begot a controversy. In
1544, John Cheke was entrusted with the education of
Prince Edward, By the prince, when he became king,
the learned man was knighted, and endowed with lands.
He had been made chief gentleman of the king's privy
chamber in 1550, and it was in the October of the suc-'

---

[1] Geniturarum Exemplar, p. 5.
[2] Ibid. p. 13.   [3] Ibid. p. 37.

-ceeding year that he was knighted. He assisted afterwards at two solemn theological disputations, and took
part in political affairs. In May, 1552, when Cardan was
on his way from Paris, Sir John Cheke was ill of a complaint which Jerome pronounced to have been peripneu-
monia. On the 25th of August of the same year, while
Cardan was in Edinburgh, Sir John was made chamberlain of the Exchequer for life. He was holding that new
dignity when, in October, Cardan tarried for some days
in London, and had for his principal friends John Cheke
(with whom he lodged) and Claude Laval, the French
ambassador[1]. In Edinburgh, too, it should have been
said, that the representative of France, the Duc du Cell[2],
had been his friend.

Cheke, who was thirteen years younger than Cardan,
was then aged thirty-eight, and already in high repute as
one of the most learned men in England. Jerome de-
duced from the stars the fact that if he could avoid public
calamities he would live to the age of sixty-one. He did
not avoid public calamities, but escaped, as we know,
the Tower and the scaffold by abjuring his religion, to
die vexed and remorseful at the age of forty-three. His
body, says Cardan, was graceful, with a yellow freckled
and thin skin, hair moderately long, and decent eyes of a

[1] De Vitâ Propriâ, cap. xv.
[2] Whom he calls Usellæ Princeps. De V. P. cap. iv.

grey colour. He was tall, hairy, ruddy enough from ex-
posure to the sun, handsome but unequally proportioned,
weak in the arms. He was, said Jerome, of a dry temperament, with active qualities. He would, therefore, soon
grow bald, and sooner grey. He would die of a lingering disease, with cold humour and pain in the lower extremities, there being also deflux from the brain. He
would be a man admirably knowing how to fit himself to
time and place. Considering his country, he would be
shrewd and ingenious. He would be always busy, grave,
liberal, wise, humane, the glory of the English people.

Cardan while in London lodged with Sir John Cheke,
and received from him the utmost respect and attention.
Yet he repressed, as he says, all pride in himself, and desired not to obtain homage for his own wit, but to do
homage to the genius of his friend; for in so doing, he
adds, there is a true happiness[1].

It was on the 2nd of April, six months before Jerome
visited the king, that Edward had been attacked by the
measles and small-pox. They left him with his health
weaker than ever. The Italian was not required to inter-
fere with his majesty as a physician in any systematic
way. The chief desire among the nobles evidently was

---

[1] Geniturarum Exemplar, p. 41.

to get, by help of one who was renowned as an astrologer, some information of the future course of politics, to have Edward's nativity calculated, and if possible to find out how long he would live. The courtiers, says Jerome, worried him, and some wished to use him as a tool[1]. He was placed in the midst of the English court life such as it was at that time, and he was greatly shocked by what he saw.

But the young king commanded his unstinted admiration and good-will. It may be that before having audience of his majesty, Cardan prepared himself by cutting the small band under his tongue. It has been said that he had a stutter in his speech, and he tells us that three or four times, even in his adult life, he attempted to diminish it by cutting at the band that seemed to tie his tongue[2]. It is very possible that he desired to speak his best before the King of England.

Edward, as described by Cardan, was "of a stature somewhat below the middle height, pale-faced, with grey eyes, a grave aspect, decorous, and handsome. He was rather of a bad habit of body than a sufferer from fixed diseases. He had therefore a somewhat projecting shoulder blade; but such defects do not amount to deformity,

---

[1] Geniturarum Exemplar, p. 19.   [2] Ibid. p. 82.

even when contracted from birth. Affections of his that were not habitual were to be called diseases, as a blindness and a deafness troubling him at times[1]."

But, says the philosopher, after having pointed out various conjunctions of the stars, and pronounced among other things that the monarch would have trouble from quadrupeds, " he was a marvellous boy. I was told that he had already mastered seven languages. In his own language, French, and Latin, he was perfect. He was not ignorant of dialectics, and in all things teachable. When I had speech with him he was fifteen years old, and he asked me (speaking Latin with as much polish and promptitude as I could use myself):

" What is there in those rare books of yours on the Variety of Things?" For I was obtaining leave to dedicate them to him.

Then I: " In the first chapter I show the cause of comets, long sought for in vain."

" What is it?" says he.

" The concourse," I say, " of the light of the planets."

But the king: " How is it, since the motions of those stars are different, that it is not dissipated, or does not move in accordance with their motion?"

But I: " It does so move, only much faster than they,

[1] Geniturarum Exemplar, p. 15.

on account of the difference of aspect, as the sun shining through a crystal makes a rainbow on a wall. A very slight movement of the crystal makes a great change in the rainbow's place."

But the king: " And how can that be done when there is no *subjectum*, for to the rainbow the *subjectum* is the wall."

Then I: " It occurs as in the milky way, and by the reflection of lights. When many candles are lighted near one another they produce between themselves a certain lucid and white medium. Therefore, *ex ungue leonem*, as they say[1]."

Having given this very candid illustration of the quickness of the king's intelligence, Cardan goes on immediately in a strain of genuine and hearty admiration. " This boy filled with the highest expectation every good and learned man, on account of his ingenuity and suavity of manners. * * * * When a royal gravity was called for, you would think it was an old man you saw, but he was bland and companionable as became his years. He played upon the lyre, took concern for public affairs, was liberal of mind, and in these respects emulated his father, who, while he studied to be too good, managed to seem bad. But the son was free from all suspicion of

[1] Geniturarum Exemplar, p. 17.

crime, his disposition was completely trained to philosophic studies."

Urged to calculate the horoscope of this boy, Cardan
provided a sufficiently long life for him, though he declared[1], what seemed certain enough, that his vital powers
would be always low. " At the age of twenty-three years,
nine months, and twenty-two days, languor of mind and
body would afflict him. At the age of thirty-four years,
five months, and twenty days, he would suffer from skin
disease and a slight fever. After the age of fifty-five
years, three months, and seventeen days, various diseases
would fall to his lot. As long as he lived he would be
constant, rigid, severe, continent, intelligent, a guardian
of the right, patient in labour, a rememberer of wrongs
and benefits; he would be terrible, and have desires and
vices growing from desire, and he would suffer under im-
potence. He would be most wise, and for that reason the
admired of nations; most prudent, magnanimous, fortunate, and, as it were, another Solomon."

The king's death followed so soon after these predictions, that Cardan made it his business to re-consider
them, and in his book, after a recitation of his false con-
clusions, he proceeded to give a dissertation headed
" What I thought afterwards upon the subject." One

---

[1] Geniturarum Exemplar, p. 19.

could desire no better evidence than there is here of Jerome's good faith and sincerity as an astrologer.

Of course his faith in the supposed science was not shaken. He entered into details for the purpose of showing that it was unsafe to pronounce upon the term of life in weak nativities, unless all processes, and ingresses, and external movements that from month to month and year to year affect the ruling planets had been carefully inquired into. If, he said, in the prognostic which he gave to the king's friends he had not made a distinct reservation on this account, they would have been fairly entitled to complain of him. But to make such a calculation would have cost him, he said, not less than a hundred hours.

He did not wish to give any opinion at all. He was compelled to write: the courtiers worried him, and strove to implicate him in their plots and jealousies. He felt the danger of predicting—if he should by chance have to predict—King Edward's death. He remembered having read of two men who predicted death to princes. One, Ascletarion to Domitian; instant death to himself was the reward of his true prophecy; the other, a priest to the Duke Galeazio Sforza; he also predicted truly, and being cast into prison, was, in the most cruel manner, starved out of the world, after he had prolonged his life in it for a few days by a wretched expedient. Jerome, had he foreseen it, would, he said, have been urged by his own natural sincerity, and by his love for the king, to predict the fate then imminent, he should have told all that he knew; and he thought, therefore, that he owed to his ignorance a most fortunate escape. He thought it also in the same way a providential thing that he had not agreed to stop in Scotland until April, for he should then not have reached London till the king was in his last disease, and so should have fallen upon evil.

The king, after Cardan's departure, kept too jovial a Christmas, and in the first days of the succeeding February there appeared the fatal cough, that never left him till his death in the succeeding July. It was in April that those matches were agreed upon which formed part of Northumberland's designs, and it was on the 11th of June following that the Lady Jane Grey plot became manifest. The king was induced to disinherit in favour of that unhappy victim, not only his sister Mary, on account of her religion, but also his sister Elizabeth, against whose creed no fault could be objected. The part played by Northumberland, as the first mover in these schemes and the most powerful among the nobles, was no worthy one, though there is much room for differences of opinion as to the extent of his criminality and the exact aim of his policy. Of course there is no just reason for supposing, as Cardan and many others did, that King Edward was poisoned. Cardan imputed too much evil to the duke;

but the following passage is not uninstructive as showing
the opinion formed by that philosopher of English politics,
after a week or two of Court experience in London.   He
chronicles impressions formed during the autumn that
preceded the king's death.   The passage also, in the final
sentence, illustrates very completely the candour with
which Jerome spoke always the truth about himself.   He
is speaking of his false prediction[1]:—"I could indeed,
after the manner of some astrologers, affect to have known
what was about to happen, and to have been silent through
fear, an easy thing in so conspicuous a case, but I was so
far even from thinking of such an event, that I was far
enough surely from foreseeing it.. I did, indeed, foresee
it, but in another way, when I perceived that everything
lay in the power of one man,—the boy, the fortresses,
the exchequer, the parliament, the fleet.   Children whom
he could not rule he made rulers; and the power was
with him whose father the king's father had beheaded,.
while he who had lost also two uncles by the mother's.
side successively condemned and executed, was misguiding
everything, being urged, not more by hate than fear, to
plot the king's destruction.   And when all were silent
through dread (for he condemned judicially as many as
he chose), and he had conciliated to himself most of the
nobles by distributing Church property among them, so.

that all things might be done according to one man's
decision, and at the command of him who was most
hostile to the king, I, proving a better prophet through
my mother wit than through my knowledge of this
science of astrology, at once departed, for I saw the omens
of a great calamity and was alarmed."

The failure of the astrologer could scarcely have been
owned more frankly. The method of accounting for the
failure was in no respect evasive. According to the
science of astrology, as taught by Ptolemy and by Cardan,
it never is enough, for perfect accuracy, to predict a whole
life from a single horoscope. The nativity of a man's
wife, for example, and the nativities of each one of his
children, together with many other aspects and conjunctions, have the most direct influence in modifying and
sometimes completely altering his fortunes. As one person's life upon earth influences the life of another, so one
person's stars influence the stars of another, and the calcu-
lations necessary for an accurate prediction thus become
extremely complex, and may well cost the labourer a
hundred hours of work. A good astrologer, says Jerome,
ought to be another Argus.

In that book on the Variety of Things, which Edward's
death prevented his design of dedicating to him, Cardan
spoke again of the young king, who had won so largely
upon his esteem: " If Edward VI, that boy of wondrous

hope, had survived, he would have contributed not a little to the establishment of the whole kingdom. For, as Plato says, that is a true republic whose kings are philosophers[1]."

The stranger, of course, carried away with him from England certain impressions of a people among whom he had for some months been sojourning. "It is worth consideration," he reported[2], "that the English care little or not at all for death. With kisses and salutations parents and children part; the dying say that they depart into immortal life, that they shall there await those left behind; and each exhorts the other to retain him in his memory. Cheerfully, without blenching, without tottering, they bear with constancy the final doom. They surely merit pity who with such alacrity meet death, and have no pity on themselves."

But what do they look like, asks a speaker in the dialogue through which Cardan relates familiarly his impressions; what do they look like, and how do they dress?

"In figure," he replies, "they are much like the Italians; they are white—whiter than we are, not so ruddy;

---

[1] De Rerum Varietate, p. 285.

[2] The succeeding account of the English people is collected from Cardan's dialogue De Morte, printed at the end of the book Somniorum Synesiorum, pp. 371, et seq.

and they are broad-chested. There are some among them
of great stature; urbane and friendly to the stranger, but
they are quickly angered, and are in that state to be dreaded.
They are strong in war, but they want caution; greedy
enough after food and drink, but therein they do not
equal the Germans. They are rather prone than prompt
to lust. There are great intellects among them—witness
Duns Scotus and Suiseth[1], who rank second to none. In
dress they are like Italians; for they are glad to boast
themselves most nearly allied to them, and therefore study
to imitate as much as possible their manner and their
clothes. And yet, even in form, they are more like the
Germans, the French, and the Spaniards. Certain it is,
that all the barbarians of Europe love the Italians more
than any race among themselves. We were all nearly
killed in Belgium, because I had a youth with me who
looked much like a Spaniard. But perhaps these people
do not know our wickedness.

" The English are faithful, liberal, and ambitious. But
as for fortitude, the things done by the Highland Scots
are the most wonderful. They, when they are led to execution, take a piper with them; and he, who is himself
often one of the condemned, plays them up dancing to
their death."

---

[1] Richard Suiseth, an English arithmetician, whose " Calculator,"
edited by Victor Trincbavello, had been issued at Venice in 1520 by
Cardan's first publisher, Ottaviano Scoto.

And you penetrated, says the questioner, as far as Scotland.—" I did, and it was a great pleasure to me to see so many provinces; this is at any rate one pleasure open to the living."—But the questioner then urges the discomforts that he must have endured; for example, those resulting from his ignorance of the language. " Truly so," replies Cardan. " And I wondered much, especially when I was in England, and rode about on horseback in the neighbourhood of London, for I seemed to be in Italy. When I looked among those groups of English sitting together, I completely thought myself to be among Italians: they were like, as I said, in figure, manners, dress, gesture, colour, but when they opened their mouths I could not understand so much as a word, and wondered at them as if they were my countrymen gone mad and raving. For they inflect the tongue upon the palate, twist words in the mouth, and maintain a sort of gnashing with the teeth. But then what pleasure could be taken there by one whose thoughts were with his children? I was so racked by the thoughts of those whom I had left at home, that for that cause only I was ready at once to seek and beg for leave to go on with my journey."

The stay in London was not, therefore, very long; but an offer was there made to Cardan by which, if he had accepted it, his departure might have been still more hastened. Laval, the French ambassador, and also another confidential agent of the King of France, were offering him eight hundred gold crowns a year; and further, promising a chain of five hundred gold pieces if he would kiss hands and at once leave the court of London. There were others also who endeavoured to secure his services for Charles V, who was at that time besieging Metz. Jerome declined both offers. He would not go to the emperor because he was then in a position of the utmost difficulty, where he, indeed, lost the greater part of his army through cold and hunger. He would not go to the King of France because he thought it wrong to forsake his liege lord and to give in adhesion to the enemy[1]. His spirit shrank also from court servitude, because, as he said, he thought it foolish, life being so short, to become a dead man for the sake of a livelihood, and to be unhappy for a long while, in the hope of being some day happy[2]. Resisting, therefore, all temptation, Jerome set his face in a determined manner towards Milan. Another temptation also he resisted. He steadily refused to acknowledge the title of King Edward to be styled Defender of the Faith, in prejudice of the Pope, and took from the court a reward of a hundred gold crowns, rather than of five hundred or a thousand which

---

[1] De Vitâ Propriâ, cap. xxxii. for the preceding.
[2] De Libris Propriis. Lib. ult. Op. Tom. i. p. 131.

he was told that he should have if he would overcome his scruple[1].

In this mood he quitted London. Our capital itself does not seem to have made any great impression on him. In a chapter upon cities that he had seen, written soon afterwards, he says of London only that it is about fifty miles from the sea, upon the river Thames; but that to confess what he thinks, it is not by magnificent buildings or by walls that towns are made illustrious, but by men, brave and excellent, who cherish virtue. Fine buildings for a foolish people are a handsome body for no soul[2]. That is the whole opinion given by him.

Determining, for reasons before stated, not to go home through France, Jerome left London for Dover[3], meaning to take ship from that port and cross the Channel. He was detained there, however, for nine days by adverse winds. Now he had conceived a desire or whim to carry home with him to Italy an English boy, and as he was talking of that whim on the evening before he sailed, the person with whom he lodged showed him a boy named William, twelve years old, honest, sensible, and obedient to his parents. His grandfather Gregory still lived, his father's name was Laurence, and they came of

---

[1] De Vitâ Propriâ, cap. xxix.

[2] De Varietate Rerum (ed. cit.), p. 672.

[3] For this, and the succeeding facts, see the preface to the Dialogue de Morte, at the end of the book Somniorum Synesiorum, p. 344.

a good family[1]. The boy's father may, perhaps, have
thought that here was a fine opportunity for getting his
son out into the world. " The fates," says Cardan,
" thrust him upon me. Neither I nor his friends took
time to remember that the boy could not speak either
Italian or Latin: if I had thought of that, which was the
beginning of all his misfortunes, I should scarcely have
taken him away. But next morning, when there had
passed only some words on the preceding evening, the
father brought him down in haste, the ship then being in
a hurry to depart through fear of pirates. The poor boy
fell down upon the shore, so that he could scarcely rise
again even when helped; and when I was told of that
omen I almost refused to take him." Nevertheless, seeing
with how much alacrity the boy was pressed into his
service, Cardan says that he did not like to send him
back. William himself was far from manifesting any
reluctance to leave home. Hastily, therefore, it was
decided that he should be taken, and the philosopher,
taxed with a new responsibility, set sail across the narrow
Channel for Cape Grisnez, meaning, when he reached
land, to turn aside directly into Belgium.

---

[1] The surname of this family is called in the last book De Libris
Proprus, Lataneus, in the preface to De Morte, Cataneus; one of
course being a misprint. It was not, perhaps, of English origin
Cardan says of the father, " erat Ligur."

CHAPTER VII.

THE PHYSICIAN AT THE SUMMIT OF HIS FAME.

WHEN fairly across the sea, Cardan discovered that the English boy should have been left behind. He was not the son of poor parents. His paternal roof soon afterwards was thought worthy of sheltering Queen Mary and Philip of Spain, and he had been sent with the great philosopher under the impression that he would return to his own soil another Theophrastus[1]. But there were no means of communicating with him otherwise than by signs. He could speak only English, and the only English that could be made available in his case—it belonged to the store of one of Jerome's followers—was in vain put into requisition. He could have been sent back by one of the physician's friends, Gianangelo Anono, who offered to take charge of him if needful; but it was Jerome's wish that he should go back of his own accord.

[1] De Morte.   In the dialogue.

He therefore took pains to disgust him with the enterprise on which he was engaged, by whipping him for nothing on the naked skin. At the same time, the follower who had picked up some knowledge of our tongue stood by to improve the occasion, asking the boy, while he still smarted, "Volgo Doura?" (which is English for Will you go to Dover?) but the little Spartan answered only "No." Then the attendant asked him, "Volgo Milan?" and he signified a positive assent. Therefore, by no means meaning that the youth should come to harm, Cardan abided by his first intention. While they were on the way from England, William's father died, and there is a story of a ghostly head and dead face that appeared to the boy and frightened him when they were on the water[1].

Jerome Cardan, in his route homeward, passed through Gravelines, Bruges, Ghent, and Brussels, to Louvain. At Louvain he talked with Gemma Frisius, properly named Reinerut, but entitled Frisius from his birth in Friesland. Gemma Frisius was professor of medicine in the Louvain University, and, like Cardan, excelled in mathematics. He had been often summoned to the court of Charles V, but had refused every invitation, much preferring the tranquillity of academic life. He was a remarkably small man, of the most insignificant aspect;

---

[1] Preface to the Dialogue de Morte, for the preceding.

AT LOUVAIN—ANTWERP—BASLE.

and when Jerome talked with him at Leyden, forty-five years old, and only two years distant from his death.

From Louvain the travellers went by Mechlin to Antwerp, and at Antwerp they remained a little time, for no pains were spared there to detain them[1]. In that town Jerome met with a slight accident. Going into a shop to buy a gem, he fell over the brasier, was hurt and bruised in his left ear, but the injury was not more than skin-deep.

Antwerp was the first place at which any long halt was made, and to visit that town Cardan had diverged slightly from his track. The original route was afterwards resumed, through Liege and Aix-la-Chapelle, to Cologne. From Cologne the travellers went up the Rhine, by Coblentz, Mayence, Worms, Spires, and Strasburg, to Basle.

At Basle, if Cardan had not received timely warning from Guglielmo Gratalaro, he would unwittingly have put up at a house infected by the plague. That town was the second place at which he tarried for a little time, and there the learned Carolus Affaidatus (who had published a work on physics and astronomy at Venice in the year 1547) received him into his villa. That liberal

---

[1] De Vitâ Propriâ, cap. xxix. for much that follows on Cardan's route, for the next incident cap. xxx. of the same work. Whatever is said in the text more than may be covered by these references, will be found in the Geniturarum Exemplar, pp. 138, 139.

man, at his guest's departure, used great effort to compel
him to accept a valuable mule, worth nearly a hundred
gold pieces. In the course of the same journey, a noble
Genoese, named Ezzelin, offered also to the traveller an
ambling horse (the English, Jerome says, call it, in their
language an Obin—does he mean Dobbin?); but he was
ashamed to take it, though he had never seen an animal
that he thought handsomer. It was quite white, and
there were shown to him two of the kind, from which he
might have made his own selection.

On the horse given by Affaidatus, Jerome turned aside
to Besançon, where he again stayed for some days, that
being the last place at which he tarried on his way.
There he lodged with a liberal and courteous scholar,
Franciscus Bonvalutus, and met with a Church dignitary,
by whom he was hospitably entertained and sent away
with gifts. His was indeed a triumphal journey home
to Milan, for his fame abroad was at the highest, and
good gifts awaited him at almost every stage.

From Besançon he travelled into Italy, through Berne
and Zurich, of course visiting at Zurich Conrad Gesner,
who kept open house there for all learned men who came
into his neighbourhood. Gesner was not only the best
naturalist among the scholars of his day, but of all men
of that century he was the pattern man of letters. He
was faultless in private life, assiduous in study, diligent

in maintaining correspondence and good-will with learned men in all countries, hospitable—though his means were small—to every scholar that came into Zurich. Prompt to serve all, he was an editor of other men's volumes, a writer of prefaces for friends, a suggester to young writers of books on which they might engage themselves, and a great helper to them in the progress of their work. But still, while finding time for services to other men, he could produce as much out of his own study as though he had no part in the life beyond its walls. Cardan therefore records, as we might have expected, that on his way through Zurich he was Gesner's guest.

So then travelling on into Italy and there sailing across the Lake of Como, Jerome re-entered Milan on the 3rd of January, 1553, after an absence of three hundred and ten days. How different that entry from the former one, when he and Lucia came in from Gallarate paupers! He had been called, for the sake of his skill, to a remote part of Europe. He had been sought by the emperor himself, by the King of France, and for the Queen of Scotland. He had been honoured by the King of England. The foremost men for rank and learning in many foreign countries had been eager to obtain his aid as a physician, or his personal acquaintance as a friend. He came back into Milan loaded with honours and rewards to take his undisputed place as chief physician in the city

by which he had been despised. He became by right
the medical adviser of the great men of the place. The
governor, Gonzaga, courted him soon after his return, on
behalf of his relative, the Duke of Mantua. He proposed to buy his service to the duke in perpetuity, for
thirty thousand crowns, of which the first thousand were
displayed at once: Cardan refused them. Gonzaga saw
no harm in such an offer, but to the philosopher it sounded
like an insult. He refused it steadily. Ferrante was
astonished and displeased. Having in vain laboured to
persuade Jerome, he betook himself to threats, but the
physician, who refused to sell himself into a kind of
bondage, explained boldly why it was that " he would
rather die than be disgraced." To the credit of the
governor, it is to be added that he liked him afterwards
the better for his self-assertion[1].

From this point in Cardan's career we may glance
back upon the past, and illustrate the change in his condition by referring to a few small objects of ambition not
yet specified, which he had in the days of his adversity
failed to attain. When he was leaving Sacco he had
some designs upon the village or town of Caravaggio;
where he would have received something less than a
stipend of eighty crowns a year. He had been willing
to take fifty-five crowns for a like position at Mazenta,

_____
[1] De Vitâ Propriâ, cap. xxix.

but the plague raged so much in the place, that he would probably himself have been one of its victims; having looked over the ground, therefore, he prudently withdrew. At the same time he had thoughts of a hundred crowns a year at Bassano, whither his friends advised him not to go. In those days of his poverty Cesare Rincio, a leading Milanese physician, thought it no shame to recommend that he should settle in a village of the district of Novara, fifty miles from Milan, on a stipend of twelve crowns a year! Salaried physicians, settled thus in the plague-smitten and impoverished Italian towns and villages, fulfilled functions similar to those belonging now in England to an union surgeon; and their services were as inadequately recompensed. Cardan names two physicians, one of them at Gallarate, who married upon incomes of twenty gold crowns, hoping to perpetuate their families. He doubts whether either of the two would be disposed to marry twice. Later in his own life, when he was thirty-seven years old, and still struggling in Milan, he was a rejected applicant for the office of medical attendant on the hospital of St. Ambrose, which would yield a yearly profit of between seven and eight gold crowns[1]. His condition was much changed,

---

[1] De Vitâ Propriâ, cap. xxxiii. He himself claims credit for the next fact in balancing his own account of vice and virtue. Others observed upon it. An example of such an opinion from without will occur in the course of the present chapter.

but he was the same man still; he had not changed his
manner with his fortunes.

After his return from Scotland, Cardan occupied himself upon the emendation of his Books of Subtilty, and
in the further preparation of his work on the Variety of
Things. The extent of his practice interfered with his
desk labour. In the year following[1], however, he wrote
two books, containing nearly three hundred fables, designed for the pleasure of children and the use of men.
These fables have, unhappily, remained unpublished.
They would have formed an interesting portion of his
works. We have to regret also that the familiar letters
which he arranged for publication have escaped the press.
In 1554 he wrote little or nothing; he was prosperous
in his profession; indeed, he says, overpaid. Every year
works of his were being printed or reprinted in one or
other of the literary towns of Europe. In 1555 his commentaries upon Ptolemy, written on the Loire, with
twelve horoscopes appended, in a separate work published
at the same time in the same form, appeared at Lyons.
Therein, speaking of himself, he wrote: " What I have
not, I might have had; what I have has been not only
spontaneously offered, but in a manner thrust upon me,

---

[1] The account of these books, written between 1552 and 1557, is
from the end of the Liber de Libris Propriis, published in the latter
year.

yet all in accordance with my earliest ambition[1]." The
dreams of his youth were realised.

In 1555 Jerome wrote on the Uses of Water, and,
having been lately ill, wrote a work called Ἀλήθεια, or De
Dedicatione.   In 1557 he wrote a summary of medical
science entitled "Ars Curandi Parva," other medical
books, and some miscellaneous essays.   He wrote, also, a
letter to his old patient, Gaddi, then in prison—an Oration
in Praise of the Milanese College—quite in good faith, to
that had he come at last—and, among other things, a
Declaration of the Size of Noah's Ark.   From this list I
have omitted the reply to Scaliger, published in 1556,
because that is part of an affair that will require separate
consideration.

In the year 1557 Cardan published, also, for the second
time, a little work "On his own Books," which included
many biographical details, and made good up to that year
the register of all his writings In the same year happened
a domestic event that gave importance to the date.   I
take it, therefore, as the next point up to which the
several threads into which this narrative occasionally
divides itself have to be brought.

Before quitting the subject of these books, we should
not omit to take notice of a protest, published afterwards
by Cardan, on the subject of a liberty taken at Basle with

[1] Geniturarum Exemplar, p. 92.

his work on the Variety of Things. That elaborate
supplement to the books on Subtilty was printed at Paris,
Lyons, and Nuremberg, both in Italian and in French, as
translated by Richard de Blanche. The printer of an
edition issued at Basle, Henricus Petrus, set among reformers, interpolated in one chapter half a dozen words
hostile to the Dominicans. Jerome wrote to the printer
on the subject, who replied in justification, What did a
few words more or less matter to him so far away. The
offensive sentence was reproduced in an edition published
soon after at Avignon. Cardan therefore appealed to the
world on the subject years afterwards in the third and
last essay on his works, and made that interpolation the
occasion of one of the very few allusions to the religious
movements of the time that were suffered to escape his
pen. Few as they are, they are all consistent and distinct.
" As the writings of Saint Jerome himself," he says,
" were interpolated by men who did not agree with his
opinions, so, lest any person be misguided or deceived by
others in my works, let it be known to all that I nowhere
play the theologian, and that I wish never to stick a hook
into another man's mass. But so far as regards my own
way of life and my religion, I desire to follow what is
safest, to obey that law, and use those rites, ceremonies,
and customs under which I was born, which have been
obeyed and used for so many centuries by my forefathers;

that I have no wish to sow discord, or to make a God of
my own mouth, or to know more than is needful[1]."
Perfectly tolerant himself, Cardan withdrew from all
cause of political offence.   While he was true to the
Church, and faithful to the priestly class by which he was
throughout life supported liberally, and which, it should
be observed, included his best patrons—Archinto, Sfondrato, Morone, Hamilton, and others who will be hereafter mentioned—he did not find this allegiance inconsistent with much bold speculation upon things divine
His speculation, however, was of that harmless and
fantastic kind that may amuse philosophers, but never
can infect the crowd.   It attacked no Church interest,
and did not hurt him, therefore, in his intercourse with
cardinals and bishops.

"In the year 1557," says the physician, "I began
some writings, but they were continued with the greatest
difficulty on account of the assiduous care of sick people,
most of them magnates, so that I had scarcely breathing
time.   For I had about that time ascended, as it were,
without will of my own, to the highest point of my authority and influence, though there were many refusing
to acknowledge it, and even plotting against me."   Finding it difficult to make time for his pen to work out all

[1] De Libr. Propr.   Lib. ult.   Op. Tom. i. p. 112, *et seq.* for this and
the citations following.

the ideas passing through his head, he resolved then to establish a method for the more ready finishing of books that still remained upon his hands. To hasten the completion of five or six works, he began, therefore, a sixth or seventh, and in that way arose his volume upon Dialectics, which treats of the essences of things. He began, also, then in his most prosperous day, another book on a matter of which he had had much experience, the Uses of Adversity.

Of his prosperity as a physician we have had many illustrations, and among the incidents of practice that occurred at Milan, between the date of his return and the year 1557, one only is necessary to this narrative. It will be remembered that Cardan left Edinburgh with a promise from Archbishop Hamilton, that at the end of two years he would send word how his treatment had succeeded. Jerome had, in the interval, both written and sent to him, but for two years no tidings of the archbishop were received at Milan. At the end of two years and one month there arrived a Scotchman, known to Cardan, with a letter from the reverend lord, running as follows[1]:

"Your two most welcome letters, written in former months, I received through the hands of an English merchant; another was brought by the lord bishop at

[1] The letter is printed in the book De Libris Propriis, ed. 1557.

Dundee, with the Indian balsam. Your last letter I
had from Scoto, with your most choice commentaries on
the very difficult work of Ptolemy. To all these I have
three or four times amply and abundantly replied. For I
had addressed very many letters to you, but am uncertain
whether they have reached your hands.

"Now, however, I have given orders to a servant
whom you know, and who is travelling to Rome, that he
shall pay a visit to your excellency, and, saluting you in
my name, thank you, not only for your various and very
welcome little gifts, but also for my health, that is in
great part restored, for the almost complete subjugation of
my disease, for strength regained; in fine, I may say, for
life recovered. All those good things, and this body of
mine itself, I hold as received from you. From the time
when I had your medicines, prescribed and prepared with
so much art and dexterity, the disease that is peculiar to
me has made its visits with much less frequency and
violence; the accustomed attacks now scarcely occur once
a month, and sometimes once in two months; then too
they are not urgent and pressing, as they used to be, but
are felt very slightly.

"It would look like ingratitude (and I confess to it) if
I did not acknowledge all those many and great benefits
and send you back thanks. But now I despatch to you a
living letter (namely, this Michael), and entreat and pray

your excellency, from my heart, that if I can be of use to you in anything, with aid, service, or money, you will send word to me by him; he will, without delay, send me intelligence, and the moment I have tidings of it consider the thing done.

" Besides, Master William Cassanate, the physician, went home last year to his father's house, and has not yet returned. A man certainly worthy of great name and honour, whose daily offices and house companionship are very pleasant to me. I would much urge and beg your excellency not to fall short of your usual kindness in writing to me, that the separation of our bodies may not be a separation of our minds, but that we may be always present to each other. I wish you, in my name, to salute those who are of your household. Farewell. From our metropolitan seat of St. Andrew's. October, 1554."

Michael was the archbishop's first chamberlain, and he came privately authorised to offer to Cardan large payments if he would take office as Hamilton's physician. But those offers were refused[1].

Though rude of speech, Jerome, as has been seen, was not rude with the pen; his just and high notion of the dignity of letters, and of the courtesies due by literary men to one another, not only kept all anger out of his

---

[1] Geniturarum Exemplar, p. 193.

printed works, but caused him to establish and maintain, by correspondence, friendship with many people whom he never saw. His recent tour had added to the number of his friends, and there were others with whom he was in his best days personally very intimate. Among these were two brother physicians, Montagnano Cavallo and Aurelio Stanno. There was also a Milanese patrician, Francisco Vimercati, skilled in philosophy, who acknowledged himself a disciple of Cardan. He had been called by Francis I. to Paris, and there made professor of philosophy; afterwards he was summoned to Turin by the Duke of Savoy. Vimercati was a good Greek scholar, and was the best interpreter of Aristotle in his own generation. Another of Jerome's friends was Boniface Rhodiginus, jurisconsult and astrologer, related probably to the great Cœlius Rhodiginus, who had taught at Milan, and had ranked the elder Scaliger among his pupils. The friendship felt for Cardan by his fellow-professor, Alciati the jurist, was maintained by his heir, Alciati the cardinal. Cardinal Alciati had power to become another strong supporter of the great physician's fortunes, and he thus again acquired a patron in the Church.

To this list of friends we must not delay to add the name of Gianpietro Albuzio, who might have been named in a former chapter as fellow-professor with Cardan at Pavia. Albuzio had, like Jerome, struggled a little while

at Gallarate, but at the age of twenty-five obtained the
chair of Rhetoric at Pavia, and from that time remained
for forty years, through all its trials and its struggles,
true as a lover to his university.   He became popular,
and was invited to Bologna and to Pisa, but no prospect
of greater gain could tempt him from his post.   From
the chair of Rhetoric in Pavia he passed to the chair of
Logic, and when a vacancy occurred, his faithfulness was
rewarded with the senior chair of medicine.   He was a
very learned physician, versed not only in polite letters
and history, in Greek and Hebrew, but also a deep
theologian.   With him Jerome became more intimate in
later years[1].   Among other friends, Jerome names also
Melchior, a Milanese physician, and one Thomas Iseus,
towards whom he maintained always a great good-will,
though it was met with an unsparing enmity.

Cardan was rarely without one or two youths under
his care.   In Milan, after his return, he had three pupils
in succession—Fabrizio Bozio, who became a soldier;
Giuseppe Amati, who became a political functionary; and
Cristofero Sacco, who became a notary public.   His old
pupil and relative, Gaspar Cardan, had commenced practice in Rome[2].   His elder son, Gianbatista, having with

---

[1] The preceding names of friends are from the fifteenth chapter De
Vitâ Propriâ.

[2] De Vitâ Propriâ, cap. xxxv.

much trouble after two rejections obtained his degree at
Pavia, practised at Milan under his father's auspices, but
even then it was not easy to procure his reception into
the Milanese College of Physicians[1].

This son, in spite of his father's praises and fond par-
tiality, does not seem to have been particularly clever.
His simplicity verged, perhaps, upon stupidity; he had
acquired that taste for dice which Jerome himself only
set aside when he had attained the position sought so
restlessly; he had a taste not acquired at home, for he
was a glutton. Certainly he and Aldo gave Cardan
much trouble after his return ; now, he says, he was
distressed by one, now by another, and sometimes by
both at once. Aldo was becoming very fast a hopeless
reprobate. Gianbatista wrote a very little book while he
was in his father's house at Milan, but it did not go to
press during his lifetime. It was " Upon the fœtid foods
not to be eaten[2]," and arose out of the domestic supper-
talk. Upon the appearance of the usual salad, the young
physician threw out a professional remark concerning
onions, that Galen had forbidden any physician to use

---

[1] De Libris Propriis. Lib. ult. Op. Tom. i. p 92.
[2] Authorities for the preceding will be cited in the sequel. The account of the origin of Gianbatista's book is taken from the introduc-
tion to the book itself, De Cibis fœtidis non edendis, appended by
Cardan to the first edition of the work De Utilitate ex Adversis
Capiendâ.

fœtid articles, as onions, garlic, or the like in food. Jerome contradicted that assertion. His son was surprised, and thought that he must intend some joke or trick, for Galen was particular upon the point in more places than one. Finding his father to be serious, Gianbatista began next morning his little treatise, addressed "by a Physician to Jerome Cardan, Physician of Milan." He attended poor people and others, to whom it was allowable to introduce him, and effected, as his father declared afterwards, some great cures. He began also a little tract "On Lightning," but that was not a kindred subject, for it is evident, I think, that he himself was not particularly quick or brilliant

"My nativity and that of my daughter," Jerome said, in a book published after his return from England, "decree to me many calamities and little good, but the nativities of my sons promise me much good and little harm[1]." Libellous stars! The daughter, Clara, never gave her father any pain. While he was practising in Milan, after his return from his great journey, an excellent and wealthy young man, Bartolomeo Sacco, a Milanese patrician, courted her, and married her, and received with her from the hands of the great physician a befitting dowry. In after life she never gave him any

[1] Geniturarum Exemplar; p. 122?

reason for an hour's regret, except at the fact that she continued childless[1].

But there was another member brought into the household of Cardan—the English Boy. When he reached Milan, unable to explain what were his own wishes or what promises his father might have made to him, little or nothing could be done till he had picked up a knowledge of Italian. The physician became full of occupations, and the luckless William suffered great neglect. At the end of a year and a half he spoke Italian well enough to complain that he had not been sent to any school, that nothing had been done for him. He had, however, been put under a music-master, because, says Cardan, " the people of his country seemed to have aptitude for music," but the master took small pains to teach, though he received in one year ten gold crowns, and the boy seemed to be very quick at learning. Then, when Jerome bought a book, William did not appear at all solicitous to learn to read it, for he was immoderately fond rather of playing with companions of his own age. In the crowd and hurry of his daily practice, Jerome forgot, culpably it must be said, his duty to his charge; he did not fulfil the trust he had too thoughtlessly accepted. When his conscience was uneasy at the boy's neglected education,

[1] De Vitâ Propriâ, cap. xxvii.

he consoled himself with the reflection that the youth
seemed to have no taste for study. But he was faithful,
obedient, honest, and clever; he was gifted with remarkably acute vision, was patient in enduring labour, and
was never querulous. " Wherefore," the physician adds,
" he was so loved by me, that he could not have been
loved better; and that made me feel more heavily that
I appeared to be deficient in my duty to him. But in
the .mean time, so many impediments were raised in my
way by my sons, that I could attend to little else. Now
one troubled my waters for me, now the other, sometimes
both at once[1]."

Very incidentally and without giving any date, Cardan
says, that "in those days a person wrote against my
books on Subtilty, in reply to whom I wrote an Apology,
which is added to the third edition of the work. It is
very useful to assist the comprehension of the books
on Subtilty ; expositions of some difficult passages are
therein given, and demonstrations not commonplace,
though few[2]." So lightly the philosopher thought it
proper for the dignity of scholarship, that he should pass
over the violent and unprovoked assault upon his credit
next to be chronicled.

The assailant was the elder Scaliger, who had begun

[1] Preface to Dialogue de Morte for the preceding.
[2] De Lib. Prop. Lib. ult. Op. Tom. i. p. 117.

life as a fighter among soldiers, and closed it as a fighter among scholars. He was born seventeen years before Cardan, on the banks of the same lake of Guarda within which Jerome had once been nearly drowned, and from which Brother Luca had drawn the delicious carp that were to him not less agreeable than mathematics. The birthplace was the castle of Ripa, belonging to his father, Benedict, who had done good service in war to King Mathias Corvinus. Two days after his birth he had felt the pressure of the times; the castle was attacked by the Venetians, taken and plundered, the mother, with the infant just born, and the other children, saving their lives by flight. At twelve years old the future scholar, Julius Cæsar Scaliger, became page to the Emperor Maximilian. Him he served for seventeen years, proving himself a fine soldier on all occasions, and particularly at the battle of Ravenna, wherein he lost his father and his elder brother, Titus. He was not then named Scaliger, and it is doubtful whether he had at any time a right to take the name. He claimed to be descended from the princely family of La Scala to which Verona had belonged, and considered that Verona was his heritage whenever he could get it. On the other hand, it is declared positively that the Scala family had been extinct for some generations. His father, Boniface, "a terrible man," the grandson calls him— indeed the whole family was terrible—Boniface called

Julius Cæsar, after his place of education in Sclavonia, Da
Burden, in order to distinguish clearly between him and
his brother Titus.   Enemies of Scaliger made light, afterwards, of the Verona story, and undertook to prove that
he belonged to a family of humble tradesfolk, bearing the
name of Burden.   Julius Cæsar, rightly or wrongly, held
himself to be a prince born to a principality that was
maintained against him by the enemy, Verona being in
the hands of the Venetians.   To get his own, he thought
that he could do nothing better than become a pope, and
declare war with Venice.   He, therefore, at length quitted
his post in the army, and began a bold push for the pope-
dom by betaking himself to Bologna with a view to preparation for an entry into the Franciscan order.   He studied
at Bologna logic and scholastic philosophy—especially
the works of Duns Scotus—but a little closer knowledge
of Franciscans soon disgusted him, and he forsook their
company.   At Bologna he had made himself remarkable
by having his hair cropped, while other Italians wore it
tolerably long on each side of the face, as the monks used
to do.   He became known, therefore, by his crown among
the Bolognese as Tonso da Burden.   That name he retained when he left study, and, resuming his old profession as a soldier, served under the King of France in
Italy.   He was diverted at last from a military life by
love of knowledge and, by gout, and having been suf-

ficiently disgusted with the notion of a monk's life, turned physician. He received his doctorate at Pavia, then bearing the name of Burden. In 1529 he accompanied the Bishop of Agen to his home, as medical adviser, on condition that he should not be detained at Agen longer than eight days. Within that time, however, at the age of forty-five, he fell in love; it is said, with a young woman of thirteen. Her youth must, I think, have been maliciously exaggerated; at any rate her charms were powerful; they detained the physician, caused him to settle in the town, and very soon to marry her. Julius Cæsar Scaliger thus became fixed at Agen as M. de l'Escalle, an eminent practitioner who prospered greatly. He and his wife had fifteen children, of whom seven survived; and the boys seem to have been all terrible, like their grandfather and their father. " My father," said his son Joseph Justus, the scholar, in familiar talk[1]—" my father was honoured and respected by all those court gentry. He was more feared than loved at Agen; he had an authoritative way, a majesty, a presence —he was terrible; when he cried out he frightened all of them. Auratus said that Julius Cæsar Scaliger had a

[1] The preceding sketch is amplified by reference to, and all the succeeding traits are taken from, the first good edition of the Table-Talk of Scaliger the Younger. "Scaligerana. Editio altera, ad verum Exemplar restituta, et innumeris iisque fœdissimis mendis, quibus prior illa passim scatebat diligentissime purgata." Cologne, 1667.

face like any king's.   Yes, like an emperor's.   There is
no king or emperor who has so grand a way as he had.
Look at me; I resemble him in every respect perfectly,
the aquiline nose.   I was but eight years old when I held
my little sister at her baptism, and on the same day
my father gave me the birch—birched me, his fellow-
sponsor.   My sister is a poor creature, a beast[1]."

A terrible man was Julius Cæsar Scaliger when he
girded up his loins to birch Jerome Cardan.   He believed
that he had a familiar demon—his son says a devil[2]—that
urged him to write and gave him understanding.   He
had two daughters—I do not know which of them was
the beast—but they must have differed from each other
much; one died a nun, the other died the widow of two
husbands[3].   His sons all had the spirit of the family.   One
of them, Constant, was called, commonly, the Gascon
Devil.   He was so terrible, said Joseph Justus, that once
when he engaged for sport in lance practice with eight
Germans, he killed some, hurt others, and fled to Poland,
where he was armed afterwards by Stephen, the king, but
destroyed by the envy of the nobles.   They stabbed him
during a hunt.   My brother Leonard, too, was killed by

[1] Scaligerana (ed. cit.), p. 229.   ". . . . Il estoit terrible et croit
tellement . . . ."
[2] " Erat Dæmoniacus, habebat diabolum ut credebatur." Ibid. p. 233.
[3] Ibid. p. 228.

twelve men: I never could have justice. Condé would do nothing[1].

M. de l Escalle made money at Agen, bought houses, and acquired property which he could not hold securely as an alien; he therefore obtained letters of naturalisation, and became a Frenchman. In the deed he is entitled Jules César de l'Escalle de Burden[2]. The new adoption was no shock to his patriotism, for the son says, " My father thoroughly hated the Italians, and they hated him[3]." We may as well know something too of Madame de l'Escalle from her son Joseph: " My mother was very eloquent in Gascon. My father used to say, that if she had been a man, and they had made a lawyer of her, she would have won all the bad causes." What weapon she had, therefore, she also was prompt to use. " My father," says the son, who became famous—" my father called me Justus, and my mother Joseph. He used always to say to me, 'I want you to be more learned than I am.' " So indeed he became; but the elder Scaliger, with a bold and striking character, had talents of no mean order,

---

[1] "Qui dicebatur Vasco Diabolas, tam terribilis fuit . . . ." Scaligerana, p. 233.

[2] The letters of naturalisation were first printed by Bayle in his Dictionary, where they may be seen in a note to the article " Verona."

[3] Scaligerana, p. 234. The succeeding citations are all selected from the same work, and may be found scattered between the pages 227 and 243.

although they were not equal to a contest with Cardan.
He was not so good a scholar and a critic as his son, but
he was a better poet, and a justly eminent physician.
During the first forty-seven years of his life he published
nothing; then he began to print, and thenceforth poured
out writings in a flood.　He had a wonderful memory,
and understood Hungarian, German, Italian, Spanish,
French, Greek, and Latin; he accomplished a feat that
had been achieved by no other alien, and by few French-
men not to the manner born—he caught the Gascon dialect
most perfectly, and talked it like a native.　He was kind
to the sick, and hated liars.　He thought it no lie to
declare that Xenophon and Massinissa rolled together
would not make a Scaliger.　He was well made, tall, and
robust, of course.　How could he have been puny?　At
the age of sixty-four he could carry a weight that four
ordinary men would barely lift.　" My late father, in
walking, was so bold and erect, and yet he was gouty;
that belongs to us by race, bold and erect walking."

I must add, upon the same authority, two or three
minor characteristics, to complete our picture of the man.
" My father painted perfectly, both in the Greek and
Latin style, yet only with two fingers, the thumb and
ring-finger, on account of gout, old pictures and new
ones. · · · · Neither my father nor I ever have needed
spectacles.　My father did not mend his pens, they were

made for him; I cannot mend mine properly. My father wrote his copy very carefully, and that is why his books were so well printed. He once imitated exactly, with his pen, an old Arabic manuscript. My father replied to the sixth edition of Cardan on Subtilty. His book was very well printed at Paris; it did not contain one misprint. The second German edition was dedicated to me. . . . . My father always said that he should die in the month of October; so he did. . . . . My father, four years before his death, was half a Lutheran; he saw abuses more and more every day, and he wrote epigrams against the monks, whom he detested."

The energetic Scaliger the First, of course, soon made himself famous, and it need scarcely be said that his main notion of literary laurels was, that they were to be earned by fighting. He must win them in tilt against renowned knights of the quill; and so it happened that he began his literary career with a violent assault upon Erasmus. Erasmus had published two orations upon Ciceronian Latin[1], the object of which was to show what most literary men of the time, and Cardan among them, also asserted and acknowledged, that the Latin of Cicero was insufficient for the purposes of scholars in that day, and that it must be modified and amplified for use in Europe

---

[1] Desiderii Erasmi Ciceronianus, sive De Optimo Dicendi Genere. The preface to the first oration is dated 1531.

[handwritten note:] y Jortin's Erasmus 1521. For Cardan's opinion of Erasmus, and for ... regarding Cardan see Jortin 2, 709

as the universal language of the learned. It was also too cumbrous to suit itself to modern idioms of thought. Scaliger raised the cry of Cicero for ever, and asserted that the language, as used by that orator, sufficed for every purpose, and should to the end of time never be departed from by any scholar who had proper principles of taste. The attack upon Erasmus was quite unprovoked, wrong in the matter, and rude in the manner; but as it was Scaliger against Erasmus, the two names were placed in opposition as the names of rivals. On the same principle, after some years of warfare against men of lower mark, Scaliger aspired next to be talked of as the rival of Cardan. That physician had been travelling through France, and was just then perhaps the most renowned and popular of all contemporary philosophers. His books on Subtilty were being talked of by all learned men. Was there a better thing that Scaliger could do than fight Cardan in presence of the world of letters, and make him confess in his throat the books on Subtilty to be all nonsense?

He therefore addressed Fifteen Books of Esoteric Exercitations upon Subtilty to Hieronymus Cardanus[1], which were prefaced by an address from Joannes Bergius, physician, to the candid reader. Joannes Bergius ex-

---

[1] Julii Cæsaris Scaligeri Exotericarum Exercitationum Libri xv. de Subtilitate ad Hieronymum Cardanum. Paris, 1554.

plained that the fame of Cardan's work having induced
him to get it, he, when he had read it, sent it on to
Scaliger, and Scaliger, for his own private amusement,
battled with its errors. Being urged then to reply to
the book more amply, he displayed his willingness to do
so, but was unwilling that his comments should be
printed. But he was urged at last to suffer that; for he
was grieved at Cardan's errors, thought that he should
have put an Italian curb upon his runaway wit, and
felt it proper to admonish him as a father—now and then,
when the occasion required, with severity. Occasion
seems to have required that on every page, if severity be
implied by railing, jeering, and rude personal abuse. It
was a thick military book, full of hard fighting, with no
quarter and no courtesy. At the end, Scaliger himself
abjured all imputation of a desire to raise himself upon
the ruins of a brilliant reputation. His book, certainly,
if it had that object, failed. The contest was unequal,
and the opinion of the learned, as reported by Naudæus,
was, that though there were faults in Cardan's book,
Scaliger committed more errors than he attempted to
correct. By Jerome's dignified reply the attack was
made to look extremely pitiful. A standard historian of
Italian literature, Tiraboschi, compares the spirit shown
by Cardan in the dispute to that of a giant fighting with
a girl. "Upon matters of philosophy and mathematics,"

he says, "Scaliger was not worthy to come into contest
with Cardan; and all the learned, while they acknowledge that Cardan erred on many points, at the same time
agree that he achieved a perfect victory over his rival[1]."
The tone of Scaliger's book may be shown by the quota-
tion of one little exercitation; it is one of those in which
he had the sense on his own side, selected only for its
shortness[2].

"We confess, too, from this that you are divine. You
say that silver has a pleasant, sweetish taste. And that
gold has a far better taste, but does not yield it. Are
you not clearly divine, who alone know what no man
ever knew? For if it is not yielded, it is not perceived.
If it does not act, you are not acted upon.. If you are
not acted upon, you do not perceive. If you do not
perceive, you do not know that there is anything per-
ceptible. If you do not know, do not enunciate. If
you enunciate, the Aristotelians, whom you call too rash,
will say you lie."

Jerome did not trouble himself very much about this
onslaught, which was based, Joseph Scaliger says, on the
sixth, Cardan himself says on the second[3], edition of his

[1] Tiraboschi. Storia della Letteratura Italiana (Milan, 1824), vol.
vii. p. 689.

[2] Exotericarum Exercitationum (ed. cit.), p. 160.

[3] He says that he added his answer to the third. Scaliger may have
replied, however, to the sixth impression, as there were piratical
issues in some towns which Cardan would not reckon with his own.

celebrated book: In what temper an answer was prepared will presently be stated. In the mean time, no answer having come to the hands of Julius Scaliger after the lapse of many months, I think it must have been some jester practising on the vanity of the disinherited Prince of Verona, quintessence of Xenophon and Massinissa, who told him that the renowned philosopher of Milan had expired under the terrors of his criticism—that Cardan was dead, and that his death was caused by the Exercitations. Scaliger believed it, and what was more unlucky, acted upon his belief. He thought reparation due to the public for the harm he had unintentionally done, and put forth an oration which was published with some letters of his[1], and which, as an illustration of vanity, belongs to the curiosities of literature. Cardan survived by seventeen years the author of the succeeding funeral harangue:

"When the cruelty of fate had pressed on me so miserably that with my private glory was combined the bitterness of public grief, and my efforts so eminent and laborious were followed by a calamity so dire: I thought that I must not neglect to leave a testimony to posterity that the distress of mind occasioned to Jerome Cardan by

---

[1] Julii Cæsaris Scaligeri Epistolæ aliquot nunc primum vulgatæ. Accedunt præterea alia quædam opuscula, &c. Tolosæ. Typ. Raymundi Colomerii, 1620 It was published as an appendix to the Ciceronian Orations of Erasmus, and the attack of Scaliger upon them.

my trifling castigations was not greater than my sorrow at his death.

"For even if his life had been a terror to me, yet so great was his merit in all departments of letters, that I, who am but a citizen of the literary world, ought to have preferred the common good to my own personal convenience For the republic of letters is bereft now of a great and incomparable man: and has endured a loss which perhaps no after centuries may know how to repair. I, who am but a private man, have lost a witness and a judge, and even (immortal gods!) an applaudei of my lucubrations: for he approved of them so much, that he rested all hope of his own defence in silence, despairing of his own power, ignorant of his own strength: for in strength and power he so much excelled, that there could escape his knowledge no possible way in which my castigations might have been turned to the increase of his own celebrity.

"But he was so great a man as to be able to show to students that if he had judged truly, he would have seen the truth of all the things that I had written contrary to his own doctrine; if he had felt otherwise, the same presence of mind would have determined him to confirm what he had once asserted, so far as he had asseited what could be confirmed. I who in that mind and hope wrote to this man, of whom I heard commonly that he was, of

all mortals, the most ingenious and erudite, trusted indeed
that he would not vanquish me, but who does not see
that I expected hard-earned praise out of his life, through
his assent, not idle quiet through his death, and as it were
desertion of the argument.

"Especially, illustrious men, might I have been allowed
to enjoy the benignity and beneficence of one whom I
knew to be most acute and confident in his own greatness. For it was easy to obtain from him, the most
courteous of men, even by the simplest little letters an
exchange of friendship. Was it for one long exercised in
battles or accustomed to meet with audacity all perils, for
one almost worn down among incessant disputations, con-
sumed with daily cares of writing, to dispute supinely
with so great a hero? in so great a conflict and so great a
dust, it was not likely that I should have set my heart
upon the winning of a sleepy victory.

"Such victory is not in reason absent, nor in the opinion
of judicious men should it be absent, but it is of no use
to my fame. For to this opinion my mind always has
adhered, that every man (since we are all of us but little
more than nothing) is so capable of fault that he might
contend, if he pleased, even against himself. But if this
be the case with a most consummate man—as it is often
with me and some others,—his slips from truth are not to
be set down in the register of errors unless he shall after-

wards determine to defend them. Obstinacy must needs pass for firmness, fierceness for courtesy. He does not err through anything that falls from him too hastily, until he supports his fault with an unworthy defence. Therefore, if while he was living, from a consciousness of their truth, he received my endeavours to correct him silently, what could have been more to my honour? For he would have received my words as from a teacher or a father with the most modest assent. But if he had embroiled himself in a more pertinacious disputation, who cannot now understand, from the agitation of mind already produced, how that would have gone near to madness?

So much that divine man shrewdly considered. What he could not bear, he bore; what living he could not endure, dying he could. And what he could have borne he did not bear, that is, the communion of our minds and studious judgments for the public good. Wherefore, I lament my lot, since I had the clearest reasons for engaging in this struggle, the most explicit cause of conflict, but instead of the anticipated victory I obtained such a result as neither a steadfast man might hope (for who would have anticipated such an end to the affair?) or a strong man desire.

" My praise of this man can scarcely be called praise of an enemy. For I lament the loss suffered by the whole republic, the causes of which grief the herd of literary men may measure as they can, but they will not be

measured in proportion to the merits of his real divine-
ness. For whereas learned men ought to excel in three
respects—in integrity, in erudition, and in wit joined to
solidity of judgment, these three points so completely met
in him, that he seemed to have been made at once by
nature wholly for himself and solely for the world. For
no man was more humane and courteous even to the
lowest, no man was more ready for all dealings with the
greatest men. Royal in lenity, popular in the elevation
of his mind, he was the man not only suited for all hours,
but also for all places, for all men, for all changes of fortune.
Forasmuch as concerns his erudition, I ask you to look
round on the most consummate world of letters in this
happiest of ages; many and great men will display each
his own merit, but each occupied only on this or that
part of philosophy. He, however, so joined with the
profoundest knowledge of the mysteries of nature and of
God an acquaintance with humaner letters, and expounded
them with so much eloquence, that he appeared to have
devoted his entire life to their study. Truly a great man,
great if his power were not more than this. But if we
consider the surprising swiftness of his wit, his power, as
of fire, to master anything, embracing equally the least
things and the greatest, his laborious industry and his
unconquered perseverance, he may be called shameless
who should venture to compare with him.

" I had not, therefore, a mind hostile against one whose footprint I had never seen, nor was I envious of a man whose shadow never had touched mine; but on account of the famous arguments, many and great, recorded in his works, I was impelled to learn something about them. And when the Commentaries upon Subtilty were finished, there came out a sort of appendix to the former work, the book on the Variety of Things. Then I, before I heard anything of his death, after a custom certainly common with me, imitated myself, and composed, in three days, an excursus on it in exceedingly short chapters. After hearing of his death I formed them into one small book, that I might lend my aid also to his labours; but it was done as he would himself have wished it to be done, if he had first talked over his work with me, or with some person my superior in learning."

How far Cardan was from counting Scaliger among the sorrows of his life, the preceding narrative, and his slight mention of "a person's" book against him, will have already shown. It has been said more than once, that although rough of speech, Jerome held very exalted notions of the courtesies due between literary men. He kept all personal dispute out of his books, and in his reply to Scaliger, who had been hunting him by name, and crying out at him with lusty vilification through page after page, beginning with the title-page, Jerome not only abstained from all mere abuse, but (no doubt to Scaliger's great mortification) he did not once mention the name of his antagonist. The book was superscribed simply " In Calumniatorem[1]," and the name of Scaliger does not occur in it once. When, however, Jerome heard of the kind things his censor had said, when he supposed him dead, the name of Scaliger appeared in a succeeding work, coupled with friendly words and free acknowledgment of courtesy. The younger Scaliger cited Cardan's answer to his father as a literary curiosity, because it was a reply that never once named the assailant[2]. The motive for that reservation certainly was not disdain, but a conviction that injurious personalities ought not to be allowed to find their way into the deliberate productions of a scholar who desired an immortality of fame.

[1] Actio Prima in Calumniatorem.
[2] Scaligerana, p. 243. "Cardan a respondu a Scaliger et ne le nomme point, mais dit, adversus quendam conviciatorem."

CHAPTER VIII.

INFAMY.

JEROME CARDAN is speaking[1]. "It was on the 20th of December, in the year 1557, when all things seemed to be prospering that I lay awake at midnight. When I wished to sleep the bed appeared to tremble, and the chamber with it. I supposed there was a shock of earthquake. Towards morning I slept, and awaking when it was light, asked Simon Sosia, who has since followed my fortunes, and was then lying on a little chair bed near me, whether he had perceived anything. He replied, ' Yes, a trembling of the room and bed.'—' At what hour of the night?'—' Between the sixth and seventh.'   Then I went out, and, when I was in the market-place, inquired of people whom I met whether they had observed the earthquake. When I returned to my own house a servant came running out to me full of sorrow, and announced

[1] De Vitâ Propriâ, cap. xl.

that Gianbatista had brought home. Brandonia Seroni as
his wife, a girl whom he loved, but who was destitute of
all good qualities. I drew near, saw that the deed was
done.   That was, indeed, the beginning of all ills.

"I thought that a divine messenger had wished by
night to signify to me what he knew to have been settled on
the evening before.   At dawn, before he quitted my
roof, I had gone to my son and said (not so much admonished by the portent as by his manner, for he was not
like himself), ' Son, take care of yourself to-day, or you
may be doing some great harm.'   I remember the spot
from which I spoke, for I was in the doorway; but I do
not remember whether I named to him the portent.

"Not many days afterwards I again felt the chamber
tremble; I tried with my hand, and found that my heart
was palpitating, for I was lying on my left side.   I raised
myself, and the tumult and palpitation ceased: I lay down
again, and then when both returned I knew that they depended upon that.   It must have been so on the former
occasion; but I thought that the trembling might have
had a double cause, partly supernatural and partly natural."

As usual, in Jerome's superstition there is no dishonesty.
So, when he had read among his father's papers that
prayer to the Virgin at a certain time on a certain morning in the year would be a cure for gout, he tried it, and
he adds, that a few months after trying it he was relieved,

but that " at the same time he employed remedies according to his art[1]."

The marriage of his eldest son with a girl who was of the worst repute, and who could bring to her husband and to himself, too, if he should harbour her, nothing but disgrace, was the beginning of Cardan's great sorrow. He refused to admit the new wife to his home. Father and son parted in anger; but the physician's heart ached for his foolish boy. Care gathered about him, and the months of separation, during which Gianbatista struggled weakly in a sea of trouble, were not less miserable to the father than to the son. " In one word," he once said of himself, " I embrace all. I have been immoderate in all things that I loved[2]." For about nine months he maintained the battle with his feelings. During that time a grandchild had been born to him, but its mother was no honest wife; and Gianbatista had found bitter reason to deplore his rashness. Then Jerome heard that his boy was living with Brandonia in destitution, and his heart could bear no more. He therefore wrote to him, and his letter was as follows[3]:

" As I feel rather pity for your fate, my son, than anger against the offence which you have committed, not

---

[1] De Vitâ Propriâ, cap. xxxvii.
[2] Geniturarum Exemplar, p. 91.
[3] De Libris Propriis. Lib. ult. Op. Tom. i. p. 117.

only against yourself, but against all who belong to you, I write to you these words. If you will fairly give your mind to them, and obey them to the letter, there is yet hope of saving you. That you may bring your mind to do that (if there is any power in the prayers of a father for a son) I entreat and again entreat God as a suppliant.

"For how can I help being moved to pity when I see you beset with so much calamity that you want all things of which mortals stand in need? At the outset, advice, money, strength of frame; and now, at last, your health. O Heaven! If you had not sought all this by your own will, this sorrow would be more than I can bear. But since you have compounded for yourself this cup of all miseries, among which I have lately understood that you are contemned even by my friends, and that (I think) through your own fault, I can do nothing (for I know their great influence and their good-will towards you and me); but I have resolved to bear with equal mind whatever is in store. Nevertheless, so great is my anxiety, that in the depth of night (though I was not used to rise before the day, now I rise long before it) I write to you this.

"I call God to witness that I am moved by no anger; that I would in any way have helped you, and received you into my house; but I feared (as was most likely) that to do so would have been rather my own ruin than your

help.   For you are several and young, ready to destroy; ;
I am already seized by age, and am alone. . I have no ;
property ; you, with a prodigal.. mind, have no. wit. ..
Therefore, it was far more likely that I should have fear. '
on my own account than that I should have hope of .
redeeming you by my advice.

"Consider too your deed which cannot be undone; the
evil mind that is in those people ; for aged parents, if .
they were not evil-minded, never could have permitted in .
their daughter conduct that was of the worst example, in
defiance of the laws of God and man, and precepts of the .
senate.   They supposed that my small professional returns, .
which they took to be greater than they are, would be.
brought to the rescue ; they had profligately wasted their..
own goods, what wonder that they gaped after the goods..
of others ? If they had had anything else in view, they '
would not have driven you so hurriedly into these nuptials.   It was not to be hoped, therefore, that I could at
once transform your fortunes and hers; that would have .
been the labour of a very wealthy man, as they supposed..
I was: how I feared that I should fare worse through .
them than through you, if I received you, do you (who.
are now, I think, more placably disposed) consider with
yourself.   A father, without any fixed.. property; with .
income from a precarious art, entering upon old age; surrounded by the great envy of many, and therefore with .

uncertain hold of reputation, with weak health, and a
prospect of scarcely more than maintenance among so
many taxes, in face of the great dearness of everything,
surrounded by so many wars; of which an end is scarcely
to be hoped: I am to go without, or lose the little gains
derived out of my printed books, which form no small
proportion of my income; to abandon hope of office; and
to support you, numerous, impotent, without a calling,
or without repute in any, without sense, with the most
ruinous habits of indolence, luxury, and prodigality.
What say you?   To have done that would not have been
to avoid danger, but wilfully to send for it.   But, lastly,
if there was or is any hope in our affairs, it may be that
you, living outside my house, without being in any way
an impediment or cause of danger to me and (what I
count as infinitely more important) without being a
cause of grief or care, can obtain a subsistence if you
will obey my commands.   How that is to be done I will
now tell you:

" In the first place, I seem very opportunely to have
written two books of which you both are in much need;
one is entitled Consolation, and the other, much more to
the purpose, I am now finishing, upon the use that is to
be got out of Adversity: they are of use, too, to me, as
it is fit they should be.   First, then, for the assistance of
which you perhaps stand in present need ; it will be two-

fold: from me and through me.   For myself, I will take
care that you shall have your full income, for I promised
you a moiety of the present year's receipts, and I will
give you the same share in the coming year; now also I
permit you to obtain supplies at once for your immediate
support.   If I can beg anything at court, you shall share
it, and have half the income it may bring; and so, however the matter may be, you will have more than I, who
from the first had to support my family.   Let it be your
business to arrange with your father-in-law that when, in
a future year, the letting shall expire, the woods be afterwards separated into as many lots as possible, either by
sales or by the letting of the trees, for either half of this
will come to you with a stipend from the court, or the
whole without a stipend, should fortune oppose my endeavours.   But what will be done through me you know
already; all receipts from the common people, or those
inhabiting the many-storied houses, and those who,
having shown their excretions, ask to be visited, shall
become yours.   Whatever I can beg from friends, to
your advantage, you shall have.   The Venetian ambassador gave me five ells of silk; he will either give the
same to you, or you shall have the half of what he sent
me.   So much concerning help.

" As for the books on Consolation, your mind is in want
of moderation.   In the first place, do not cherish sorrow

at past deeds, or present fortune: for all the ills that now hang over you, your poverty, your wife, your ill-repute, your absence from your father's house, all these I say you have prepared for yourself willingly and knowingly. Wherefore, bad as they are, you must not bemoan them. Of what belongs to fortune you have nothing to bemoan: your nature is human, not brutish; you are a man, not a woman; a Christian, not a Mahometan or Jew; an Italian, not a barbarian; sprung of a renowned city and family, and—if that be anything to the purpose—of a father through whose work (if you do not go utterly to ruin) your name will endure for many ages: do you think fortune has been hard to you in these matters? You have only to bear with infirm health and a weak body; one was your hereditary right, the other (if you were prudent, and abstained from excessive pleasures) you could meet and remedy. Reflect upon this, that through your errors God punishes me, and through mine you; for you could not have gone astray except with His permission. For the mind that is within us comes from God, and that, too, momently. And things which seem to be calamities, if you could look a little forward into coming events, you might understand to be vain things, such, too, our seeming pleasures would be found. While, therefore, congratulations over happiness are the business of a man ignorant of human nature: still less does a man.

need to be condoled with over sorrow, because there is one end to us all. And although contempt of money would be foolish, and in these times (if ever) hard, nevertheless even for money to contemn God would be a great deal worse. Therefore your grandfather Fazio imposed upon me two main precepts: one, daily to remember God and think of his vast bounty and of all his benefits; the other, to be thoroughly intent on anything I did while I was doing it.

" As for the Uses of Adversity, they teach you these things:—First, never to be angry. Anger impedes the mind, and hinders it from seeing truth. There is grief in anger, and it corrupts the habit of the body, making a man in face and manner like a lunatic. Therefore when Aristotle was asked what anger was, he replied, A temporary madness. Do not be a liar: that is not only commanded by Scripture and philosophy, but the liar suffers this loss, that his truth is not afterwards believed. Do not live in idleness, but study perpetually, mindful of the saying of the holy man: When the mind is idle, evil thoughts come into it, as weeds and snakes abound in the uncultivated field. Do not indulge in games of chance: it is written, Fly from the dice; gamblers of all kinds used to be infamous. You lose time, the dearest of things, and estimation: you lose also your money. Never believe that your fortune will change for the better if you do not free

your mind and body from impediment: you cannot set
your body free until you free your mind from vice, and
shall adorn yourself with virtues.   Believe me, we must
all begin with that, for even usurers and highway robbers
get the happiness they have from virtue—usurers from care-
fulness and prudence, robbers from fortitude.   With these
virtues there are vices mixed by which they are made
hateful in the sight of God, and of the law, and of all
honest men.   But if in such men any good that they have
springs out of good, that is, depends upon some virtue,
how much more is it the case in others!

"Do not envy those, my son, who have become
rich or powerful through evil deeds, and are attired in
gold and silk.   The far more opulent empire of the
Romans and the kings of Persia God has destroyed, with
many other princes, so that of all those mighty forests not
a twig remains.   But on account of the justice of Abra-
ham, and because he pleased Him, out of the one twig
Isaac many forests have sprung that remain still, and very
many more would have remained, and they would have
been greater and more flourishing, if impiety against Christ
had not hindered.   The shadow of God's finger glides
over the whole surface of the world.

"Keep your mind sedate, and manage thus your affairs.
Do not lie down too late; for our race is of a warm temperament, and somewhat subject to stone.   Sleep for nine

hours. Rise in the first hour of the day, and visit the
sick, silent with all, and saying nothing that does not concern the case before you. Do not exert yourself so as
to become heated, certainly not so as to perspire. Set out
by help of a horse, and return on foot. When you have
returned put on a warmer garment. Breakfast on bread
and a little meat or dried fish. Drink very little After
breakfast, if your engagements let you, study for four
hours: studies delight a man, obliterate his cares, prepare
for him renown, adorn his mind, and help him to perform
his duty in his calling. Then visit patients again, as before:
but before supper" (Cardan used and advised only two
meals daily, and we may call his early supper a late dinner, if we please), "ride and visit groves, copses, and
pleasant places, walking or riding in the suburbs of the
town. If at any time you become wet with rain or per-
spiration, when you return home you have only to see that
you have a change of linen dry and warm, and hang up
your wet clothes near the fire. Sup your fill. Retire to
bed ten hours before the first hour of the day, your hour
of rising. When the shortness of the nights makes that
impossible, supply the deficiency of bed-time by a sleep at
noon.

"From seven things abstain wholly: from summer
fruits, from black wine, from vain and copious speech,
from falsehood, from gambling, and do not reveal any

secret to a woman, or indulge her more than is proper.
For a woman is a foolish animal, and therefore full of
fraud: if you bestow over much endearment on her, you
cannot be happy, she will drag you into mischief.

"Avoid as much as you can bleeding and purging.

"You have the book on Consolation, you shall receive
also the book on Water and Æther, and, after a time, also
that on the Uses of Adversity.

"Derive instruction from admitted error, live frugally,
be content with a famulus and a horse, do without a nurse:
for Phocion who ruled Athens had even a smaller family.
Be moderately flattering towards all, and give your mind
to study. Now enough of this, since it has all been specially
set forth by me in the volumes named, as well as in the
books on Wisdom and some others. Above all things,
never dwell on empty promises or empty hopes. Consider
that you possess only what is in your hand, and reckon
only on your actual possessions. Farewell.

"I would have sent you also the little book of Precepts,
but my copy of it is too much engaged.

"September the Fifth."

Upon the many little illustrations of Cardan's daily life
and of his character contained in the preceding letter, it
would be superfluous to dwell. The son of course gladly
became indebted to his father's overflowing love, and we

must not censure Jerome too severely, if his love exceeded
his discretion. By crippling his own means, he further
hurt the prospects of the English boy, then a fine youth,
full of affection, whom he called tenderly his Guglielmina,
and who had been with him six years to little purpose.
The troubled physician said that he was ashamed in the
sixth year to send him away untaught and unremunerated
for his loss of time, but he could spare nothing, he said,
" on account of the many expenses into which I at that
time was plunged by my sons[1]." He had loved them
both, but he had been incompetent to educate them properly, and they had too soon lost their mother. They
were, indeed, partly his own sins that were being punished
in him through his children.

The intention to seek office again mentioned by Cardan
in his letter to his son resulted in his return, four months
afterwards, at the beginning of the next year, to the
University of Pavia. A professorship was again accepted,
the offer of which had been obtained through the good
offices of his friends the Cardinals Alciati and Borromeo.

Cardan then sought to provide for the boy William,
whom he had held bound to him by daily kindness, while
he dared not send him home, and could not afford to
establish him in life   He resolved to put him into busi-

---

[1] For this and the following, see preface to the Dialogue de Morte.

ness, and proposed that he should either learn a trade, or learn to read and write, or sing and play, either of which he could have done easily, for he already could read a little, and sing reasonably well. Jerome undertook to provide for him, if he chose to study, maintenance in the house, with proper clothing. William chose to be taught a trade, and Cardan, when they went to Pavia, had in his mind shoemaking, as a business that would be tolerably light, and not too mean.

Just before quitting Milan, Jerome having resumed, according to his promise, his old kindness towards his son, had given him a new silk gown of the kind usually worn by physicians. On a Sunday, Gianbatista having put it on, went out beyond the Porta Tosa. "There was a butcher there," says the philosopher[1], "and as usual outside that gate there were pigs. One of them rose up out of the mud, and so defiled my son by wild running against him, that not only his servant, but the butchers and neighbours had to run out with weapons and drive off the pig, so that the thing seemed to be a prodigy. When the animal was at last half wearied, and my son ran away, it left him. On account of that occurrence he came back to me sorrowful beyond his wont, and told me all, and asked me what it might portend to him? I answered, that he should take

[1] De Vitâ Propriâ, cap xxxvi.

care lest, by leading a hog's life, he came to a hog's end.
And yet except a love of dice and of good eating he was
an excellent young man, and of unblemished life."

The father went to Pavia. The son remained in Milan,
and by him unhappily this narrative must for a time abide.
Before proceeding further, however, two or three political
changes in the Milanese world, that will have an important
influence upon the future course of Cardan's life, must now
be chronicled. In the year 1557, on the 15th of November, Ferrante Gonzaga, Prince of Molfetta, and Signor di
Guastalla, governor of Milan, died in Brussels. He had
been no bad friend to Jerome, though he was but a hard
soldier, who believed that the simplest elements of knowledge were as much as a prince needed, and had been
persuaded with some difficulty to permit the education of
his children. As often happens in such cases, the ignorant parent left a daughter Ippolita, who became noted
for her genius and her learning, and a son who was a lover
of letters, and of whom it may be said incidentally that
he was friendly enough towards Cardan to be made the
object of a dedication. Don Ferrante being dead, one or
two great Spaniards had brief and temporary sway in
Milan until King Philip, in March of the succeeding year,
sent a new governor in the person of Gonsalvo Ferrante
di Cordova, Duke of Sessa. He was another military
chief, a bold man, able to hold the town against all comers.

In Milan, the most eminent among the doctors naturally became his physician, and, indeed, after he had gone to Pavia, Jerome was summoned back to prescribe for this duke, on which occasion he received as his fee a hundred gold crowns and a piece of silk.

Another of Jerome's friends, his first Milanese patron, Fillippo Archinto, who had finally become Archbishop of Milan, died in June, 1558, after two years of absence from the see. His place was taken for a time by Ippolito II. d'Este. On the 18th of August in the same year Pope Paul IV. died dropsical, and was succeeded by the Cardinal de' Medici, who took the name of Pius IV. This pope was a Milanese, and very kind to his own town and to his townsmen. It happened also that the Churchmen who had most influence with him were Cardan's friends, Morone and Borromeo, the last a young man of immense wealth and influence, moreover nephew to his holiness. At the end of the year 1560, Cardinal Ippolito resigning, Borromeo was appointed Archbishop of Milan, but he did not repair directly to his see; he remained at Rome, acting as secretary of state to his uncle, and it was not until the 23rd of September, 1565, that at the age of twenty-six he celebrated the assumption of his episcopal functions at Milan with a pompous entry. Carlo Borromeo was not only an archbishop, but, by his munificence and other good qualities, attained also permanent rank in the

Church as a saint. It was well for the fortunes of the sinner Cardan that he had a firm friend in Saint Carlo Borromeo. Of that great man I trust that I shall say enough if I sum up his character in the words of a Frenchman who wrote in the succeeding century:—"It may be said of Saint Carlo Borromeo that he was an abridgment of all the bishops given by the Lord to his Church in the preceding ages; and that in him were collected all the episcopal virtues that had been distributed among them[1]."

Gianbatista Cardan had grown up from a miserable childhood. "He felt," his father said[2], "all my adversities, and little of my success." He was born, as it may be remembered, at Gallarate when his parents were extremely poor, and he was at first entrusted to a good nurse. But that nurse had a jealous husband, who compelled her to desert her charge. Then, because Jerome and Lucia,

---

[1] Antoine Godeau—"Eloges des Eveques qui dans tous les siecles de l'Eglise ont fleury en doctrine et en sainteté" Paris, 1665. Eloge 98 Quoted through Count Verri's Storia di Milano. I should here acknowledge myself to be indebted now and then to Verri's History for information upon the affairs of Milan.

[2] The succeeding narrative is drawn chiefly from two sources: 1. The last chapter of the work on the Uses of Adversity, entitled De Luctu, written just after the events, and a fair statement of facts. 2. Cardan's defence of his son before the senate, written in the midst of the trouble, and of course a one-sided version of the case. The defence was appended to the first edition of "The Uses of Adversity," paged continuously. The narrative here given is based throughout on the chapter De Luctu, and authority will, therefore, be cited only for interpolated incidents.

on account of poverty, found. few who cared to accept their hiring, the infant fell next into the hands of a dissolute woman, by whom it was fed sparely with old milk, and more freely with chewed bread. In its third or fourth year it had a tumid belly, and was seized with a fever, from which it recovered with much difficulty. After his recovery he was found to be deaf on the right side, in consequence of a discharge that had, during his illness, broken through that ear. As Jerome's affairs mended, his son came to be better nourished, and received abundant education. He became in a manner learned, and was especially a good musician, both playing on the lyre and singing to the cymbals. At the age of twenty-two, having failed previously, he obtained his doctorate, and two years afterwards succeeded in obtaining his enrolment among the members of the Milanese College of Physicians. He lived with his father, who took pains to introduce him into practice.

Personally, he had grown up into much resemblance to his grandfather Fazio. He had the same small, white, restless eyes, and a fair skin. He had large, broad features, and a big, round forehead, foxy hair, and a beard that came late, for it had only begun to form a reddish down upon his face in the year at which we now arrive. He was small of stature, even somewhat smaller than his father, who was a man of but a woman's height. He had more than his grandfather's round shoulders, for there was a hump on his back that amounted to a positive deformity. It has been already said that he was born with the third and fourth toes of the right foot joined together, " a defect," notes Cardan, "of evil augury, which, if I had observed it in time, I should have removed at once by a division of the digits."

Though this young man was usually moderate in speech, yet he was wonderfully voluble when he became excited, and then poured out such a torrent of words that he seemed to be a madman. That fault helped him to his fate. He was wanting, too, in common sense, and Jerome, fearing that he might fall into mischief through his hot temper and his simplicity, was very desirous that he should be allied in good time to some prudent woman. The father, therefore, had taken much pains to persuade the son into thoughts of marriage, and suggested to him many noble maidens among whom he might make his choice. To all such urging the young doctor answered, that in the first place it was requisite for him to devote his whole time to the perfecting of himself in his profession, and in the second place he wished to know how he could bring a bride to live in his father's house among the young men who were his father's pupils and attendants. When there were no young men to be her house companions it would be time enough for him to bring his wife. Besides, he really had paid court to some young ladies, who objected against his deformity.   In all this Jerome willingly saw reason; yet there was nothing in it but deceit.

In the mean time, the beloved son spent freely his father's money, kept his own horse and his own famulus, indulged in the luxuries of life and in its lusts   Three centuries ago, in Italy, and in a part of Italy familiar with the license of the camp, morality as between man and woman was extremely low.   I leave the reader to take this one fact for granted.   Jerome himself was not only prone, but, even beyond the age of seventy, prompt to lust, and I do not find that in those days even arch-bishops lived more purely than their neighbours.

One day, when Cardan and his household were at breakfast, a person came in to them who said that Gian-batista was intending to go out that morning and get married.

"Marry whom?" Jerome inquired.   The person did not know.

Then Cardan, turning to his son, said, "Why did you wish to conceal this from me?"   It occurred to him to remember four damsels, two of whom he knew that his son loved, and all good matches, therefore he said to the youth, naming them, "If it be one of those four, take which of them you will.   If any other lady is to come into the house, I beg that you will first

tell me who she is." He had before often warned him
not to be too precipitate, or take a wife without his father's
knowledge. He could not afford to marry into poverty,
it would be better than that if he should bring home a
woman without marrying her to be the mother of his
children. Grandchildren Cardan ardently desired "I
desired," he says, "to receive grandchildren from him,
thinking that as he was a copy of my father, his children
might perhaps be copies of myself."

In reply to the betrayer of his counsel, Gianbatista
simply denied all knowledge of any impending nuptials,
and said that he was as much astonished as his father at
the news. On that day nothing was done, and nothing
on the next. Then came St. Thomas's day, the day in
December on which Brandonia Seroni was brought home
as Gianbatista's wife, in the manner described at the beginning of this chapter.

The youth might have looked far before he could have
met with a less eligible person. She presented him with
herself and her lost character, and brought upon him at
the same time the burden of maintaining three unmarried
sisters and a mother. She had three brothers—common
foot soldiers—ignorant of any trade, not bad fellows, but
rough, and wild, and poor. The family to which she
belonged was not originally poor, it was a wreck made by
her father Evangelista, who was a ruined spendthrift,

and had lost all his possessions or the use of them. The woods mentioned by Cardan in his letter to his son were probably some fragments of the lost estate that had been alienated only for a term of years.

Jerome, as we have seen, refused to admit the bride into his house, or to take upon himself the support of the Seroni family, and for nine months Gianbatista lived upon what he could earn, or by the sale of superfluous possessions. He was unable to clothe properly himself or his wife, and even after his father had taken pity upon their state, and supplied liberal means, they were still pinched by want. The young physician went on foot about the streets of Milan, wearing his summer clothes for want of others in the winter weather[1]. Gianbatista had no prudence, and his wife was represented by a hungry family of idlers. Even the wedding-ring that Jerome had given to his son—Lucia's perhaps—Brandonia gave secretly to her father with a piece of silk that he might pledge them to raise money for himself. Husband and wife lived thus together for about two years, quarrelling daily, and helped stoutly in their quarrelling by the wife's mother. The soldier brothers-in-law also plunged into the domestic war, and one of them once went to bully Jerome, and so get more money for his

[1] " Defensio Joan. Baptistæ Cardani, filii mei, per Hier. Card. Med. Mediol." Passages in the same document contain the facts stated in the next five sentences.

sister. Against him appeal was made to the authorities.
A daughter was born, and as her father was named after
John the Baptist, she was named after the Queen of
Heaven, Diaregina.   Next there was a son born, soon
after Jerome went to Pavia.   At that time the troubles
of the wretched family were at the worst, and Gianbatista
bought some arsenic.   He even made a faint attempt to
kill Brandonia by mixing some of it with her food, but
that failing, he relented.   Thereafter, whenever he became enraged—they quarrelled daily—he resolved to kill
her, and relented as he cooled.

Before the birth of their second child—a son, called
Fazio[1]—Brandonia was ill, and after his birth her health
was very feeble, though she was strong enough to scold
her husband.   The infant had not been born many days
when, in the course of a great quarrel, she told Gianbatista that neither the infant nor the girl Diaregina were
his children.   Her mother backed the assertion vehe-
mently, and the two women not only repeated it, but
named other men who were their fathers.

Then Gianbatista went to his famulus, a youth who was
his partisan in the domestic war, and with whom he had
plotted mischief.   He promised him money and clothes,
gave him the poison, and told him to put it into a certain
cake which was to be made, and which his wife would eat.

[1] Paralipomenon, Lib. iii. cap. 17.   ". . . Nepos meus ex filio
Facius. . . ."

The day before the crime was committed he redeemed his fathei-in-law's pledges, and took not a part only, but the whole of his wife's family into the house to live with him[1].

For a few minutes we must change the scene to Pavia, where Jerome was happily established in his professorship with a salary of six hundred gold crowns, clipped money indeed[2], but the payment of congenial labour that at the same time did not withdraw him wholly from his practice as a popular physician. He had just resumed his lectures, and if he was tempted into formal disputation he was quite able to silence an antagonist. So he overwhelmed at Pavia Branda Porro[3], who omitted the word "not" from a citation. He was accused mildly but firmly of his error by Cardan, who adhered to the accusation, "at the same time expectorating freely," he says, "as was my wont." Branda, who scorned the imputation of having made so vital a mistake, called for the book from which he had been quoting, and out of that he was convicted and defeated.

Now it happened that seven days before the commission of the crime in Milan, Jerome's younger son, who was at

---

[1] Def. Filii mei, for the last sentence.
[2] Ibid.
[3] De Vitâ Propriâ, cap. xii. for this incident. The next resumes the story from the chapter De Luctu.

Pavia with him, became restless, and determined to depart. Whether he was in any way privy to the designs of his brother it is hard to say, but he contrived fairly to incur suspicion. Cardan objected wholly to the youth's departure, and when he found that he could not persuade him to remain at home, being unwilling to use force, he consulted the stars, and discovered that his son would be imprisoned, and was threatened with grave harm. Interpreting that omen as having reference to Aldo, he then warned him privately of his discovery. When that warning proved to be of no avail, he said to him, in the presence of the entire household, that if he went he would be wanting to return when he would not have power to do so. It was then vacation-time, and Jerome could have travelled with this son to Milan. He was really on the point of doing so as a relief to his anxiety. If he had done so, his whole life might have ended differently, he might have been in time to snatch his other son from the abyss of crime into which he was about to leap. The fates, he says, kept him at Pavia.

Aldo had come into his brother's house. The cake was made, and a piece of it was given to the sick wife, whose infant was but a few days old. She vomited at once. The mother-in-law took some of it with a like effect. Gianbatista thought, as he alleged afterwards, that the poison had not been used, partly because his sister's husband had been at the house, and, noticing the cake when it was in making, bade them see that it was large because he too should eat some of it. Whether he really thought so matters little to the actual offence, but if he did not think it, possibly he meant more mischief than he perfectly achieved, for he offered the cake to his father-in-law, and then also took a piece himself. They, too, were sick, and the criminal himself was for a few days unable to go about. One of the soldier brothers entering the house soon after the cake was eaten, found his father, and mother, and his sister violently sick. Instantly suspecting them to have been poisoned by the Cardans, he drew his sword, and in a fury rushed forward to kill both Gianbatista and his brother Aldo[1]. They were perfectly defenceless, and by no means of warlike nature. The soldier's fury, however, overcame him. He fell down in a fit before he had completed his design, and it was some hours before he again came to be master of his actions.

The old people recovered, but the weak Brandonia had received a fatal dose. Doctors declared that she was dying of a fever called by them lipyria, which she had had before the child was born. She was of broken constitution. Jerome himself, before he left Milan, had cured her of a disease implying taint of blood. While the poisoned woman was still lingering in life, her mother

[1] Def. Filii mei.

one day set up a fierce quarrel with the nurse who attended at the bedside. The mother ran at the nurse to
box her ears, the nurse endeavoured to avoid the blow
by scrambling over the sick bed, and in so doing fell with
her whole weight upon the patient. When the fight was
at an end, Brandonia was dead[1]. The day was the 14th
of February, 1560. On the day following, Gianbatista,
Aldo, and the famulus were seized[2].

Again the scene has to be changed to Pavia. One day,
in the month of February, chancing to look into his right
hand, Cardan observed a mark at the root of his ring finger
like a bloody sword[3]. He trembled suddenly. What more?
That evening, it was on a Saturday, a person came to him
with letters from his daughter's husband telling him that
his son was in prison, that he must come at once to Milan.
Lines upon hands differ of course; but whoever looks
into his own probably will see that straight lines run
down from the roots of each of the two middle fingers,
and it is likely that one of them may have a short line

[1] Hier Card. Medic Mediol. Responsio ad Criminationem D. Evan-
gelistæ Seroni (appended also to De Ut. ex Adv. Cap.), p. 1145.

[2] De Vitâ Propriâ, cap. xxvii. Where the date is said to be the 26th
of February. The correction in the text is from an incidental statement in Cardan's defence of his son that the eleventh day before Brandonia's confinement was the 25th of January. This was said when
the facts were recent, and leads to the true date of the murder; one
that harmonises with all other portions of the story.

[3] Ibid. cap. xxxvii.

crossing it in the place necessary to suggest a sword hilt. The blood implies no more than redness of the line, and it is not hard to understand how, as the case went on, while he was working for his son in Milan, Jérome's excited fancy traced the growth of the sword upward along his finger.   On the Sunday morning after he received the message, since night travelling was hardly possible, Cardan hastened to Milan.   There he learned from his daughter and his daughter's husband the extent of the calamity that had brought shame and ruin on his house.   It was not for him then to stand aloof, or have regard for reputation.   The glory and hope of his life were gone; he cared no more for his credit in the town; he was a father, nothing else, sixty years old and grey-headed, with no object before him but the rescue of his son.   He threw the whole of his personal influence and reputation at the feet of his child.   A physician, high in reputation, could not safely lavish love and time and money on a murderer.   Cardan was to be seen labouring night and day for a villain whom few men thought worthy of compassion, and not content with hired and formal advocacy, standing up with all his wretchedness in open court to plead for him, eager to ensure to him the use of all good and bad arguments that wit could devise in extenuation of his villany, cleaving to him as his son, and making common cause with him; he could not be seen doing that and remain in the world's eye the great man that he had been.

But he did not go to the prison. He did not visit the offender[1]. His heart reproached him with the memory of his own wrong training of his children, the gamblers and the singing people by whose presence he had suffered them to be defiled. In the midst of such grief Gianbatista lay so callous in his cell that he could mock the old man's heart by sending a special message with a request that he would be bail for him in ten thousand gold crowns, in order that he might go out of his prison for two hours to see a show. There was to be a sham fight under the castle, and he had a great desire to see it. His father, therefore, who was not worth two thousand gold crowns, was to be bail for him in ten, that he might not miss the spectacle[2]. He was a simpleton, said Jerome, always well-disposed, and learned, but his simplicity of character had been his ruin.

At his first examination Gianbatista kept his counsel, and Cardan was not without hope that he had escaped actual bloodguiltiness. Vincenzio Dinaldo, who had attended his son's wife, said that she died of lipyria[3].

---

[1] The chapter De Luctu.

[2] Defensio J. B. C. filii mei.

[3] Responsio ad Crim. D. Evang. Seron.; and, for what follows, the Defence, where it is implied that the physicians all gave evidence at the trial. See also the chapter De Luctu.

Five physicians declared that she had not died of poison, for the signs of it were wanting on the tongue, and about the extremities ; her body was not black, her belly was not tumid, neither her hair nor her nails had fallen off, and there was internally no erosion. Against that conclusion people set the facts in evidence and the circumstance that the accused was a member of the College of Physicians, of which the respectability would be in some degree tainted by his conviction. Evangelista Seroni and the three brothers of the deceased were also the bitterest of prosecutors.

One day when Gianbatista had been imprisoned for about three weeks, during which Jerome had been straining all energies on his behalf, the old man was studying in the library of some friends with whom he was then staying in Milan, the Palavicini, and while he was so sitting there sounded in his ear some tones as of the voice of a priest consoling wretched men who are upon the verge of death. " My heart was opened," he says[1], " torn asunder, broken. I leapt wildly out into the court-yard where some of my friends stood, well knowing how much hope there was for my son's rescue if he had not pleaded guilty to the crime, or if he was really innocent. ' Woe is me,' I cried, ' for he is guilty of his wife's death, and now he has confessed it and will be condemned and fall under the

[1] De Vitâ Propriâ, cap. xxxvii. for this incident.

axe!' At once receiving my cloak, I went out to the market-square. When I was nearly half-way there, I met my daughter's husband looking sorrowful, who said, ' Whither do you go?' I replied, ' I doubt whether my son, conscious of the deed, has not made full confession. Then he replied, 'It is so. It has lately happened.' A messenger whom I had sent then ran to me and told me all."

Gianbatista, who had at first maintained reserve, was unable to restrain himself during a subsequent examination, when he heard the evasions of his famulus. That youth declared that he had received the powder from his master, understanding that it was to be given to Brandonia for the purpose of increasing her milk, because she was ill able to suckle the infant. When presently the person was introduced of whom the poison had been bought, the criminal confessed freely all of which he was accused, and even more. For he said that he had held the deed two months in contemplation, and that it had been twice before attempted[1].

[1] De Luctu.

CHAPTER IX.

THE FATHER IN THE DEPTH OF HIS DISTRESS.

BEFORE the Milanese Senate and its President Rigone[1] the formal trial of Gianbatista shortly afterwards came on. The administration of the poison not being denied, the pleading for the defendant could be directed only towards the mitigation of punishment. Sixty-four pleas in mitigation were devised in his behalf[2].

The accusation against Aldo had not been maintained, but against Gianbatista the proofs apart from his own confession were convincing. Cross-examination showed the existence of such provocation as has been already detailed, and Evangelista declined to aver that his daughter's character was unstained when she married. The case against the character of the dead woman was not, however, closely pressed. Physicians testified, on behalf of the defendant, that poison had not caused Brandonia's death.

[1] De Vitâ Propriâ, cap. xlii.
[2] Respons. in Crim. Evang. Seroni, *ad fin.*

The feeling of the President Rigone was strongly against the criminal. Jerome hoped for merciful intervention from the governor, who was his patient[1], and for help from the great men who were his patients and his friends ; it is, however, natural that they should have felt unable to extend any of their friendly feeling to his son. It is not easy or desirable to mitigate the universal detestation due to a man who can poison his wife while she has a ten-day infant at her breast. . For Jerome, the miserable father, we may feel true sympathy ; for Gianbatista none.. Jerome himself, though he struggled painfully on his behalf, only excused the offence when he stood up formally to be the young man's advocate. The physicians said, and he believed, that his son's wife had not died of poison ; since, therefore, many a foul crime had by help of interest been favoured with a lenient sentence, Cardan, having as fair a right as any man to favour, thought himself entitled to expect, not that his son would be acquitted, but that he would be condemned simply to. exile. To condemn him to the galleys would be cruelty, he thought ; to kill him would be murder.

Through all his after sorrows Jerome Cardan never wrote angrily of the Seroni family. He was not really. the apologist of crime. Standing before the senate in the. character of advocate, to plead for the life of his son, he

---

[1] Evidence of this will appear fully in the sequel.

was there to urge all that an advocate could say, not to
express his individual opinions.   He had exerted all the
wit of which he was master and all his powers of disputation—such powers as he had spent once for sport on
an encomium of Nero—in the manufacture of a formal
and elaborate defence.   It was not for him to consider
what arguments he himself thought tenable, but what
arguments might by any chance weigh upon any person
who had a voice in his son's fate.   He understood the
casuistry of the schools, and practised it.   His speech for
his son, of which an outline is here given, contains much
strange folly that the world has now outgrown.   How,
completely the puerilities of the old logicians were a part
of their own sober and earnest life, how little they saw
what was absurd in their established way of arguing,
may be gathered even from the brief outline of this.
speech, in which a scholar of the sixteenth century,
although a man of quick wit and strong feeling, handled:
a question of the very gravest moment to, himself..

Seven things, he said[1], were to be considered in the.
case: public example, the deed, the instrument, the cause,
of the deed, the mode of doing, the person, and external
circumstances.   He arranged his argument under these:
heads:

[1] What follows is a reduced outline of Cardan's speech for his son,
published at the end of the first edition De Ut. ex Adv. Cap. (Basil,
1561), where it fills forty pages.

Having stated briefly the occasion of his son's crime,.
and pointed out the special provocation that consisted in
the shamelessness of a wife, who not only was unfaithful,
but who boasted to her husband of her faithlessness; and,
having cited examples of men who were pardoned for
destroying their detected wives, he proceeded to urge that
those learned men were wrong who state that to kill by
poison is a worse crime than to kill by steel, because the
deed is more traitorous, and the chance of escape that it
gives is less.   More men, he said, had been slain by the
sword than by poison.   Crime so perpetrated caused less
scandal; and, therefore, the public example was less dangerous.   He quoted Plato's Phædo, in which poison is
said to have required two or three separate administra-
tions, even when no antidote was used.   He cited authorities to prove the superior dignity and respectability of
poison as an instrument of death.   It was said of poisoning, that it should be repressed by additional severity,
because it was a crime easy to perpetrate, hard to detect.
Was that a just ground for severer punishment?   Mar-
tianus taught, that small thefts by domestics were not to
be brought at all to public trial; yet of all offences they
were the easiest; why were not they punished the most
severely?   Then, again, what was the offence punished?
A contempt of law.   If no law was offended, why was
the man imprisoned?   But is not open contempt of law

by the sword worse than the tacit respect for the law implied by the poisoner when he endeavours to deceive it?
There is no petulance in the act of poisoning. He who
kills by poison, kills from some necessity. He who kills
by the sword, kills through anger, ambition, or licentiousness, and means to kill. He who uses poison, swaying
between anger and just grief, means and means not to
kill, and, in the end, leaves the result very much to
chance. Of fifty that are poisoned, only one may die.
He who drinks poison, need not drink; he who is stabbed,
has the knife thrust upon him, whether he will or not.
But it is urged that poison is more certain of its victim
than the sword. Not so, argued the casuist. It is necessary of poison that the dose be fatal, that it be all taken,
that remedies be absent or be neglected, and that the
taker trust a person whom he has capitally injured. Does
he die, then, through a trust betrayed? Say rather, that
he is punished for his rash and impious confidence. But
poisoners in the eye of the law, were not they who gave,
but who killed by poison. The old Cornelian law, too,
instituted among such criminals a rule of dignity. The
common people were given to wild beasts; persons of
higher grade were exiled. "Therefore," the father said,
" my son, graduate in medicine and member of the
college, and the son of a graduate and member, at the
same time the grandson of a jurisconsult and member of

the college, and the descendant of a noble race, even if
he were guilty, if he did this deed without a cause, if he
were not a youth, if he were not so simple-minded as he
is, ought not to incur the ordinary penalty, but only to
be exiled."

Concerning the deed the pleader argued that murder
by poison had not been committed, and therein he urged
what he then and afterwards believed to be the truth.
Brandonia died, he said, from natural causes.   Her physicians stated that from the beginning of the fever under
which she had been labouring she had coldness of the
extremities and shivering fits, and four or five most com-
petent physicians, deputed by the senate to investigate,
reported that no signs of poison had existed either before
or after death, either without the body or within it.   But
people do not die of poison without showing symptoms of
it ; if they do, why are investigations entered into and
decisions based upon them ?—why are bodies inspected ?
Again, urging the evidence of the physicians, Cardan
quoted to the senate the opinion of Galen on the ease
with which it was possible to diagnose cases of poisoning.
Besides, he added, there can be no wonder that in this
case traces of poisoning did not exist, the quantity of
arsenic administered being so small.   Only an ounce was
used, divided into three parts, of which the deceased took
only one, and that she vomited.   " It would require," he

said, "twenty times the dose she took to kill a man. If it
be vomited scarcely a pound of arsenic will kill, as may
be seen in the mountebanks who devour daily a great deal
of it, and suffer scarcely at all[1]. An ounce will not kill a
dog, because he vomits it."

From these statements we must infer that the general
term arsenic was applied, as Dioscorides applied it, to the
yellow sulphuret which we call orpiment. This contains
much free arsenious acid, and is a decided poison, but is
much less active than white arsenic, of which a few
grains kill. Even of white arsenic, however, horses have
been known to take fabulous quantities without fatal result, and there are cases of human recovery from half-
ounce doses taken upon a full stomach and speedily rejected. In the case of Brandonia, vomiting was speedy,
and as it was not, according to the medical jurisprudence
of the day, possible to detect traces of the poison, Cardan
was not without grounds for believing that the deceased
had not been actually murdered.

Again, Jerome pleaded that it was not proven that the
poison in the cake taken was put there by his son's wish.
He himself denied that it was ; he was at that time re-
penting of his purpose. "That, too," he went on to

[1] "Si evomatur vix una libra arsenici interficit hominem, sicut
apparet circulatoribus qui magnam quantitatem ejus devorant quo-
tidie et nihil penitus læduntur." Op. cit. p. 1117

urge, " is clear from the reasons which my son has adduced, for he said, if I had known of the poison I should not have given the cake to others, should have eaten none myself: and also when I heard that I was detected I should have taken flight, especially as I was advised by many so to do. But I was innocent and ignorant of this deed, and, as I said, already penitent. My servant did it, in the hope, I think, of reward." Having cited this statement (which it must be owned was not worth much), Cardan returned to the medical evidence, and laid stress on the testimony of three physicians who had visited the deceased when living, and who all agreed that she died of natural disease. One of the three, a man of no common erudition, named the disease, and said that it was a fever called lipyria. Having spoken further upon that head, and again adduced the authority of Galen, Cardan next urged the fact that the other persons who had eaten of the cake recovered after a day or two from its effects.

A witness said that arsenic was given to the deceased on the tenth day after her confinement, and then, not succeeding in its purpose, was again administered. By reference to the apothecary's books, it was to be seen that she had been ill from the eleventh day before her confinement; that is to say, from the 25th of January till her death.

It might be suggested that the poison, which was not enough to kill a healthy person, was sufficient to destroy a woman who was without it dangerously ill. If there were only the doubt, said Jerome, it should be decided on the side of clemency. But there was not doubt. Poison that in its operation resembles the disease would hasten a sick person's death, even though not given in a dose poisonous by itself. If it should prove to have a contrary operation, it would prolong life. So the common people use the flesh of vipers against elephantiasis, euphorbium against palsy. But arsenic or white orpiment[1] is warm and dry, since, therefore, lipyria is cold and moist, such poison would in this case rather be a benefit than a hurt; its effect would in fact be to prolong life, not to destroy it. It is therefore clear that neither did the poison alone in this case cause the death, nor was it, as the physicians say, a concomitant cause.

Having pleaded on his son's behalf so far according to scholastic forms, the anxious advocate proceeded to discuss the argument from other points of view. He turned next to the mood in which the attempt was made, the animus of the accused criminal. It was asserted that he killed deliberately and with malice aforethought. The accused himself made confession that he renewed and dropped the idea as he and his wife alternately quarrelled and made

[1] "Arsenicum seu auripigmentum album." Op. cit. p. 1119.

peace. But why speak of deliberation? A man with an unfaithful wife, a man who is in constant grief, cannot deliberate. His mind is never calm enough for the use of such a faculty. Gianbatista also, as it was proved, had begged Brandonia's father to take her away from him, lest harm might happen. Had he deliberated murder would he have wished for the removal of his victim? He urged it again after she had spoken those shameless words. If she had not spoken those words, no crime would have been attempted. "The youth," said Jerome, "acted simply. Out of his simplicity he has confessed the whole truth, without torture, without threats. We have shown, by witnesses produced, that he is a young man of the simplest character; this fact is most notorious. If any of you have known him, such persons will know that I do not lie. Ask even his accusers. If I lie upon a matter that is very manifest, can I ask you to credit me on doubtful points? By simplicity he was led to take a wife without a dowry, by his wife's relatives he was drawn into hostility towards me; he has been guilty of innumerable errors, but of no crime. His nature is the better for its simpleness. He swears in confession as if criminal judges would put faith in him as a wife in her husband, a parent in his child. By that you may be sure that he tells truth to you, though, indeed, you are not bound to believe him."

Turning next to the cause of the offence, the scholar
dwelt upon the Roman laws concerning murder following
the provocation given by unfaithful wives. He urged
that an act of disloyalty unblushingly confessed was
greater provocation than an act detected, because the
latter might be excused in a variety of ways, " as is shown
by Boccaccio." What could be greater horror then, than
to hear mother declaring before daughter, and daughter
before mother, a dishonour that they were determined
should not pass unknown and unconfirmed. The laws
provide for no such case of provocation, because it was
never contemplated. Many wives are unfaithful, but they
respect themselves, their husbands, and their children, so
that even though they should be killed by a just wrath,
they leave the reputation of their house preserved, they
do not blast the prospects of their children; but this
woman cut off from them all hope. Upon this subject
Cardan dwelt with emphasis and with keen feeling. He
had himself suffered in boyhood from the reproach attaching to his birth, and moreover the desire of his old
age was to live again in grandchildren, to found again his
family, but upon all such hopes Brandonia's confession
rested like a curse. Stung to the quick by this view of
the subject, he exclaimed:—" If Brandonia had been my
own daughter and Gianbatista but my son-in-law, and if
it had been proved, as it is proved by two witnesses, that

Brandonia had made such a proclamation, and that my
son-in-law had poisoned her, though he had prepared the
poison a whole year before, I swear by the Throne in
Heaven that if he bade me to supper the day afterwards
I would go in to him. For what can be more vile?
What punishment can be too great for her who violates
the rights of her own offspring." Immediately Jerome
turned, however, from that strain of anger to allude to
letters in Brandonia's hand, and witnesses that had been
produced testifying that her parents were the cause of all
her sorrows; "she, perhaps, did not sin of her own will,
and did not merit so much misery."

   " But we are asked," he said, " to produce the evidences
of her guilt. Too much is known. The times are known
and the persons; they are known to the senate, if it will
recognise such common knowledge. We know more
than we should. We know the panders and the pro-
curesses, and the entire shame. I would that we knew
nothing. It is worse for us, perhaps, known than unknown, the youth may deserve to be condemned."

   The advocate then turned to arguments for mercy.
Gianpietro di Meda, who upon mere suspicion of un-
faithfulness destroyed his wife with twenty-five wounds,
had been acquitted by the senate that was trying Cardan's
son. The son of the rich Gianpietro Solario, for the
sake of wealth, had attempted to poison his father, his

three sisters, and his nurse, but at the intercession of his father, who had promised to take care of him, he escaped punishment.

A father was excused by the law for the slaying of his daughter. This was a like case. For why was the father held excused? Because his love could be relied upon. And what love had not Gianbatista shown towards his wife, when he had married her dowerless, and it was proved even from the lips of hostile witnesses, that he abandoned for her sake wealthy maidens, any one of whom he might have married? How long and patiently he lived with her in misery, and was prepared to live not only in misery, but even shame, pointed at by his neighbours! And as it was, had he gone on enduring, he must have been deprived of the honours of the college, shut out from all decent intercourse, deprived of all that usually is taken from the infamous. After such degradations, might he not himself have been killed, if not by his wife, by one of her paramours? If he had gone to the judges for a remedy, how much laughter would have been excited, how much hate among relations, public talk, and private irritation! If he had sent her away, he incurred peril more manifest and imminent. While they were sitting there, a man in the town was dying of the wounds inflicted, because he had put his wife away. But he might have killed her by stabbing. That was the point

upon which most people insisted. How so? He was a
peaceful doctor who had never carried arms; she had
three brothers, soldiers, already privately given to prac-
tices which were against the law, but "which," said
Jerome, "I pass over, because I am not here to accuse
them, but to defend my son. They are known once to
have secretly threatened me for not doing what I could
not afford to do for the support of their dowerless sister,
and that fact may be seen in the public records. It is on
record also, that one of the brothers, Sforza, threatened
my son in my presence. In my absence, what might
they not do? What law, then, can be so Scythian, as to
urge men whether they act, or do not act, to death and
infamy?" Moreover, he observed, that poison was an
agent which it was more honourable to use, since it respected the woman's family, and removed from them the
occasion for an open scandal.

He further entreated that the senate would not be
influenced by the bitterness of spirit shown by his son's
accusers. He quoted from ancient history a case decided
by the Areopagus, to which body he likened the most
learned senate. The boy had been despoiled by his wife's
family. He had been so preyed upon by the avarice of
his father-in-law, the poverty of his sisters, the petulance
of his mother-in-law, and of his wife, that in the bitterest
days of winter he had been forced to travel out on foot

in summer clothes. Let the senate reflect how much he must have patiently endured! The advocate opposed to him was a clever man, and he had suggested many things that Gianbatista should have done, but they were all absurd. And what could a boy then do, tried as he was, if so learned and acute a lawyer had himself no sensible alternatives that he was able to suggest?

Speaking next of the person of the offender, the advocate became lost in the father. Surely the youth was worthy of excuse and pardon—a youth, simple of wit as any in the state—and for his age, the Scripture pleaded, Remember not, O Lord, the sins of my youth. How few of the most sacred senators had not erred gravely as young men! Had not all reason to be thankful, as he himself was, that they had been spared that hard test of their strength under which his child had fallen? He spoke of his own past errors, and, forgetting his advocacy for a moment, cried, "I thank God, by whom I am chastised through my son, that I may be reserved perhaps for greater mercies."

"But he was so simple that he had no more prudence than a boy of ten years old, though not without aptitude for study. He was deaf of one ear, and in a miserable childhood endured much, for he was the partner of all my days of hardship." And the advocate then became nothing but the grey-headed old man, the father strug-

gling for his child, earnestly pleading again and attesting
that he was but as a boy of ten. But he could sometimes think well and reason as a man ? He owned that
he could ; but would they inflict death on a lunatic who
killed a man because his lunacy had lucid intervals. The
law inclines to mercy, and would say that he sinned when
not in his right mind. As for his boy, he was so simple:
"I take more thought," the old man urged, "in the
buying of my shoes than he took in the marrying of his
wife." Was it not folly to wish to get rid of her? Could
he by so doing better his condition ? If he meant murder, was he not foolish in using insufficient poison ; in
having a confidant, and that confidant a boy ; in waiting
to be taken when he was detected ; in confessing when
he might have escaped by silence, and in confessing more
than was suspected, or than any man desired to know ?
He told as proof of his son's simplicity how he had sent
to him to be bail in ten thousand gold crowns, that he
might have two or three hours' liberty to see a show.

Then he dwelt upon the claim to consideration established by the social rank of the accused—a graduate, a
man honoured by the college, noble by ancestry, " for no
artificer or person of ignoble rank," he said, " is to be
found among our forefathers." He was a student, and
was the head matured and educated by so many nights of
toil to be cut off like the head of a man ignorant of yester-

Then Jerome pleaded on his own behalf that as a father he might not be bereft. How, he asked, shall I be able to smile upon a grandson whose maternal grandfather thirsted for my son's blood? Will he not, when he becomes my heir, arm himself to avenge his father? How much discord and future trouble might be sown by Gianbatista's death? He ended the speech with a portent which he held significant of the divine will. The hand of Brandonia's brother Flavio had been arrested when he rushed forward to slay Cardan's sons. He had fallen in the manner already described. Divine help had been afforded when there was none human near. Then let the august senate next save father and son from the hands of cruel enemies.

That is a brief outline of Cardan's speech for his son, in which the argument was from time to time applied to his desire that Gianbatista's sentence should be not death, or the galleys, but perpetual exile. Pardon he did not ask.

In a second shorter address, or probably a document handed into court, Jerome replied to the statements in the formal crimination of Evangelista Seroni[1]. That Seroni's daughter died through no man's crime, that the proximate cause of death was the falling of the nurse over

[1] Responsio ad Criminationem D. Evang. Seroni (published in the same work) for what follows.

her body, in a quarrel with her mother, as has been already related ; that her health had long been bad, and that he had himself attended her when labouring under a constitutional disease, as an indication of which there remained a scab upon her head when she died[1]. He laid it down as "most certain" that arsenic after it has been cooked ceases to be a poison. He pointed out that the servant denied having been corrupted by his master's bribes. He said, "I solemnly swear that although stung by so many wrongs, affected by so many losses, I have attempted nothing more than has concerned the preservation of my son. Many things that I could have proved I would not suffer to appear in public depositions, nor would I persecute those with my hate who are indeed most worthy of it, but this wrong I leave to the Just Judge to vindicate." He said that it was a false accusation against himself to assert that he had not helped his son's household. Gianbatista had received from him in seventeen months, as had been shown, ninety gold crowns, being a sum equal to the whole of his own real income for twenty-seven months. "The reason why he could not clothe his wife, if I must confess the truth, was I believe partly a defect in himself, for he was so simple, and trifled

---

[1] "Repente obiit, tum maxime quod diu comitiali morbo ex quo à me liberata est laboraverat; cujus indicio fuit fovea in capite mortuæ puellæ ut in actis apparet. Quid fovea cum veneno?" Op. cit. p. 1145.

so much, that he could earn little money. And he was kept poor too by the prodigal life (to use a modest term) of his father-in-law, of whom it is within the public knowledge that he has wasted his own money and estate, which I am told were ample means enough, and more beside. And the mother-in-law and the sisters-in-law gnawed to the bone that miserable boy of mine, who never knew how to deny. Oh, you will say[1], that was but a little matter! Granted. But that little was all to a poor man earning not much, and maintaining a large household."

A random charge had been inserted in the crimination which accused the father of a guilty knowledge and complicity in his son's crime. The ground for the accusation was that a short time before the murder Jerome Cardan quitted a large practice at Milan, and removed to Pavia, where he accepted smaller gains. This accusation Cardan in a few words showed to be absurd; but he said, "I take it to be a spark thrown from the hot wrath of Dominus Evangelista, rather than a conjecture stated by his counsel ; it would be too clumsy for that."

He replied briefly to the accusation against himself of cruelty. I have left it to be stated here, that after his return from England, while struggling against the reprobate courses of his son Aldo, he had on one occasion been

---

[1] "Oh, dicetis, parum erat hoc! fateor. . . ." P. 1149.

stung during supper to the infliction of a barbarous chas-
tisement, not wholly out of keeping with the roughness
of the times—he cut off one of his son's ears. He referred
to that act afterwards as one of the misdeeds of his life.
It was remembered against him in the town, and found
its way into Evangelista Scroni's act of crimination.
"He calls me cruel," said Cardan, "and cites what
should be a proof rather of drunkenness than cruelty. I
am cruel if it be cruel to hate wickedness. I hate not
only evil-doers, but those who wilfully turn into the way
of evil." Truly it was a rough kind of reprimand with
which to hope that a son might be turned out of the way
of vice, and Aldo was not made less wicked by his father's
wrath.

These were the points upon which Evangelista's document of inculpation compelled Jerome to speak. He
ended with a personal appeal to the senate. They could
not condemn his son to the galleys without condemning
to a worse fate the father, who was innocent ; death to
his son would be far worse than death to him. He besought, therefore, that his son might be sentenced only
to perpetual exile.

There were members of the senate, as he thought, influenced in their judgment by hostility towards himself[1].
He had meditated over the defence of his son that has

[1] De Vitâ Propriâ, cap. x.

been here sketched, hoping not much from the judicial court, but something from the friendly intervention of the governor, the Duke of Sessa. He rose before the senate, as he tells us[1], with his heart shocked by the recollection of his son's grief, aghast at the impending peril, enervated by the past course of events, anxious for the future ; but the speech was delivered, the struggle for the life of his first-born son was maintained by Cardan to the end, and in the end was unsuccessful. No man stretched out a hand to rescue the philosopher from an old age of sorrow. Gianbatista was condemned to death. This mercy was shown, that if peace could be made with the prosecutors, the life of the condemned man would be spared.

No terms could be made. The foolish son had bragged to his wife's relatives of treasures that his father certainly did not possess. The Seroni family, therefore, demanded as the price of their relenting, sums that it was in no way possible to raise.

The red mark, like a sword[2], that seemed to be ascending Cardan's finger, on the fifty-third day after his son's capture, seemed to have reached the finger tip, and shine with blood and fire. Jerome was beside himself with

---

[1] " Ego memoriâ doloris filii perculsus, imminentium attonitus, præteritorum enervatus, futurorum anxius, sic tamen exorsus . . . ." De Vitâ Propriâ, cap. x. The same chapter contains authority for the statements that occur between this and the next reference.

[2] De Vitâ Propriâ, cap. xxxvii.

anguish and alarm. In the morning, when he looked, the mark was gone. During the night his son had perished. He was executed by night in his prison on the 7th of April, 1560, being then twenty-six years old[1].

The mutilated body was delivered to the old man, who had taken to his heart the orphan children of Brandonia. Thrusting aside all question of legitimacy, he had received them as his own blood. But the girl, Diaregina, died almost at the same time as her father, and within the week there died also the nurse who had come with the infant boy. These all had to be buried, and three funerals[2] in one week crossed the threshold of Cardan. The old physician and his little grandson were thus left alone together. To that infant, three months old, his solemn charge, his consolation in the bitterness of his affliction, the philosopher transferred all love that was not buried with his son.

The stroke that fell so heavily on Cardan's heart destroyed at the same time his local reputation[3]. He had poured out his money in his son's cause. Thus from the very summit of his fame he had been thrust suddenly into poverty, contempt, and wretchedness ; but it was only of the wretchedness that he was conscious. Time

---

[1] De Ut. ex Adv. Cap. p 1105.

[2] De Vità Propriâ, p. xxvii.

[3] Evidence of statements here made will appear in the sequel.

never. healed his grief; even his reason was impaired by
it. "I was told," he says, "that some of the senators
privately confessed that they condemned my son with the
hope that through grief I might perish or go mad ; how
barely I escaped one of those ends God knows." The
narrowness of the escape is visible in all his after life.
He could write still, according to the habit of the philosopher, and be beguiled from sorrow by the pen, though
into his books, upon whatever theme they were composed, there almost always crept through some chapter or
paragraph, a cry of wailing for his child.   But in his
conduct in society he was no longer always master of his
reason.   Mistrust became habitual; he seems to have felt
like a stag at bay, and seen in nearly all his neighbours
hounds watchful. for an undefended spot upon. him into
which to fix their teeth.   Superstitions darkened heaven
for him like a night, and through the midst of the night
there came in every form the voice of the old man
lamenting for his son.   Sometimes it took the form of
verse.   One metrical effusion, which seems to have arisen
naturally out of the first sense of bereavement, Cardan
published in a. philosophic treatise, to the writing of
which he at once betook himself, as to an opiate.   It was
a book that he undertook for the expressed purpose of
supplying medicine to sorrow.   In it he printed not only
his Latin verses, but the notes for harp music, to which

his friend Giudeo, a composer who was then ninety-seven years old, set them. These are the verses put into an English form[1]:

> " A purple flower cut by the hard plough
>   Droops, so to me my dying son appears ;
> Worthy a Nestor's life, I see him how
>   Under the axe, and long upon mine ears
> Murmurs a voice,
>   ' O pitiable sire !'
>   It says, ' O infant born hard years to know !
> ' Three souls at once under one stroke expire,—
>   ' My own death is the least part of my woe.

[1] Theonoston, Lib i Op. Tom. ii. p. 346. The poem itself is here appended:

> " Ut flos purpureus duro concisus aratro
> Languescit: sic illa mei morientis imago
> Filii, nestoreos heu digni vivere in annos,
> Qui postquam suculam vidit sævamque securim
> Exanimis jacuit, diu tandem voce receptâ:
> ' Heu:—miserando pater,' dixit, 'miserandaque proles,
> Nunc tres concordes animâ moriemur in unâ,
> Sed mea mors mihi jam minima est pars certe doloris.
> Infantem miseror parvum, patrisque senectam,
> Languescentemque animum sternit pietatis imago ,
> Et quanquam moriar primis juvenilibus annis,
> Quosque mihi sensus olim tribuere parentes
> Carnificis dextra eripiat, cum vestra nefandos
> Jura tegant, lætique trahant per crimina vitam:
> Immemorem tamen heu pietas facit' O dolor ingens.
> Nobilis heu pater, en quis te solabitur inde ,
> Mœrentem ? laterique hærens comitabitur ultro ?
> Infantem commendo tibi nostrum, rogo vive,
> Obdura in sœvos casus, curamque nepotis
> Suscipe, meque putes florentem vivere in illo.
> Verum utinam possem moriens amplexier ambos.
> Non licet; et postquam votis vos stringo supremis,
> Per tenebras nunc vado æternas· jamque valete'—
>
> Condidit auditis cœlo his Deus astra sereno:
> Saxaque fleverunt, ulularunt undique feræ."

A DIRGE.

' My little child, my father's age, I mourn,
   ' The piteous image fills me with alarm ;
' Though I die young, and give the senses born
   ' For loving nurture to the headsman's arm,
' While evil-doers sheltered by your laws
   ' Drag life with gladness through the ways of crime,
' I heed not that. A keener sorrow draws
   ' My spirit downward. In the coming time,
' My noble father, solace who shall give
   ' To your great sorrow,—who, firm to your side,
' Will be your comrade onward? Ah, yet live!
   ' To you our helpless infant I confide.
' Harden his soul to bear the hurts of fate.
   ' Cherish the grandchild; in his bloom behold
' Your son again—Oh, wish that comes too late!
   ' Could but my dying arms you both enfold!
' In vain. I tell my last desires, and fade
   ' Departing through eternal shades.—Farewell !'

God covered up the stars when this was said,
Brutes moaned, and, dropping from the rock, tears fell.'

CHAPTER X.

AFFLICTED and ashamed, Cardan returned to Pavia, where his sensitive mind suffered a daily torture. Infamy had fallen upon his house. He either was endured uneasily by his associates at Pavia, or he tortured himself with the belief that he was no longer honoured. " I could not," he says, " be retained with credit, or dismissed without a reason; I could not live safely in my own country, or quit it without risk. I wandered in despair about the town, conversed with people who despised me, shunned ungratefully my friends; I could not devise what to do, I knew not whither to go; I do not know whether I was most wretched or most hated[1]." Nevertheless he remained at Pavia two more years.

He had bought a house there, near the Church of Santa Maria di Canepanova[2]; he had, of course, by right of his position, been enrolled a member of the Pavian College of Physicians; and before the late catastrophe he had

---

[1] Paralipomenon, Lib. iv. cap. vi.
[2] De Vitâ Propriâ, cap. xxiv.

always found that there was a great contrast between his
position at the two towns of Milan and Pavia. In his
own town he always was beset by petty scandal and un-
kindness, but in Pavia he had been generously used and
treated with respect[1], until the events lately detailed
shattered his reputation. He then found that a man with
an ill name was spared no more in the one town than in
the other. He had in his house successively three pupils
during the last two years spent by him in Pavia. One
was Ercole Visconti, an only son, entrusted to Cardan
by his father Galeazzo[2]. The youth belonged to a great
family, that had in a former century filled an important
chapter in the history of Pavia. The Galeazzo Visconti,
by whom the existing castle of Pavia was built, probably
was the grandfather to Jerome's pupil. Ercole was young,
handsome, affectionate, and a good musician. He often
shared the night-watches of the afflicted father, and with
him also Cardan sought to kill care by playing with the
dice. The other two pupils were Benedetto Cataneo, of
Pavia, who became a lawyer, and Gianpaolo Eufomia, a
musician, who acquired considerable erudition[3]. The
pupils, we shall find presently, were made a theme for
scandal.

[1] De Vîtâ Propriâ, cap. xxxiii.
[2] The father's name is incidentally stated in Cardan's Defens. pro
Fil.
[3] De Vîtâ Propriâ, cap. xxxv.

Unwillingly retaining his professorship, Cardan betook himself assiduously to the writing of books. The work on the Uses of Adversity, which he had commenced in his most prosperous days, was nearly finished; and he completed it with a chapter upon Grief, of which the . text was a narrative of his son's story, and the moral was a philosophical, or it should rather be said scholastic, enforcement of arguments, to show that this was no real cause of sorrow to his father His stoicism was not more genuine than his adhesion to some of the arguments that he had thought proper to the disputation in his son's defence. The book was published, and the defence spoken by Cardan for his son was printed at the end of it, together with a fragment of the young man's writing " Upon Fœtid Foods," and a fatherly laudation of his skill as a physician, which, in the case of certain Spaniards, had enabled him to effect a cure that even Jerome had in vain attempted. The work on the Uses of Adversity was divided into four books, of which the first treated generally of all kinds of adversity, and of the preparation of the mind against imminent ills; the second treated of bodily adversity, as deformity, disease, age, death; the third book treated of adversity in fortune, as through poverty, envy, exile, anger of princes, prison; and the last book treated of adversity through one's relations, as through wife and children. It was thus naturally closed with the history of his misfortune through his son. The whole work is written in the temper of a follower of Epictetus, and contains many allusions to its author's private history. It was first published at Basle, in 1561.

Jerome had been engaged also when his son died upon the fourth book of a work on Secrets[1], which included such topics as occult speaking and cipher writing; medical problems, for example, stone, hernia, deafness, &c.; philtres, and the natural vision of demons. Sixty-six secrets were explained in it; and of the explanations six were approved by personal experiment, two had not been tried, the rest were half tried. After his son's death he had no heart to test them any further.

He sought relief rather in philosophic meditations, and began to console himself with the writing of a bulky work, entitled Theonoston, in five books. The first book, all written at Pavia, was upon Tranquillity, and was begotten of the struggle to find rest for his own troubled mind. The second book was on the Prolongation of Life, a medical treatise. The third book, partly written at Pavia, but some of it ten years later, was on the Immortality of the Soul; the fourth on Contemplation; and the fifth on the Life of the Soul after Death, and its Felicity.

The only medical work written at this time by Cardan was a comment on the Anatomy of Mundinus. Mundinus was the text-book upon which, until Vesalius broke

---

[1] The account of works written in these years is from the last book De Libris Propriis. Op. Tom. i. p. 118.

through the rule, physicians commented, if they had any
anatomy to teach. The anatomist, instead of writing a
new work of his own, edited Mundinus. Cardan admired
Vesalius, as we have seen ; but he considered him to have
erred in certain respects, which he named. The object of
his comment on Mundinus was to discuss some philosophical points of anatomy that had been much neglected,
bearing particularly on the connexion and use of parts,
and on the application of anatomy to the diagnosis and
cure of disease[1]. He wrote also, soon after his son's death,
a philosophical dialogue, entitled Tetim, in which he
dwelt mournfully upon his sorrows ; and, among other
things, said that he had lived happily under Ferrante
Gonzaga, who was a harsh man, while under the mild
rule of a liberal successor he had lost his son[2].

Considering the execution of his son to have been a
crime on the part of all concerned in it, he watched the
fates of those who had afflicted him ; and noted afterwards[3]
that the President Rigone lived to expel his own wife
from his house without any provision, and to lose his only
son. Only a few days after Gianbatista's execution, his
harsh prosecutor, Evangelista Seroni, had been put
into chains ; and losing some small office, of which he had
endeavoured to enlarge the profits by extortion, he became

---

[1] See the preface to Mundinus. Opera, Tom. x. p. 129.

[2] Dial Tetim. Opera, Tom. 1. p. 671.

[3] De Vitâ Propriâ, cap. xlii. De Varietate Rerum, Lib. xvi. cap. 93.

a common beggar. His favourite son was hung in Sicily.
The prince, by whom Cardan was deserted in his hour of
need, though otherwise, says Jerome, generous and humane, was distressed gravely both as a public man and
through his family. All others who took part in the
boy's death suffered, some more, some less.

There is one particular in which the growth of Cardan's
superstition after his son's death came to be very distinctly
marked. Before that date he had not adopted the superstition of his father, or the hint then misapplied by many
of the learned from the ancients; he had not believed that
he was aided by a demon. Scaliger, as we have seen, had
such a faith; and it arose in that age not unfrequently out
of an unspiritual reading of some of the later Greek philosophers, and chiefly, I think, of Plotinus, for whose
works Cardan and many others had a very high respect.
Very few years before his great misfortune, in his book
on the Variety of Things, Jerome had been discussing
this subject, and had said, "I truly know of the presence
near me of no demon or genius; this I well know, that
for my good genius there was given me reason, great
patience in labour, courage, a contempt of money and
honours, all which I make the most of, and count such
gifts better and ampler than the demon of Socrates."

After his son's death, in the dialogue entitled "Tetim,"
we find his opinion in a transition state. He tends to
believe in a demon, though the belief he expresses is

half the expression of an allegory. But in his last years
the belief was real. He thus wrote in the dialogue,
speaking of himself through his imaginary character:

"*Ram.*—So many and such great marvels have happened to him against his will, that I am forced to suspect,
and he too with whom I am very intimate, himself thinks,
that he has a genius, and a great, powerful, and rare one;
so that he is not lord of his own actions, but what he
desires he does not have, what he has he did not desire,
or even hope for. But he turns with horror from this
thought, and acquiesces in it only when he thinks that
all things are prepared by God.

"*Tetim.*—But what is its nature? For some are said
to be saturnine, others jovial, and so of others.

"*Ram.*—It is suspected to be under Venus, with a
mixture from Mercury and Saturn.

"*Tetim.*—All such live miserably and perish, though
the name of some grows to be great.

"*Ram.*—I do not know that, because I know no one
who has had a familiar genius of this sort except the man
of whom I speak, and his father, and Socrates."

The sudden loss of character and fortune that had fallen
on Cardan deprived him of the power of assisting properly
the English William who still dwelt in his house, and had
grown up to be a young man twenty-two years old, for
whose future career the provision had been still from year
to year delayed. Cardan had strong affection for him,

loved his winning ways, and often called him in the
household Guglielmina. When, after Gianbatista's death,
it became requisite that William should be put out in
life, nothing was found better than to put him with a
tailor in Milan, paying for his board, that he might have
instruction in the trade. The end of William's story is
thus told by Jerome[1]. (He has just adverted to the fate of
his son) ".... by which I was compelled to work all the
year through at Theonoston; besides I had to lecture upon
Galen's art of medicine, and was intent upon it, so that I
again forgot my pupil. After six months, a good deal of
Theonoston being written, especially that part which
treats of the immortality of souls, I again thought of my
design that William should learn a trade, for he had been
eight years away from Dover. Then for reasons which I
at the time thought substantial, but which I now think
light (for he was a youth, a pupil, a friend who loved me,
and who for love of me thought little of his distant kindred), I proposed that he should board out of the house.

"I said then, 'William, you grow to be a man, and have
learnt nothing; that I may show how much I love you,
now that, as you know, I must go to Pavia, if you like I
will place you in the house of some tradesman; I will pay
him for your keep, and provide you with clothing, so that
you may learn a trade. You shall then either go home,

[1] In the preface to the Dialogue de Morte.

taking money with you, or I will supply you with the means of opening a shop and establishing yourself here in trade, so that you may earn a comfortable living.' He was pleased at what I said; but I added, ' On holidays you must learn reading and writing.'

" He agreed.

" ' But what trade will you choose ? (And then I made a great mistake in offering to a simple youth the most laborious.)   Will you be a tailor ?'

" He agreed to that, and the more willingly, because he had been in the habit of talking with my tailor, Messer Antonino Daldo.   I proposed him to that person, who at once agreed about the price: that I was to pay at the end of six months thirty-two gold crowns. That was my second error.   I ought to have paid every year (we agreed for three years) only a third part. But I committed a third error.   I should have placed him to be taught by somebody at Pavia, where I was residing, not at Milan.   The fourth mistake was, that I did not retain, lodged in my own house, regardless of youthful errors, which concerned neither my life, honour, or fortunes, so faithful a pupil, who had been entrusted by his father with so much confidence to my good faith. If I had not kept him with me, I should have sent him to no place but his own home.

" The six months expired: the crafty man flattered the excellent youth ; I saw that to be out of policy ; but, suspecting no fraud, paid the thirty-two gold crowns. Daldo then throughout the summer, having a little country farm, took the youth out to play, so that from tailoring he went to the custody of vineyards; at the same time, if there was necessity, they came back in the evening— the place was about two miles out of town—and spent the night in sewing. The boy danced about among the rustics, and made love to all the girls. Thus it happened that when I chanced to be at Milan he was taken with a fever.

"He came to me, and I neglected the matter, for many reasons : partly because he did not complain much, partly because I did not know that the disease was caused by improper and excessive labour, partly because, when he had been with me, he had two or three times had a similar attack, which passed away in about four days ; and, finally, because my son Aldo and a boy had run away. What more? I ordered him to be bled ; and four days afterwards I was sent for in the night to visit him, because he thought he had not long to live. He was seized with convulsions, and had lost all consciousness. I nevertheless battled with the disease, and he recovered.

"After that I was compelled to return to Pavia to lecture ; but he, when, after he had risen from his bed, his master was celebrating some wedding, was compelled to sleep in the shop: there, on account of cold and bad food, the boy became miserable, and was about to come to me at Pavia, when the disease returned upon him. Then his impious master ordered him to be taken to the poor-house[1]; where the next morning he died of the disease and of distress of mind, and night chills. By this misfortune I was so overcome, that I seemed to have lost another of my sons."

Thus William died; and the philosopher was again smitten in conscience when he saw that another being whom he had loved was ruined by his carelessness. He accused himself most justly, and not in a word too heavily for his neglect of duty. He had assumed lightly a grave responsibility, and it was well that he should grieve when he saw the wretched end of the boy, well-born and quick-witted, who had been confided to him by strangers as to the most learned man in Europe, in the hope that he too might become learned and famous. If William had lived, he would have become an idle tailor; but he perished of neglect. Cardan went back to Pavia full of grief, and set to work upon the only act of atonement that occurred to him. He would compensate in some measure for the youth's death by conferring upon him literary immortality, and for that express purpose wrote a Dialogue on Death, of which the English William was the theme. In the preface he told candidly the story of his conduct in the matter, concealing nothing that told hardly on himself, acknowledging the full extent of his neglect. The

[1] Xenodochium.

dialogue itself was meant to be the literary monument on which Jerome would inscribe for the instruction of all ages, the youth's name and the grief of the philosopher by whom he was so much loved and so much neglected. The essential part of the youth's name, however, obscured by translation into Latin, and further perplexed by a misprint, it is hard now to determine. I suppose it to have been Latombe[1].

Beset by miseries, and shrinking at Pavia from the face of men who had known his son and did not share a father's pity for his fate, Cardan sought relief in change of scene. He desired a removal from among the people who had seen his house degraded. He had been known always to the Borromeo family, and the young cardinal, who was so great and truly excellent a man, had grown up in good-will towards him. His mother, indeed, Margaret de' Medici, the first of his father's three wives, had once been indebted to the skill of the physician for her life. It has been said that Carlo Borromeo was at Rome, but his activity was felt in other places. He

---

[1] In Hasted's Kent the only family names that seem likely to have been transformed into Lataneus, are Latombe and Latham. The Lathams mentioned are clergymen in out-of-the way places; but Thomas and Jane de Latombe are said to have held early in the next century Brambery Manor, ten miles from Dover. William's family was good, and of foreign origin. I suggest the name for want of a better. It may be possible to ascertain whether Philip and Mary ever were lodged in Kent by a Latombe, and if not, by what other family whose name might be rudely Latinised into Lataneus.

was a man of influence even at Pavia, where he had
studied under Alciat, and where he founded, early in
his after life, a splendid college, called by his own
name, of which the edifice was raised from the designs
of Pellegrino Pellegrini, at a cost of sixty thousand gold
crowns.   That college was founded in June, 1564 ; but
already, in 1562, he was engaged in a like work at
Bologna.   There he was the most munificent contributor
towards the erection of the university building that at this
day ornaments the town.   Though the university had
prospered under Papal patronage, its accommodation had
been very bad ; for that reason, in the year 1562, the
building of the present edifice was begun, and as it was
begun chiefly through the munificence of Borromeo, the
influence of that cardinal's voice in the affairs of the
University of Bologna was almost that of a master.   To
this good friend and patron, therefore, Cardan turned, in
the hope of obtaining through his interest a chair at
Bologna, for which he could resign that which he held at
Pavia.   Escaped from among the gossip that surrounded
him, and from the stigma that had been attached to his
name since Gianbatista's execution, he might hope to find
friends, and again meet with due honour out of his own
country.

   Borromeo's answer gave him all the necessary hope.
Morone, too, was influential at Bologna; therefore, relying

on the friendship of the cardinals, Jerome at once consulted his own feelings, and endeavoured to throw up his
appointment in the University of Pavia. The senate delayed for some time the acceptance of his resignation.
He had then no other appointment offered him, and they
seem to have supposed that he was acting rashly on the
spur of his unhappiness, and that it would be most
proper to interpose delays, and force upon him that time
for mature deliberation which, in the disorder of his mind,
he seemed to be unwilling or indisposed to take.

It was then that the afflicted old man was exposed to
town scandal and insults, which he begins in this way to
record[1] :—" I was professor at Pavia, and reading in my
house. I had a nurse and the youth Ercole Visconti, and
two boys, and a famulus, as I believe. Of these boys,
one was an amanuensis and musician, the other a page.
It was the year 1562, in which I had made up my mind
to leave Pavia, and resign my professorship ; but the
Senate took that ill, and as if I decided angrily. Then
there were doctors, one, a hot man, who had once been
my pupil, the other Extraordinary Professor of Medicine,
a simple man, having, I think, no harm in him. . . . . .
My rivals were most anxious that I should leave the city,
doing all they could, as it seemed, to bring about their

[1] De Vitâ Propriâ, cap. xxx.

wish. Then, when they did not hope to get my dismissal
from the senate, though I myself was asking for it, they
resolved to kill me, not with the sword, for they feared
the infamy and the senate, but with a scandal. They
wrote to me first a vile and filthy letter, in the name of
my son-in-law and in the name of my daughter, saying that
they were ashamed of their relationship with me, that they
were ashamed for the senate and the college, which were
likely soon to remove me from connexion with them. Be-
wildered by this audacious censure from my kindred, I did
not know what to do, what to say, how to reply; for I could
not interpret the meaning of these things." After a few
days, the distressed physician received also a letter signed
with the name of Fioravanti, a most modest man and his
friend, opening his eyes to a charge so vile, that he reverted instantly to the letter of his son-in-law in grief and
amazement at his children's rash belief of it. He went at
once to Fioravanti, who confessed the letter to be his;
and being asked upon what grounds the accusation rested,
answered upon common fame, and the opinion of the
rector. Now the rector was a partisan to Delfino, Cardan's nearest rival. Fioravanti, who had at first been
influenced by the reports, readily did justice to his friend,
and a check was opposed to the filthiness of scandal.
Fioravanti was the hot friend, and Delfino the simple
rival, who desired to succeed to Cardan's vacated chair.

The libel had been founded on the fact that Cardan, whose love for music was a ruling taste, generally maintained in his house, according to a custom of the age, a singing boy, and that he was rarely without pupils. The sick mind of the philosopher had no longer the strength to despise idle calumny; and even Fioravanti could not afterwards desire the aid of his boys in a church choir, or as singers in a comedy, without exciting Jerome's anger at suspected motives. Visconti was at last swayed by the strength of Cardan's feelings into sharing the belief, that it was designed to remove all faithful attendants, that his master might more readily be poisoned.

It is evident that Jerome's intellect was greatly shaken by the suffering that followed his son's crime and execution. His superstition, increased and confirmed by age, was increased tenfold by his gloomy fortune; and his views of life were coloured as they never before had been by his sick imaginings. The next illustration of this fact is very striking.

In May of the year 1562, there was founded in Pavia the Accademia degli Affidati, which suddenly became one of the most illustrious of all Italian institutions of the kind. Writing from Pavia in August, Contile[1] spoke of

---

[1] Contile is here quoted through Tiraboschi, from whose Storia della Letteratura Italiana (ed. Milan, 1824), Tom. vii. pp. 276, *et seq.* this account of the academy is taken.

it thus: "There has just been established here an academy named 'Degli Affidati,' in which are the first men of letters in all Italy, as Branda Porro, Cardano, Delfino, Lucillo, Bobbio, Corti, Cefalo, Berretta, Binaschi, Zaffiro, and many others not less learned than these, although not equally famous. I will send you information of the forms they use, the laws they observe, the faculties in which they have readings, who are to be the readers, and the days of meeting. The Lord Marquis of Pescara is made academician, and the Signor Federigo Gonzaga. It is believed that when the Duke of Sessa comes, he will also take a place in it." In September, the same correspondent wrote:—" Thanks be to God, whom it has pleased to cause my reception into the Accademia degli Affidati, founded in this city four months since, which has in a short time made so high a name, that it may be exalted as a marvel without paragon. We are more than forty: six excellent and famous jurisconsults, ten philosophers, and about fifteen of the learned in other faculties; many knights, some princes, and among them the Lord Marquis of Pescara." The academy did, indeed, take at once so high a stand, that after four years it ranked as its academicians the first cardinals of Rome, and some of the chief rulers of Europe, including his Catholic Majesty Philip the Second.

Fifteen days after the town scandal against him had

been at its height, Cardan was asked to aid in the establishment of this academy. He did so most unwillingly; he was indignant still against his libellers, morbidly sensitive to shame, and perceptibly affected in his mind by his son's fate. Even the just homage to his reputation stung him as an insult. "Before all things," he wrote in his old age[1], "they took care that he for whom his country was to blush, and his family, and the senate, and the colleges of Milan and of Pavia, the whole body of his colleagues and his pupils, should enter the Accademia degli Affidati, in which there were several good theologians and two princes, the Duke of Mantua and the Marquis Pescara. And when they found that it was hard to get me there, they forced from me my consent by threats. What could I do, overwhelmed by the terrible fate of my son? I had exhausted the whole strength or adversity; at length I acquiesced, chiefly because they promised, after a few days definitely fixed, to accept the resignation of my office as a lecturer." "Then, after a few angry apostrophes relating to a period when Jerome felt himself to be at war with all mankind, he relates how he observed, when he passed through the doors of the academy, a beam so placed that a person might be killed by falling over it. He questioned whether that was not another foul design upon himself; and his chief occupation in the

De Vitâ Propriâ, cap. xxx.

s 2

assembly seems to have been the maintaining of a sullen watch against the hand of treason.

There can be no doubt that there was much plotting and contriving directed against Jerome, who since his son's death had been neither a reputable nor an agreeable companion. Gianpietro Albuzio, it should be said, appears to have been not only a most eminent, but a most kindly man, for with him the bereaved father found consolation in pouring out his heart, if we may deduce so much from the fact that Cardan dedicates to him a sorrowful book, and makes him, as a most generous and sympathising friend, speaker with himself in a dialogue upon the topic of his sorrows[1]. Other physicians were of a less noble stamp. One[2] whose son Cardan was refusing to take into his house as pupil with a fee, happened to be a man who boasted of his favour with the Duke of Sessa, and punished the philosopher by labouring to bring him into graver disrepute at court. His standing was already lost there. Jerome, while praising the duke in recent books, had complained that his friendship proved no blessing to him; because, trusting to it in his son's case, he had neglected help that would have served him better. Meeting Cardan in the street, the physician (who is not named) again requested that he would take charge of his

[1] De Morte.

[2] Paralipomenon, Lib. iv. cap. vi. for the succeeding story.

son, and promised that if he would, he should know how to restore him to the favour of the governor; for that he (Jerome) had retired from the duke's friendship, not the duke from his.

Jerome replied, that he needed no such good offices, and no such favour.

"Why?" asked the physician.

"Because he would not, or he could not, certainly he did not, save my son."

"Then," Jerome goes on to relate, "he cried out before witnesses that my son had perished by his own fault, not the governor's. He even added, that I was abusing the governor, and had best take care what I said. At these words people ran to us, and a ring was made about us; many who heard his accusations had not heard what I did really say. At last, when he had long held to the same tale, he added madly what I did not know before, or did not positively know, that my son perished by the fault of the governor's brother-in-law, and he named him, so that he was a maligner of princes rather than I. I answered nothing to his anger, but that I was not maligning, and had not maligned, or thought of maligning, the prince whom I served."

Afterwards this physician, with his son and two companions, meeting Jerome in the open market, told him that a relation of the prince, an angry man certainly, had

been reading his book, in which he wrote of the illustrious lord abusively, and was very near running out to
cut Cardan in two (for he happened to be in the court at
the time), and throw him down the dust-hole. But the
physician added, that he had been good enough to inter-
fere and mitigate his anger. Then he attacked Jerome,
and told him that he must speak well of. the prince, and
turning suddenly upon him, as if he were protesting that
he would not, raised another crowd. Cardan then,
" knowing," he says, " how his reputation was shattered
by the fate of his son," and what strength and law was
with the rich and powerful, felt that he was compelled to
oppose the machinations of the busybody. Entering the
cathedral, he saw one of his learned friends, Adrian
Belga, always helpful and kind, and to him told the
whole story, adding, that if Antonio Pezono, a Spaniard
doing honour to his country, were in the place, he should
know how to turn the tables on his persecutor. "He is
here," said Adrian, "just at the porch." They went to
him. He, when he heard the story, told it to a Spaniard
higher in authority, who told it, in presence of Cardan's
medical plague, to the magnate who was the hero of the
tale. The great man, who did not know the alphabet,
laughed mightily at hearing of the wrath excited in him
by the reading of a volume of philosophy, and turning
to the doctor, told him that he was a fool; smaller people

echoed this opinion, and Cardan, having seen his persecutor thoroughly chidden, went away high in the favour of the Spaniards, to whom he had furnished entertainment.

In the mean time, Borromeo having recommended his friend to the senate of Bologna, there had been sent a person from that town to Pavia[1], who on arriving got among evil counsellors, and wrote back, without having attended one of the illustrious physician's lectures, or seen any of his pupils, many bad things, and among them these: " Of Hieronymus Cardanus I have understood that he is a professor without a class, but only benches; that he is a man of ill manners, and disliked by all; one full of folly. His behaviour is repulsive ; and he knows but little of the art of medicine, expressing such sectarian opinions about it, that he is rejected by all in his own city, and has no patients."

This letter was read to the senate at Bologna in the presence of Borromeo himself, who happened then to be serving as pope's legate in the town. It was at first proposed to put an end to the negotiation with Cardan, but upon the text of that part of the letter which said that he had no patients, there rose one of those present and said: "Hui! I know that to be false. I have seen the first

---

[1] The account of these negotiations is from the Liber de Vitâ Propriâ, cap. xvii. The scraps of dialogue, like all others occurring in these volumes, are translated literally from Cardan.

men in the land using his help; and I, though not one of the first men, have also used it."

Borromeo added instantly: "I too can testify that he saved my mother's life when it was despaired of by all other people."

Another senator said: "No doubt the other accusations are as true as this." The messenger, who was present at the discussion of his own report, blushed and was silent. Cardan's enemies had overshot their mark. The unfavourable report was not, however, quite without effect. It was determined to use caution, and it was therefore resolved that a professorship at Bologna should be offered to Cardan for one year, with the understanding that at the end of that year he should vacate his office if the report sent to the senate of him should be proved correct, or if in any way his connexion with the university did not prove beneficial. At the end of the year, if his appointment were confirmed, the subject of his salary was to be re-considered. To this decision Borromeo assented; but when it was brought to Jerome by Evangelista Matuliano, he who had scorned to serve princes because they demanded from him an abandonment of independence, refused utterly to accept office upon such dishonourable terms. The stipend, too, was to be scarcely so much as he had at Pavia, and for his travelling expenses he was to have nothing. To those points he objected, but the terms attached to the offer shut out all debate; and though he had almost no income at all, because he had already resigned his post at Pavia, he summarily rejected the proposals from Bologna.   " Go," he said to the messenger; " for I account nothing baser than to be honoured on such terms, even with the best of pay."

In the year 1562, on the 11th of June, Cardan had resigned his professorship[1], and had already received the reply to his requests appointing him, on terms that he thought not honourable, to Bologna.   The prince was expected whose presence he says that he " looked forward to with horror, not as an ungrateful man, but as a man not grateful."   All his affairs were in confusion, his position was unsettled.   On the next day there was to come to him Paolo Andrea Capitaneo, a boy of fourteen, from Vilanterio.   On the forefinger of his right hand he had a ring, of which the stone was a selenite, and on the left hand a large, hexagonal jacinth, that he never laid aside.   Retiring for the night, he took off the selenite and put it under his pillow, being of opinion that it hindered sleep, he often was in the habit of so doing; the jacinth he retained, for one reason, among others, because it promoted somnolence.   Towards midnight

---

[1] Paralipomenon, Lib. iii. cap. vi.   Opera, Tom. x. p. 459, from which the succeeding narrative is taken, with scarcely any other alteration in the wording than a change from the first to the third person.

he fell asleep, and on awaking could not find the ring on his left hand. He aroused Giacomo Antonio Scacabarozio, a boy of fifteen, who was his page, and slept in the chamber, ordering him to find the rings. He found the selenite at once under the pillow. The jacinth, first Jerome and then the boy looked for in vain; they could not find it. " Sorrowful to death on account of the omen," says Cardan, " my mind desponded, for I scarcely could consider this a natural occurrence. When I had rested for a little while I gathered courage, and bade the boy go and get light from the hearth. He answered, I think because he disliked the trouble, and was afraid to be in the dark, that the fire had been thoroughly put out last evening. I bade him light a candle with the flint. He said that we were without matches or tinder." Jerome persisted, and at last got up, for he said effort must be made, "if even without hope ; because if I went to sleep upon so dire a prodigy it would portend destruction. I commanded the boy, therefore, to get light in some way. He departed, raked among the ashes, found a coal no bigger than a cherry, indeed smaller, that was quite glowing, and took it with the tongs. Then I was afraid there was no hope of getting flame; but he brought a lamp with a cotton wick, blew on the coal, and obtained a light without any emission of flame from the coal, which again seemed to me a prodigy." The boy asked whether it was not neatly done; but Jerome was absorbed in admiration at the prodigy, which he was not able to comprehend. Search then was again made for the ring with much anxious fear and care, lest the light should become extinguished; the ring, however, was soon found on the ground, under the bed. "It could not possibly have got there," Jerome adds, "unless it were conveyed by hand; its shape would have hindered it from rolling; besides, if it had rolled, it would not have been in that direction. It could not have fallen where it lay, for the pillow joined close to the bed-head, and the bed had raised sides, in which there was no chink. I expressed only wonder, but the boy himself trembled with fear. Many things may, I know, be said, but nothing likely to persuade a man, however small his superstition, that the thing was not a portent signifying the reversal of my condition and my reputation." Cardan, after the ring was found, put it on his hand, and asked the boy to draw it off, but it fitted so tightly that he could not, or did not, do so. The philosopher himself then took it off, and laid it aside for ever, after he had worn it for years as a protection against lightning, plague, night-watching, and palpitation of the heart.

Turning this prodigy to use, Jerome on the following day reflected on his dangers; and, on the excuse that his health was weak, determined that he would not set foot

out of doors. It so happened that in the morning he
was invited to the academy, but he excused himself on
the ground of ill-health. After breakfast, the rare accident happened that he was invited out to supper. The
host was to be the physician who, after Cardan's departure, taught in his place, and Jerome hints, in the
diseased spirit that had come upon him since his son's
death, the doubt whether he should have returned from
such a feast alive. He did not think his entertainer
wicked enough to do him harm, but there would be
others there glad to get rid of him. At any rate, warned
by the omen, he determined not to go. It was a festival
day[1], and all the professors and distinguished students
were to be assembled. Four or five students of Cardan's
class came to him with Zaffiro, a teacher in the University,
soliciting his presence. He said that it could not be.
They supposed it to be because he never dined that he
did not care to be present, and said, "On your account
we have had the dinner changed into a supper." He
repeated that his presence was impossible. They asked
why, and he told them of the portent, and of his determination thereupon. They were all surprised; and two
of them, talking much together, often asked whether he
would mar so famous an assembly by his absence. He

---

[1] From this point the narrative is furnished by cap. xxx De Vitâ
Propriâ.

abided by his intention. An hour afterwards came some one with more urgent entreaty; Jerome replied, that he would not break his vow, that he should not leave the house. The evening was cloudy, and he went to see a poor patient, who was a butcher, because his vow did not hinder the performance of that duty.

Afterwards dreading some evil, but not knowing what, Cardan thought of his books[1], in which there were dark passages that rivals might know how to construe to his hurt. He wrote, therefore, to the Council at Rome, subjecting all that he had written to its authority and better judgment. Through that precaution he was really saved afterwards from a position of great danger. Going then to Milan, he was there seized with a fever and weakness of the stomach. While labouring under this illness, a messenger arrived from Pavia, summoning him suddenly to his grandson, who was in extreme peril. So he was compelled to ride to Pavia in a chariot, ill as he was, under a burning mid-day sun, and it was that year the hottest summer in his memory. The grandson was cured, but the grandfather added to his other ailments an affection of a front tooth, which was soon followed by erysipelas over the face. He was near dying, and would have caused himself to be bled, if a

[1] Paralipomenon, Lib. iii. cap. vi. from this point to the end of the chapter.

conjunction of the planets had not been in opposition to
that remedy. When the disease abated, Cardan began
to write, at its suggestion, a tract " On the Teeth," and
returned to Milan, when the erysipelas had not quite
disappeared. There he had presently acute twinges of
gout in the knee, and applying those symptoms to his
written commentaries on the teeth, he tried certain experi-
ments, succeeded to his wish, and was walking about the
streets a month before he might have expected that he
should be able to leave the house. The reputation of a
new discovery in medicine brought fresh applications
from men eager to make trial of his skill; and he was
thus enabled, before leaving Milan, to recover a part of
his lost wealth and lost reputation, healing patients, and
repairing some of the loss caused by the lavishing of
money in his son's defence.

No better hope of a subsistence was then visible than
Milan offered. Pavia he had resigned, the offers that
came from Bologna he had justly scorned, and he was
finding friends and some repute again in his own town,
though it was most hateful to him ; for it was beset with
bitter recollections. Four senators in Milan severally
recommended him to seek for a professorship among themselves, and held out at the same time strong hopes of
success. He had begun accordingly to seek an honourable
appointment in his native town, when he was checked

by a rebuff of the most unexpected kind. The senate suddenly expunged him from the list of scholars qualified to lecture, warned him that he was accused of two most grave crimes, the witnesses against him being two physicians; and adding that it was only out of respect to his station in life, and his connexion with the college, that they refrained from laying hands upon him, they informed him that he was sentenced to perpetual exile from their territory. This was all hasty enough, and, in the absence of those who could by a word have proved his innocence of the crimes charged against him, Cardan wasted much time in prayers and petitions. But at last the necessary vindications came, and he escaped from his brief trouble —from beginning to end three weeks long—not only unscathed, but with a positive accession of renown. " Freed from those calumnies," he says, "I grew in fame. The citizens, indeed almost the whole state, embraced me with peculiar love, admired my innocence, and pitied my misfortunes: my books, too, were set free from all suspicion. . . . . Then there came to me from cardinals and councillors at Rome soothing and flattering letters, so that in my whole life I never met with a success greater or more splendid."

The accusations are not named, but from the last fact we may conclude reasonably that this was the occasion, or one of the occasions, on which the precaution he had taken in the submission of his writings to the Council at Rome proved the means of saving Jerome out of peril. We may also reasonably conclude, from the popularity to which he suddenly attained among the citizens on his acquittal, that in his accusation some strong public sentiment may have been touched His distress at his son's fate may have led him to say things which would be tortured into a significance of that kind of treason which the citizens of Milan might in their hearts think fairly becoming a good patriot. On this and on a later occasion, when the charge seems to have been similar, it was not set down by Cardan in his books. This I can account for only by supposing that he had been brought into collision with the ruling powers, of whom he was bound to say nothing that would give further offence, and of whose dealings with him he therefore said nothing at all. It can have had nothing to do with the scandal raised at Pavia, for of that he was ready to speak openly and bluntly, scattering it to the winds with the angriest words he ever wrote.

While reversing its decision upon this case, whatever it may have been, the Milanese senate abided on technical grounds by the exclusion of Cardan from the right of lecturing. That, however, proved to be no check to his career. The messenger returned from Bologna with a more cheerful face to tell him that the conditions against which he had protested were withdrawn, and that, although the salary was still small, he was invited to Bologna upon honest terms. " But I," he says, " because I knew of nothing worse than to endure life surrounded by the cruel faces and hard voices of the men who had torn from me my sweetest son, agreed to the conditions that were brought, though they were still unjust."

CHAPTER XI.

CARDAN AT BOLOGNA.

" In all good fortune," said Cardan[1], " and in the midst of my successes, I never changed my manners, was made no rougher, no more ambitious, no more impatient; I did not learn to despise poor men or to forget old friends; I did not oecome harder in social intercourse or more assuming in my speech; nor did I use costlier clothes than my occupation rendered necessary. But in the bearing of adversity my nature is not so firm, for I have been compelled to endure some things that were beyond my strength. I have overcome nature then by art, for in the greatest agonies of my mind I whipped my thighs with a switch, bit sharply my left arm, and fasted, because I was much relieved by weeping, when the tears would come, but very frequently they would not."

The gloom of Cardan's sorrow was made deeper by the superstition to which it became allied. Sometimes, how-

[1] De Vitâ Propriâ, cap. xiv.

ever, the allies were enemies. It would seem that the strong force exerted upon the mind by the working of a superstitious fancy was able now and then to conquer grief. Thus we are told[1], that in the first months of his misery, in 1560, in the month of May, when he was grieving for his son's death, fasting, whipping himself, and seeking forgetfulness in dice with his young pupil Ercole Visconti, who shared with him his night watches, he implored Heaven for pity; since through grief and watching he must die or become mad, or resign his professorship. If he gave up his chair he had no means of living; if he became mad he would become a jest to all men; he begged that if need were he should die. Then he fancied that a voice cried to him one night in a dream, " What do you lament? the slaughter of your son?" He answered, " Can you doubt it?" The voice then said, " Put into your mouth the emerald that you wear hung about your neck, and that will keep your son out of your memory." He followed the advice of the dream, with success he says, and he was much distressed in his mind when he could not have the stone between his lips, that is to say, when he was eating or when he was lecturing.

But no artificial aids against distress of mind had subdued Jerome's grief for his son's fate. The cloud went with him from Pavia to Bologna, when, in accepting a

[1] De Vitâ Propriâ, cap. xliii.

T 2

professorship in the university of that town, he quitted
finally his native soil.   In spite of its nominal reversal of
the decree of exile, the Milanese senate still proscribed
him as a teacher, and he appears to have been virtually
banished from the state   While he was preparing for the
removal to his new home, in the course of packing he
discovered a manuscript, that of the book on Fate, which
he had lost for three years, and after much vain search
supposed to have been stolen.   It was under a little iron
box inside his desk[1].   Reflection upon this portent caused
him to infer that he should, in the course of three years,
be restored to his country, for that would be like the
finding of the manuscript, an event of which there had
seemed to be no hope, the happening of which would be
of no use to him, but nevertheless welcome.

There is an allusion to a dream that Cardan had at or
soon after the time of his leaving Pavia, which tends to
confirm the opinion already expressed as to one of the
grave accusations under which he had then fallen.   One
part of it, he says in his interpretation[2], signified religion,
in the name of which he should suffer trials and be
brought into no slight anxiety; but he should not sustain
much hurt.

Having removed to Bologna with his son Aldo and

[1] Paralipomenon, Lib. III. cap. 6.
[2] Synesiorum Somniorum (ed. cit.), p. 219.

his grandson, Jerome established himself, against much opposition, as a professor in the university, with which his connexion was maintained during the next eight years of his life. At first he occupied a house next door to a ruined palace, of which the story was, that its owner, named Gramigna, had dug a mine in it, near some of the main pillars, for the purpose of destroying certain of his enemies, whom he had invited to an entertainment[1]. A train was set, and the mine was to explode an hour after the entertainment had commenced. The treacherous host of course made for himself occasion to depart from table just before the critical moment. At the appointed time, and after it, nothing occurred; and Gramigna, at last growing angry and impatient, rushed in with his drawn sword to ascertain the cause of the delay. When he had passed into the hall the mine exploded; and, the main pillars being broken, the whole palace tumbled to the ground. The mangled body of its owner was found dead among the ruins, and in that state gibbeted. Next door to the ruin Cardan lived. It will be most convenient here to say that he removed afterwards to rooms in the palazzo Ranuzzi, where he occupied successively two sets[2], one splendid, but with a dilapidated roof that was perpetually letting pieces fall, and threatened in the end to

---

[1] Paralipomenon, Lib. v. cap. 2.
[2] De Vitâ Propriâ, cap. xxiii.

break his head; the other lodging was less brilliant, but safe. Towards the end of his period of residence in Bologna, Cardan bought for himself a house near the church of S. Giovanni in Monte.

At Bologna he found his old pupil Lodovico Ferrari[1] lecturing upon mathematics ; but the death of Ferrari happened when he had been scarcely a year in office as professor. Ferrari, as we have seen already, owed his whole position to Cardan, and must have looked back with some pleasure to the days when he and his master worked out together in Milan the problems of "that deuce of a Messer Zuanne da Coi."

Jerome formed also a friendship at Bologna with Mario Gessio, and received into his house soon after his arrival there Rodolf Silvester, a pupil who became a good physician, and was, after Ferrari, the most notable of all his house-pupils. During the eight years of his residence at Bologna, he received also two other pupils, Giulio Pozzo, native of the town, the only youth by whom his teaching ever was abandoned, and Camillo Zanolini, also native of Bologna, a good musician, who became a notary public, and was conspicuous for elegance of manners[2].

It has been said, that in the year 1562 the building of the University of Bologna, as it now stands, was com-

---

[1] Vitâ L. Ferrar. Op. Tom. ix. p. 568.
[2] De Vitâ Propriâ, cap. xxxv.

menced, and that up to that time the accommodation for
the pupils and professors had been very bad; after that
year it was of course no better until the building works
had been so far completed as to admit of the opening of
a few halls.   Out of the difficulty that there was in procuring proper lecture-rooms, arose a vexation to Cardan
of which he writes as if it had been a conspiracy against
him.   His enemies, he said[1], to prevent his room from
filling, appointed a time for his lectures upon which
followed immediately the dinner-hour, and gave the
class-room at the same time, or just before it, to another teacher.   To him Jerome proposed that he should
do one of three things, either begin sooner and end
sooner, so that there might remain due time for the succeeding lecture, or that he should find another class-room,
or that Cardan should get another class-room, and one
of the two be left in sole possession of the room, that
could not be conveniently used by them both.   By none
of these suggestions was the difficulty to be solved ;
and therefore at an annual election day Cardan undertook formally to petition that the lecture clashing with
his own might be elsewhere delivered.   While this
quarrel was at its height, the old physician was in
other respects full of trouble, surrounded he thought,
and in some degree perhaps truly, by conspiracies.

[1] De Vitâ Propriâ, cap. xvii.

Certainly there was no lack of rivalry and heartburn-ing among professors who were in too many cases emu-lous and envious of each other. Cardan had a great name, and not a winning nature. While these quarrels were forming an under-current to his not unpros-perous career at Bologna, a student of his class at Pavia, who had become a graduate, delivered an oration in his honour before the university in that town, which, even after great allowance has been made for the rhetoric of old scholastic declamation, is of a kind clearly to imply that the fame of Cardan as a physician and a philosopher remained extravagantly great. But he had not the art of soothing jealousies; and from Bologna rumours were industriously spread abroad, especially sent to the ears of his good patron and patient Cardinal Morone, purporting that Cardan taught an exceedingly small class. There seems to have been some ground for the statement; "it was not," said Jerome, "altogether true, for I had many hearers from the beginning of the session, and they all held by me till Lent."

Cardan was first Professor of the Theory of Medicine. Practice of Medicine had other teachers; and the first Professor of Practice was Fracantiano. One day, when Jerome had not long held his new office[1], Fracantiano was dissecting publicly, and disputing on the subject

---

[1] Because Fracantiano went from Bologna to Padua in 1563, and taught there till his death in 1569.

of an internal part before the whole academy. He quoted Greek in support of some assertion, and made the mistake which had been corrected by Cardan once before at Pavia, when Branda made it. He quoted a denial as an affirmation, by omitting the negative particle. Jerome, who had been dragged to the spot against his own will by his class, said, "You have omitted *ού*."

"By no means," said the disputant.

Jerome quietly affirmed the fact, and the students, after student fashion, directly became clamorous; the book was produced, and Fracantiano silenced. But the philosopher had made an enemy. Though he was so essentially a man of books, that a defeat by him in such a form might have been borne with a good grace, Fracantiano never could forget that he had been humbled in the presence of the whole academy. From that day he avoided Cardan with so much determination that he ordered his attendants to warn him when they saw that he was near, in order that he might turn aside and escape encountering him even in the streets. Amused at this enmity, some students contrived one day to beguile Cardan into a room where Fracantiano was presiding over some dissections. The professor so interrupted rose to depart instantly, and went with so much haste that he became entangled in his gown, and fell down with his face upon the floor.

If his mind had not been crippled past all cure by the torture suffered through his son's crime and its punish-

ment, it is certain that Cardan in his old age might have
found comfort in his connexion with the University of
Bologna. Such incidents as have been just detailed
belonged only to the small jealousies of daily life, whereof
there was perhaps no scholar who had not to endure his
share. A Frenchman came one day[1] desiring to consult
Cardan in private. The physician answered, that it would
suffice if his attendants, who were present, did not hear
their conversation. The Frenchman went away dissatisfied. "What had he in his mind?" asks the old man.
"Some wickedness." The weaknesses of age being thus
aggravated, it was impossible for Cardan to enjoy the
abundant fruits of his renown that still surrounded him.
All seemed to go well with him, certainly for some years,
at Bologna. On settling in that town, he for the first
time set up a carriage[2]; until then he had ridden generally on a mule. He used to go out in his carriage and
return on foot, having made the change, not on account
of luxury, but of his advancing age.

He had become, indeed, less reckless about money
since his son's death. Before that time he had wasted
much, and it was his own fault that he had not been rich
enough, when there was yet time, to purchase Gianbatista's life. "If I were to relate," he said[3] in his old age,

---

[1] De Vitâ Propriâ, cap. xlii.   [2] Ibid. cap. vii.
[3] De Libris Propriis: Lib. ult. Op. Tom. i. p. 131.

"how much gold I have earned by my art, I fear that greater than the praise of my success would be the censure of my prodigality." At the same time, he recorded that he had cured more than ten thousand patients.

Nevertheless, except as a study, he did not like his profession. Its intellectual part had charms for him; but as a trade, as it was carried on in his day, with its internal wars and jealousies, and with the too-frequent meanness of its relations with the external public, he abhorred it altogether. "If I had money to earn," he said, "I could earn it as a doctor, and in no other way. But that calling of all others (except the glory that attends it) is completely servile, full of toil, and (to confess the truth) unworthy of a high-spirited man, so that I do not at all marvel that the art used to be peculiar to slaves[1]."

Cardan's household at Bologna was established on a moderate scale, with very few domestics, and two readers or secretaries; he had of late usually maintained several readers in his house. His general affairs also mended almost from the first. Backed by his friends the cardinals, it was not only in Bologna that he found his prospects brightening. In September, 1563, nearly a

---

[1] De Libris Propriis. Lib. ult Op. Tom. i. p. 131. "Si opes parandæ erant, medicâ arte, non aliter parare potuissem: at ea, si qua alia (gloriâ quæ illam comitatur exceptâ) tota servilis est, plenaque laboribus, et (ut vere fatear) ingenuo viro indigna, ut non mirer olim servorum fuisse hoc exercitum."

year after he quitted Pavia, Jerome found one night[1] that
the collar of his shirt had become entangled with the
string by which he suspended from his neck the emerald
before mentioned, and a written charm. He puzzled himself for a time over the entanglement, and then allowed
it to remain. Soon afterwards putting his hand to his
neck, he found that the knot had become loose, and that the
string was free. This portended, of course, some speedy
unravelment of the knot in his own affairs. Since he had
come to Bologna his little property in Milan had been
held by his son-in-law, and he himself had received none
of the returns. He had books which had been for a
long time lying untouched at the printer's. He was
lecturing without a lecture hour. His son Aldo was
in prison—he is never to be heard of incidentally, except
as party to some scrape—and there were two professors
who obstructed all his doings at Bologna. All this knot
of trouble, then, was to unravel itself. And so it did. At
the end of the next July, nine months afterwards, Cardinal Alciat, who had assisted in procuring Jerome's
appointment at Bologna[2], and who remained until the
death of the old man an untiring friend—Cardinal Alciat
caused the restoration to him of his property. He seems

---

[1] Paralipomenon, Lib. iii. cap 11.

[2] Synesiorum Somniorum. p. 252; but the previous reference covers
the other facts.

to have been deprived of it for a time by the imperfect rescinding of the sentence of banishment pronounced against him in his native town. , In the succeeding month ,of August, Jerome received from his printer a parcel of the missing books, which had at last rapidly passed through the press These changes reopened two important sources of his income. In the same month the professor by whom he was most obstructed quitted Bologna, giving up a salary of seven hundred gold crowns. There remained then only, says Jerome, the general conspiracy of the physicians.

Of Aldo[1], it will be enough to say that his foolish and abandoned conduct was the cause to his father of incessant trouble Fathers, by the law of Bologna, had then many judicial rights over their sons, and Jerome more than once imprisoned Aldo, in the vain hope of checking his misconduct. He was the son to whom the stars had been so liberal in promises of all good things,—genius, fame, wealth, the confidence of princes; he was exiled at last, and disinherited. There remained by Cardan only the grandchild Fazio.

His right as a father Jerome had exercised as a citizen of Bologna, since the senate (from whom he received always much honour) had conferred on him the freedom of the city[2]. He does not omit to tell us what he thought about his fellow-townsmen. "When I was at Bologna,"

---

[1] De Vitâ Propriâ, cap xxvii   [2] Ibid. p. 32.

he says[1], " I heard much about the manners of the people, and that they were deceitful; but that is not true. It is truer that they are ambitious and effeminate, and easily irritated. When they have begun to quarrel they are not led on by any care for equity or moderation, but they are resolved to win, even though it be against the right; for when you have offended them, they never stop to reflect whether they first caused the offence, but conceive an undying hate, so that it is doubly difficult to deal with them. Some are magnificent, beneficent, and reasonably civilised and polished. The chief thing, therefore, is to give them soothing words while pertinaciously adhering to your rights, and never slip from your main point. For when they have no right to show in a contest, they use cutting words, and put them in the place of justice. A thing certainly to be found hard, especially by those who are not used to it. Wherefore it is better to dispute with them on paper than by word of mouth, and through an arbiter than man to man."

After he had lived four or five years at Bologna, Jerome could, at least while occupied in writing philosophically, believe that his mind was tranquillised. "I am poor," he said[2], " sick, and old. I am bereaved of my best son, my best hope, the youth most dear to me, by a wrong;

---

[1] Proxenata (ed. Elzevir), p. 467.

[2] De Libris Propr. Lib. ult. Opera, Tom. i. p. 136.

from my other son I have but slight hope of happiness, or
of the continuation of my family; my daughter, now
nine years a wife, is childless.   I who once flourished so
strongly am now happy, in spite of all reverse.   I teach
with my mind bent wholly on the duty, and therefore
with a most numerous class.   I manage my affairs more
wisely than I used; my latest writings, if anybody will
compare them with my former works, will show that my
mind is fuller, livelier, and purer than it ever was before."
So, pen in hand, and with a train of philosophic meditation in his mind, he could deceive himself, and even at
times prove that his son's fate had been a blessing.   Inasmuch as he had reformed his household, and had become
more prudent in the management of money, he had
grounds for his assertion that he had improved by his
affliction.   It is true also that as a philosopher, whenever
his topic was of a purely contemplative kind, grief had
improved rather than impaired his powers.   He was
writing at that time a work " On Nature;" and admonished by his approach to the allotted term of mortal life,
was engaged upon several books under the title " Paralipomenon," in which he put down, each under its own head,
much that he had to communicate on all the subjects he
had spent his life in studying, and for which it was not
likely that room would be made in future treatises   In
this work are books on Algebra, Medicine, Natural His-

tory, Mechanics, Speculative Philosophy, embracing in fact almost the whole wide range of study to which his intellect had been devoted. The task it implied was a final heaping up before he died of all the chips that re-mained in his workshop. He wrote also at this time many shorter essays and dialogues, of a purely ethical character. A strong spirit of meditation was upon him, and it is certain that he relied in his books more practically for consolation and support upon the doctrines of Epictetus than upon those of the Church. That may have been the scholar's tendency, but it is very noticeable, and the fact is important in its bearing upon the events next to be told.

In the year 1565, on the 21st of January[1], a new governor came to Bologna. During the night Cardan's bed was on fire, and the boy, who slept on a chair-bed in his room, roused him and told him of his danger. Jerome awoke in anger, thinking the boy drunk; but seeing that he spoke truth he got up, and assisted in smothering the fire. Then being very tired, he fell asleep again; and on awaking found that more of his bed had been burnt. The painted quilt had not been injured, nor the leather cover-ing, nor any of the hangings, and only a small part of the linen had been touched; but the blankets (there were three) were burning. The fire was not easily conquered; there

---

[1] Paralipomenon, Lib. iii. cap. 52, for the following.

was flame with it and not much smoke, and little harm
done. Upon this Cardan divined that the smoke signified
infamy, the fire peril and fear, the flame great and present
risk of life. The hidden fire represented dangerous snares
laid by domestics. The fact that the bed had been set on
fire by himself portended that the danger would arise
within his own house, and that he should overcome it
without external help. The fire was the magistracy.
On account of the fire, flame, and smoke, the danger
would consist in accusation, not in violence or poison. It
would seem to be often allayed, and yet often break out
again; there would be peril, not from sharp contest, but
from flattery and bad faith, not without danger of the
loss of all his published books, of all his possessions; and,
above all, of his life. The books, however, would not be
hurt; for they were near his bed, and the fire did not
approach them. He should not judicially lose character,
because none of the hangings were burnt; nor life, because the innermost parts of the bed were safe; nor property,
because the quilt had not been damaged. He concluded,
therefore, that he should suffer in vulgar esteem, and be
put to a considerable expense through negligently having
faith in false domestics. The citizens might enter into
the matter, for they were as it were conjoined. On the
whole the loss would be little, the danger moderate, the
disturbance great.

It is hard to say whether this prophecy was considered to be fulfilled, when, five years afterwards, on the 13th of October, 1570[1], Cardan, then nearly seventy years of age, was suddenly cast into prison. He does not tell us why, but there is the strongest ground for believing that it was upon an accusation of impiety. The reasons for that opinion will appear in the succeeding chapter. In prison he was liberally used ; and after a confinement of eleven weeks, on a Friday, the same day on which he had entered, and at the same hour of the day, in the evening twilight, he returned to his own house.

He was not released, but suffered to take his own house for a prison, having given a bond in eighteen hundred gold crowns for his honesty as gaoler to himself. After the bond was signed, and the officials had departed, his faithful pupil Rodolf Silvester—who graduated the year afterwards—being left in the prison with him, and the door being left open, the afternoon sun at the same time glittering through the window, Jerome asked his friend to shut the door. It closed with a slam, and at the same time there was a sudden blow upon the window. Jerome and his friend both heard and saw it. It was, of course, the natural effect of the concussion of air, caused by the shutting of the door. But Cardan dwelt upon it as a

[1] The narrative to the conclusion of the chapter is from a comparison of De Vitâ Propriâ, cap. iv. with cap. xliii.

portent, and a sign of his own certain death that was approaching. "But afterwards," he relates, "I began thus to reason with myself: if so many princes, even in their youth, and strength, and happiness, expose themselves to certain death, that they may win approval from their kings, when they have nothing else to win by dying, why should you, a withered and almost infamous old man, not suffer for your crime, if they hold you guilty, or by wrong if you are undeserving of this evil before God, who, by His mercy, shows that He beholds all your affairs?" With these reflections he went home refreshed and fearless.

This calamity had been preceded by another portent. He was writing a medical opinion for the use of his patient, Cardinal Morone (it is published among his works), when a leaf of it fell to the ground. He rose that he might stoop to pick it up, and as he did so the paper, marvellous to behold, lifted by a gentle wind, rose with him, and flew upon the table, where it remained fast in an erect position. Jerome called Rodolf to see the marvel, and both saw that the leaf was scarcely stirred. From this he concluded that his concerns would suffer sudden overthrow, but that they would be lifted up into a right position by a gentle breeze of favour.

He had reason, therefore, to expect what happened, or he would not have thought of drawing such an inference.

The gentle breeze came to him from the expected quarter, from the friendship of the leading cardinals.' After eighty-six days of imprisonment within his own doors he was set at liberty ; but he was forbidden to publish any more books, and as a point of courtesy advised by his friends voluntarily to resign his chair. He did so; and they having then obtained for him a pension from the pope, the famous philosopher, seventy years old, left Bologna in September, and during the first week of March, in the year 1571, entered Rome.   A victory over the Turks was on that day in course of celebration.

CHAPTER XII.

THE END AT ROME.

"He cometh in with vanity, and departeth in darkness, and his name shall be covered with darkness."—*Ecclesiastes* vi. 4.

THIS mournful story of the vanity of wisdom draws now to a close. Cardan's imprisonment at Bologna had taken place under the pontificate of Pius V., a pope of pure but austere life, who had caused the strenuous enforcement of laws against heresy and blasphemy, and who combined with many noble qualities the character of a most stringent persecutor. He forbad physicians to attend patients who had passed three days without confession of their sins; he expressed disapprobation with his officials in any town that did not yield yearly a large crop of penal sentences. The imprisonment of Jerome at Bologna was a result, I believe, of this activity, and yet it was from Pius V. that Cardan received a pension, and under his wing that he spent his last years safely in Rome as a private person.

M. De Thou relates, in the history of his own times[1],
that he saw at Rome the great Cardan, walking about the
streets, not dressed like any other person, had often wondered at him and had spoken with him. He records at
the same time the character he bore: that he was " a
madman of impious audacity, who had attempted to subject to the stars the Lord of the stars, and cast our
Saviour's horoscope."

Immediately after Cardan's death, and during the succeeding century, this charge of impiety attached to him,
and he who had taken so much pains to remain on good
terms with the Church, was known traditionally as a man
who had blasphemously calculated the nativity of Christ
(Naudæus shows that he was not the first astrologer who
did so), and was occasionally named as a rank atheist.
Now it appears from De Thou that a character of this
kind attached to Jerome when he lived at Rome; and at
the same time it is a fact, that, with all his extravagant
freedom of self-revelation, any mention of such imputa-
tions has been carefully excluded from his works. We
detect their existence indirectly in one or two sentences,
already cited, as when Cardan at Pavia, dreading evil,
thought that passages in his own books might be twisted
to his hurt, and wrote a letter to Rome dutifully sub-

---

[1] Thuanus, Lib. lxii. Tom iii. p. 462, ed. Lond. 1733.

jecting them all to the authority and pleasure of the holy council, or when, afterwards, he wrote about a dream, that in the name of religion he should be put into grave peril. But in his dealing with princes and with the Church we have throughout seen that he was scrupulously prudent. During the latter years of his life the Church was subject to an ecclesiastical discipline more than usually rigid. The conflict against heresy and impiety had become, under Pius V., most earnest and severe. If Cardan's enemies or rivals brought against him in any town in which he resided accusations of impiety properly substantiated—his philosophy, and sometimes his superstition, being of a kind to provide plenty of evidence, while spies in his household might find plenty more—the authorities were bound to take sharp cognisance of the offence, and nothing less than a few strong friends near St. Peter's chair could save him.

Such accusations being made and credited, Cardan could only increase his peril by becoming contumacious, as he might be considered if he complained of them, and endeavoured to deny them in his works. He himself had stated that he did once construct such a nativity as that of which he was accused, and he had said so many things in the course of his works in a speculative way, not fearing to handle the sublimest mysteries, that, good Catholic as he professed himself to be, it was not difficult to show

that he was liable to heavy penalties. To all this operation of the age against him, to the stringency of the new
ecclesiastical spirit that had succeeded to the laxer times
of Jerome's youth and manhood, the old man could
oppose in self-defence nothing but silence and submission.

Thus he wrote of the accusation against him by which
he was cast into prison at Bologna: not that he was innocent, but that he ought to know how to endure the
punishment of his crime if he was guilty, or the wrong if
he was innocent, before God. He ventured no further than
to leave the question of his guilt or innocence entirely
open.   But even such distant allusions are extremely rare.
He took the wisest course, and as he could not write what
was untrue, and would not write what might be used for
his destruction, he wrote nothing at all upon so hazardous
a subject.   We find, therefoie, no reference in his books
to the impiety with which it is notorious that he was
charged, and it is for that reason, I believe, that we find
no precise account of the causes of his banishment from
Milan and of his subsequent confinement at Bologna.
This accords, indeed, with his expressed doctrine, for in a
Book of Advice written two or three years before his death
at Rome, in the course of a chapter on Calumny—from
which, by the way, we may infer that he was annoyed at

the accusation of insanity—we find him writing: " When the calumny is about religion (for in these days that is the most perilous kind) never confess that you have erred ; but it is best wholly to pass the subject over[1]."

At Milan he had been struck off the list of teachers, and we have seen also that for a time the printing of his books was stopped. He had, however, in good time, formally submitted all his writings to the authorities of Rome, and this precaution, as he says, saved him from peril. After his imprisonment at Bologna he was again prohibited from teaching, and was also finally prohibited from publishing his works. The prohibitions then imposed were not removed during his lifetime; and it was not until some time after his death that a few of his last manuscripts, which had been preserved, were given to the press. The cardinals who on the last occasion intervened again to protect the philosopher in his declining years, did not repeat their effort to remove the interdict upon his writings.

Though taken alone the fact is an odd one, that a philosopher imprisoned for impiety should be rescued by the leading cardinals, removed to Rome, and pensioned by the Pope, I think it may be accounted for without

---

[1] Proxenata, cap. cxi.   Opera, Tom. i. p. 455.

imputing any inconsistent or improper conduct to the Church authorities.

In the first place, of Cardan himself it may be said that he had among learned men the greatest name in Italy, and it was not natural that any rightly-disposed scholar should be content to see him die in prison. If any of his speculations had been rash, they had not originated out of any spirit of antagonism to the Church, to which he had always formally professed his desire to act as an obedient child. He was not, therefore, an antagonist whom it was proper to destroy, but simply an offender whom it was merciful to pardon. In his conduct throughout life, and especially since his son's death, it was easy to find evidence of unsound mind in mitigation of his crimes against Church discipline.

In the next place, it should be said that Cardan's friends were in the main pure-minded people, actuated by generous and worthy motives. Cardinal Borromeo was a spiritual man, a just and strict son of the Church, himself a zealous lover of good discipline, but he knew Cardan intimately, he honoured his intellect and understood his eccentricities; the physician, too, had saved his mother's life. It was not unnatural or unchristian—if I may say so, not uncatholic—in Borromeo, who worked as a trusted brother with the new Pope, to suggest, that as

Cardan certainly was not a contumacious heretic, and, being scarcely of sane mind, seemed to have gone astray unwittingly, respect might be paid fairly to his unexampled learning and the lustre of his name. He could urge, therefore, that it would be a wise and sufficient measure in his case, simply and without harshness, to take care that he should not again disseminate any opinions either by lectures or by books, and that it would be prudent to substitute for the means of subsistence so taken away a pension that would for the future keep him out of mischief, by compelling him to live at Rome, under the control of the Pope, as his immediate dependent[1].

Cardinal Morone, too, had long been indebted to Cardan's skill as a physician, and being a most intelligent and able man, had a sincere respect for him as a man of genius and intellect. Morone had been the foremost Churchman in the last sittings of the Council of Trent held at Bologna, and by writers of every creed he has always been looked back upon with a sincere respect. He was a just, temperate, and accomplished man, second to no other cardinal in influence; and the patronage was irresistible when he joined Borromeo in commending Cardan to the favourable consideration of the Pope.

[1] For the account of Cardan's patrons and friends of Rome, see De Vitâ Propriâ, cap xv., which is the evidence for all that follows till a fresh authority is cited.

Not less earnest than these friends, and constant to the last in his care over Jerome's fortunes, was Cardinal Alciat, who had inherited, with the goods of Alciat the lawyer, the strong friendship which that great man had maintained with Cardan the physician.

The philosopher found also at Rome a firm friend and supporter in another cardinal, Pietro Donato Cesio; and he enjoyed most liberal patronage from the Tridentine cardinal, Cristofero Mediuzio. The Venetian cardinal Amulio was also his friend. He enjoyed, too, the direct favour of the venerable Bishop Taddeo Massa. Of other friends of Jerome in his last years I need name only one, the Prince of Matelica, a small town in the Roman States, upon whom the old man pronounces an unusually warm panegyric for his royal qualities, his most extensive knowledge, his amenity of manners, his vast wealth, the splendour of his father's house, his wisdom, almost more than human. "What was there in me," exclaimed the old man, " that could bring me into friendly intercourse with such a man? Not benefits conferred, not hope of anything that I could do, old and despised by fortune, prostrate, no agreeable companion; if he loved me for anything, it was but for his opinion of my probity."

Jerome had also a familiar friend in his pupil from Bologna, Rodolf Silvester, who, having graduated, went at once to establish himself as a practitioner in Rome, and

often frequented the house of his old master. Cardan
lived at first in the square of St. Girolamo, afterwards in
the Via Giulia, near the church of S. Maria di Monte
Santo[1]. He had also one pupil, his name was Ottavio
Pitio, and he was from Calabria[2].

Aldo Cardan was disinherited. The child Fazio lived
with his grandfather, and was his heir. The old physician's
property had been saved to him; it included the possession
of a house or two at Milan, one at Pavia, another at
Bologna, and these, with whatever else he owned, although
they did not amount to much, and bore a very small proportion to the earnings of his life, yet formed a patrimony
four times larger than the little that he had inherited from
Fazio his father[3]. To his grandson Fazio all this was left,
and to his heirs[4]. The whole property was to stand together,
and to be subject to regulations that were equivalent to an
entail. Young heirs, by the terms of his will, were to be
kept under guardianship as long as possible, " for certain
reasons known to himself." Whatever manuscripts he left
behind him were to be corrected, and eventually sent to
press. Heirs belonging to his family who had not his
own name should take it on inheriting his property.
When succession failed, the house at Bologna was to

[1] De Vitâ Propriâ, cap. xxiv.
[2] Ibid. cap. xxxv.
[3] Dialogus cum Facio Cardano. Opera, Tom. i. p. 639.
[4] For the contents of Cardan's will see De Vitâ Propriâ, cap. xxxvi.

become the property of the University for use as a college, to be called the College of Cardan.

Another family arrangement made by Jerome when he left Bologna is extremely characteristic. The Cardans had for their arms a red castle with its turrets, the turret-tower being in the middle, and black on a white ground, by which it was distinguished from the arms of the Castiglione family. For further distinction, the emperor had added to the shield of the Cardans an eagle without a beak, and with its wings outspread upon a golden ground. The occasion of his imprisonment suggested to Cardan the substitution for the eagle in his seal of the image of a swallow singing under a shade or cloud. He took the swallow, he says, because it suited his own habits; it did no hurt to mortals, did not shun the dwellings of the poor, was always busy about the human race, yet never on familiar footing with it; it changed its dwelling often, went and came, was connubial not solitary, yet not disposed for living in a flock; it had a song wherewith to pay those who were friendly to it, and it was impatient of confinement. Other parallels were its carrying, small as it was, beautiful stones within its belly, its delight in mild air and warmth, its grateful remembrance of a hospitable roof, and its being conquered by no other bird in flight[1].

[1] De Vitâ Propriâ, cap. xxxiii. for the preceding.

Although prohibited from printing, Jerome wrote industriously, as it would seem, to the very last month of his life, during the whole six years of his residence in Rome. He carried on to the end his third and last treatise On His Own Books, which is very long, for towards the close of it he became garrulous, and not only played the part of analyst and critic on himself as a writer, but discoursed very cleverly and much at large upon the several branches of study and the principal styles of composition, adding his opinions on book-writing, with much sound and shrewd advice to authors. He supplied them also at the same time with a practical example of good conduct, for when he had been three years in Rome, and was engaging himself upon the final revision of the labour of his life, he burnt no less than one hundred and seventy of his books[1] which he thought useless, after extracting from them what was good. Yet, after all, he said, that he left behind him[2] one hundred and thirty-one works printed, and one hundred and eleven in manuscript, not twenty of which have seen the light.

His sick mind turned sometimes with loathing even from his dearest labour. Thus he sat down one day towards the end of his life, and told how yesterday he supped quite cheerfully, and after supper was seized with

[1] De Vitâ Propriâ, cap. xlv.
[2] Dialog. cum Facio. Op. Tom i. p. 639.

so deep a loathing of all books[1], whether his own or those of other men, that he could not endure to think of them, still less to look at them. And that feeling, he said, remained while he was then writing. I know, he added, no reason for this, excepting melancholy.

But there was reason for the melancholy. An ancient hope dwelt in his memory while he was arranging his books in expectation of approaching death. "My hope," he wrote in the end[2], "had been, that after my death they would be edited for me by my son, but that comfort is gone. They wished to destroy not him but me."

Nearly all his writings in the last years of his life were contemplative or admonitory; he dealt in advice or philosophic meditation. The chief exception was a copious work on the interpretation of dreams, which, together with the dialogue by which he had intended to immortalise the English boy, was published nine years after his death at Basle[3]. One of the last of his writings was a dialogue between himself and his father's ghost, in which his mind reverted to the days of his youth, while he explained the sorrows of his age, and received comfort from the other world. But there was hard comfort in one sentence that he placed upon his father's lips : " What of your sons?

[1] De Vitâ Propriâ, cap. lii.
[2] De Libris Propriis. Lib. ult. Op. Tom. i. p. 121.
[3] Somniorum Synesiorum, Libri iv. &c. 4to. Basle, 1585.

Have you not lost them by your negligence and your licentiousness[1]?" And who shall judge this old man drooping painfully under his heavy and enduring sorrow!

He was lavish of advice. Few men could teach better how to manage the affairs of life discreetly, and no man ever fell into more trouble through his own want of discretion. One of his last works, dictated at Rome, and found long afterwards in the handwriting of a wretched scribe, full of abbreviations (things which Cardan himself detested[2]), was a long treatise under the title of Proxenata, which was a guide to men who would manage themselves wisely and safely in every relation of society. When it was first issued, half a century after Cardan's death, from the Elzevir press, a second title was given to the book, and it was fairly enough said to be on Civil Prudence. In this work it is to be seen that, as a philosopher, Jerome's faculties remained to the last clear and lively. There is the old terseness in it, and more than the old wisdom. When Cardan, in his old age, wrote upon any abstract subject and forgot himself, there was no trace of the warping of his mind; he maintained perfectly the tone and spirit of a man of genius and a scholar. But in the daily business of life and in writing, whenever the

---

[1] Dial. c. Facio. Op. Tom. i. p. 639.

[2] See the preface of the editor to the Elzevir edition of Proxenata seu de Prudentiâ Civili. 12mo. Lugd. Bat. 1627.

topic happened to be personal, the wounds suffered by him in his conflict with the world could not be hidden. I cite two or three words of sense gathered at random from this book[1].

" It is manifest that he who would live to the best purpose should know what he wants, and that not only specially on each occasion that arises, but generally of the whole course of his life.

" Men rule over their fellows through religion and force, or the art of fighting, or by necessity, as with the doctors. Many men, therefore, have found it advantageous to combine the art of fighting with religion.

" In teaching youths who receive reason ill, use jests. Tell them, for example, when they prefer pleasure to truth, that they mistake butterflies for birds. In the same way you can escape out of a difficulty and give the blow you ought to take; as when it was complained against me that I had given a false prognosis when in consultation with some other physician, I said, ' It would be odd, indeed, if anything were done rightly in which he had part.'

" Instruct the mind as you bridle a horse, that it may run whichever way you turn it.

" Receive equals as your betters, paying honour to them.

[1] Proxenata (ed. cit.), pp. 63, 68, 90, 101, 113, 121, 129.

"Publish no crude books; they disarm you, and pass over to the enemy.

"Talk little. Do not relate common things that have happened to you, still less tell your secrets.

"Words uttered without thought are heavy losses.

"Do not carry out by day what you have resolved upon in the night, for by night things appear what they are not, as in dreams."

It would be easy to fill chapters with such wisdom taken from this single volume that was dictated by the philosopher in his last days. But their end is near, and there are other aspects of his life on which we now must dwell. If in his youth Jerome inherited from his father any opinion concerning guardian spirits, we have seen that in his maturity he rejected the idea that he was attended by a demon. After his son's death he manifested a disposition to maintain it, but in his old age he was to be found firm in his persuasion of the fact. He had been long persuaded, he said[1], that he was attended by a presiding spirit, called in Greek an angel; such spirits had attended certain men, Socrates, Plotinus, Synesius, Dion, Flavius Josephus, and himself. All had been fortunate except Socrates and himself, though he, too, was in a condition of which he ought not to complain. In what way he was admonished by the spirit he could

' De Vitâ Propriâ, cap. xlvii.

x 2

scarcely tell, but that he had been often secretly prompted
he was unable to doubt.   Thus, when he was walking one
day in the streets of Milan, without any reason known to
himself for doing so, he crossed the road, and immediately
afterwards there fell from a roof, near an upper window
of the house under which he should have been passing if
he had not changed his course, cement enough to kill
eight oxen[1].   Another time, when riding on his mule, he
met a coach, and had an instinctive thought that it would
be overturned, for which reason he passed on the wrong
side of it, and as he was passing it did overturn, in the direction contrary to that which he had chosen.

Invited to a supper at Rome[2], Cardan remarked, as he
was sitting down among the guests, " If I thought that
you would not take it ill, I would say something."

" You mean to say," one of the company inquired,
" that one of us will die?"

" Yes," the old man answered, " and within the year."

On the 1st of December following died one of the
party, a young man named Virgil.

" Bring me a paper," Cardan said to an old pupil of
his, Gianpaolo Eufomia, who was then at home—" I have
something to write for you." The paper was brought, and
the physician wrote under the young man's eyes, " You

---

[1] De Libris Propriis. Lib. ult. Op. Tom. i. p. 150.
[2] De Vitâ Propriâ, cap. xlii. for the three next incidents.

will die soon if you do not take care." He was taken ill eight days afterwards, and died in the evening. But, says Cardan, I saw that in no mysterious way; it was plain to me as a physician.

Though treasuring up every incident of justified foreboding that arose out of the incessant watchfulness for omens, Jerome was conscientious in his superstition, and where there had been no foreboding he did not claim as a mystery the chance fulfilment of words lightly spoken. An instance of this he set down in his old age: "I remember," he said, "when I was a youth, that a certain Gian Stefano Biffo had been persuaded that I was a cheiromancer, when I was nothing less. He came and asked me to predict to him something of his life. I told him that he was befooled by his companions; he urged me; I then begged his pardon if I should predict him anything too serious, but that he was in great danger of being promptly hung. Within a week he was seized and put under torture; he pertinaciously denied the charge against him; nevertheless, in six months he died by the cord, after his hand had been cut off."

It is not at all necessary to doubt any of the marvels that Cardan relates. A man who sees in almost every occurrence of the day a portent upon which to speculate, who is thoroughly and honestly superstitious, may be able, in the course of a long life, to store up a very large number of extremely curious coincidences upon which to feed his faith. Of this fact we will select as a final illustration the story of a morning spent by Cardan at Rome[1] only six months before he died, he being then seventy-five years old. It seemed to him so wonderful, that when he went home he set it down at length in his book " Upon his own Life;" an elaborate thesis on his own career and character, which he had just time to complete before he died:—On the morning of the 26th of April, 1576, he mounted his carriage—for he used it at Rome as at Bologna—to go into the forum. On the way he got out, because he wished to dive into a narrow court that led to the house of a dealer in gems, with whom he had business. As he left the carriage, he bade the driver, who, he says, was a torpid fellow, go and wait for him at the Campo Altovitaro. He answered " Yes," but mis-understood the direction, and the old man, when he him-self went to the place appointed, found no carriage. He was loaded with bags which he had brought from the jeweller's, considering that he should not have far to carry them. With these in his hand he walked towards the residence of the governor of the castle, to the vicinity of which he thought it likely that his driver had gone by mistake. On the road he met an old friend, Vincenzio, of Bologna, a musician, who was surprised to see the feeble

---

[1] De Vitâ Propriâ, cap. xlix.

old gentleman with his hands loaded and without his carriage. Jerome went to the castle, and not finding his man there, was compelled to journey back again over the bridge. He might, he said, have begged a carriage from the governor, but in so doing there would have been risk. Commending himself, therefore, to Heaven for the gift of patience, he went back over the bridge, and when he had crossed it, obtained rest at the other end by going into the house of the banker Altovito, professing to ask something that he wished to know about a late change in Neapolitan money, and sitting down to recover strength while he was being told about it. While he was so sitting, the governor came in, and Jerome at once rose and departed. Outside he saw his carriage, the driver having been met by Vincenzio, who told him of his error. Still the old man was in doubt whether to go home, or what to do, because he suffered not only from fatigue but from long fasting. But then, having mounted into the vehicle, he found three raisins in his pocket, and so his difficulties were entirely ended. " Here," he said, " you must observe the sequences: the meeting with Vincenzio, his meeting with the driver, my going into the bank, the governor's coming in, my going out, and because I went out just at that time, my meeting with the carriage, and upon that the finding of the raisins. Here were seven things, of which it was necessary that every one should fall out

exactly when and where it did for the attainment of the
required result. Such things do not happen to every man."

Jerome Cardan was not forbidden to exercise his profession during those last days at Rome; but at the period to
which this last incident refers, after his seventy-fifth year,
he had abstained from all labour for the sake of money,
unless he liked the people with whom it was desired that
he should deal[1].

Looking back upon the life that was almost completed,
and conscious that its leading events had all been more or
less revealed in his past writings, either by scattered hints
or by brief narratives, Cardan, in the book upon himself
which occupied his latest leisure, and was the summing
up of his intellectual accounts with this world, rather pre-
supposed a knowledge of his career than engaged himself
upon the composition of a distinct autobiography.   Brief
narrations in earlier writings had been so contrived, that,
as he said when giving one of them, " What I have told
elsewhere diffusely I tell shortly here; what I have told elsewhere shortly I tell here at length[2]." In the last book, therefore, devoted wholly to his life[3], there is one short chapter

---

[1] De Vitâ Propriâ, cap. xxiii.

[2] De Ut ex Adv cap. ii. 112.

[3] It was first published in 1643 by Gabriel Naudæus, who prefixed to
it a judgment on Cardan that has done much to disseminate a false
opinion of his character   The same "judgment of Naudæus" is unluckily prefixed also to Cardan's collected works.   Its narrow reason-
ings have therefore influenced most readers of Cardan's last book.

of rapid narrative, and all the rest is self-dissection; it contains a chapter on his vices and another on his virtues; one on his honours, one on his disgraces, a long one on his friends, a very short one on his enemies, of whom he will not speak. One chapter compiled by the old man is a long list of the illustrious contemporaries who had named him in their works. The book abounds, of course, in personal information and self-revelation; but his mind was bowed down to the dust when he was writing it. He was the sorrowful old man whose hopes were wrecked, and who was to be met in the streets of Rome walking with the strange, unsteady gait of a lunatic[1], dressed unlike other people, a man to be wondered at by strangers, and by his own friends apparently considered mad. His book contains everywhere traces of the rack on which his spirit had been tortured. Grief for his dead son is still the ruling thought, and one of his very latest writings is a Nænia[2]—a funeral song—placed near the end of his last

[1] De Vitâ Propriâ, cap. xiv.
[2] Ibid. cap. l. The lines translated in the text are these:
   " O sanctissima conjunx,
Felix morte tuâ, neque in hunc servata dolorem!
Ipse ego, nate, tuum maculavi crimine nomen:
Pulsus ob invidiam patria, laribusque paternis,
Debueram patriæ pænas, odiisque meorum;
Omnes per mortes animam sontem ipse dedissem,
Contra ego vivendo vici mea fata, superstes.
Sed tamen æternum vivet per sæcula nomen,
Nate, tuum: notusque Bactris jam notus et Indis·
Mortuus es nobis, toto ut sis vivus in orbe."

book, to the memory of Gianbatista. The old man, too, from the edge of the tomb looked back to the wife who had shared his earlier and lesser sorrows:

> " O hallowed wife, most happy in the gain,
>   By death, of freedom from this weight of pain!
>   O son, whose name is stained by my own sin,
>   I too neglected suffer through my kin.
>   From home and hearth thrust out, I conquer fate.
>   Hurts from my country, from my kindred hate,
>   Of envy born, kill me, and yet I live.
>   But through all ages shalt thou, son, survive;
>   For Ind and Bactria shall his tale rehearse,
>   Who quitted me to fill the universe."

Such were the latest thoughts of Jerome Cardan in his desolate old age. Beyond them there was in this world nothing but the grave. He died at Rome on the 20th of September, 1576, when he was seventy-five years old, and his body was deposited in the church of St. Andrew. Afterwards, probably by his grandson in fulfilment of his own desire, it was removed to Milan, to be buried at St. Mark's[1]. There he again slept with Fazio his father.

[1] Thuanus, loc. cit.

INDEX.

CARDAN, JEROME.
Leading Events of his Life.

VOL. I.

THE END.

Lightning Source UK Ltd.
Milton Keynes UK
UKHW052105230223
417342UK00011B/226